journalism

EUROPEAN *COMMUTER*

BOOKS BY WILLI FRISCHAUER

Twilight in Vienna
The Nazis at War
The Rise and Fall of Hermann Goering
Himmler
The Navy's Here (with Robert Jackson)
The Man Who Came Back
European Commuter

Willi Frischauer

EUROPEAN

COMMUTER

The Macmillan Company, New York

Contents

Contents

EUROPEAN *COMMUTER*

I | *Wedding in Vienna*

*I*t must have been a very moving occasion. A thousand candles illuminated the vast nave of Vienna's old Catholic Schottenkirche. Before the altar my mother and father were about to enter into the holy state of matrimony. She, elegantly buxom in the true image of her day (the year was 1902), wore a white veil framing her classically beautiful features; he, rough and tough in appearance, with a pugilist's nose, had the faintest trace of a tear in his sharp, steady eye, and a forbidding brow topped by a menacing, virtually unkempt mop of dark hair. . . . Not far behind them little *alte* Anna, emotion agitating her toothless jaw, attended to the unruly brood of my parents' four sons: Leo, about nine years of age; Edi, eighteen months younger; Fritz, another couple of years behind; and Paul who (if I remember rightly) was born in 1898. Their immaculate white sailor suits, with short pants, white socks, and black patent-leather shoes, contrasted markedly with their mischievously belligerent countenances, molded, it would seem, by a subconscious compulsion to rival their father's permanently aggressive attitude. The organ playing, the choirboys singing, the wedding guests clearing their throats nervously, incense sweetening the air, the priest intoning: "Whom God has joined together let no man put asunder."

If this first paragraph of my story here and there betrays an element of uncertainty, the explanation is not far to seek. I can relate only what I was told. I was not there at the time, which is not surprising because I was not yet born, although it would seem odd that my four brothers were present. Were they then all bastards? And was I, born in 1906, the only legitimate scion of this branch of my family? Not at all.

I have introduced my story with this little enigma because it is symbolic of much I have to tell. But before I explain it, I want to say that my private and professional what-makes-Sammy-run kind of life only disguises my true inclination which, vaguely, corresponds with that of the famous rabbi's adolescent son who, in the old Jewish tale, implored his father year after year to let him sit and think, sit and think without any specific purpose or practical expectation.* My busy life has done nothing for me but to interrupt this delightful and absorbing preoccupation.

In the absence of photographs to satisfy my curiosity, I have, for instance, spent much time and thought trying to visualize my father as a young man—in the 1880's or thereabouts (he was born in 1862)—when he came down from the University of Graz in the Austrian province of Styria and, a newly graduated Doctor of Law, decided to settle in Vienna. He must have been quite a person. Even when, after several years' interval, I saw him for the last time, in Vienna in 1938, he was still, at the age of seventy-six, a powerful figure, although bent by rheumatism, a little unsteady on his feet and, as a result of a double-cataract operation, almost blind. But his booming voice with its angry intonation still rings in my ears, echoing, as it always did, strong and mostly unconventional and unpopular views, and betraying an irresistible urge to voice them come hell or high water.

No, sorry—not hell. Hell he feared—or there would have been no occasion for the wedding in the Schottenkirche, a sub-

---

* The eventual conclusion: If all the saws in the world were one saw with which to fell the tree which is all trees, which then dropped in the ocean which is all oceans, imagine what a splash there would be!

ject which, incidentally, caused as many laughs at home as it raised eyebrows outside. As I see him in my mind's eye he was as yet some distance from this unusual appointment at the altar, a tall, heavily built, contemporarily moustachioed young man with an inexhaustible capacity for work and a head full of ideas—but also dented at the top of the skull from a saber blow suffered in the course of a students' duel. (As a result of this injury he could not wear the heavy shako of his exclusive regiment, and was discharged after a few unhappy days in the army. Never again in his life did he don a uniform, as if to prove that one can be belligerent without being military.)

By the time Father—one of four brothers—arrived in Vienna, his own father was dead. He had been the owner of an unimpressive but not unprofitable brown-coal mine in the German-speaking part of Bohemia which eventually became better known (and rather troublesome) as the Sudetenland. Two of Father's elder brothers held a watching brief over him. The third had emigrated to the United States, was never heard of, but survived in our imagination as the proverbial potential source of a vast dollar inheritance. What folly. Of my family I am, I think, the only one who is convinced that my lost uncle's American descendants live somewhere in the region of Pittsburgh, totally impoverished, calling themselves Freshfield or some such name, and sustained only by the hope of tracing me one day, and with me some legendary Frischauer fortune of which their forebear boasted in his declining years, and to a share of which they regard themselves entitled.

The only treasure, alas, which I can share with them is a rich fund of lore associated with the name—but not without sounding a note of caution. Since my father, in turn, has had five sons, each endowed with a vivid sense of drama, these tales, like the Odyssey, were bound to—if not always improve—at least change with retelling. In the versions that have percolated to a latecomer like myself, my father's brother, Dr. Berthold Frischauer, for instance, lawyer, journalist, and "confidant of the great," was such a grand liberal that, in contemporary terms, the British would have sent him to the House of Lords and the Americans to a series of congressional investigatory committees.

Uncle Berthold has come down to me as one of the small

circle of "progressives" who hovered around Crown Prince Rudolf, the heir to the Habsburg throne, and provided him with ammunition for his campaign to wrest some small liberal concessions for the country from his obstinate, reactionary, absolutist imperial father, Franz Josef. To me Berthold Frischauer was represented as a premature central-European Aneurin Bevan, always encouraging poor Rudolf to harass the Kaiser, to fight for the liberation of the Czechs, the Hungarians, the Poles, the Serbo-Croats from the Habsburg yoke—in other words, to preside over the liquidation of the Habsburg Empire. The way these topics were bandied about at our dinner table, it was not wine and women or his hopeless morganatic love for the pretty little Countess Vetsera which led Rudolf to Mayerling and to death (providing countless novelists and film scriptwriters with a perennial theme), it was, less romantically, Berthold Frischauer with his political prodding, pushing, and shoving. In this version it was impossible to imagine Crown Prince Rudolf and Berthold Frischauer except with their heads close together. Yet when I examine the historical facts, what do I find? Before me, as I write, I have an early reference to Berthold Frischauer in a letter from the Crown Prince to a third party (dated January 13, 1883): "Do you absolutely trust Dr. Frischauer?" asks Rudolf.

To meddle with the monarchy was, of course, a hazardous enterprise. To think in terms of liberation was dangerous, to talk about it high treason, to discuss it with the heir to the throne *lèse majesté* to boot. It would have been surprising if Berthold Frischauer had put all his eggs in one basket. Hence the Crown Prince's reservation. But it is quite true that Rudolf took a fancy to Frischauer, whose regular beat included the Prince's imperial tours. Whenever Rudolf appeared at a public function, his first words were: "Where are the gentlemen of the press? Where is Dr. Frischauer?" This, by the way, was excellent public relations long before McCann-Erickson or Colman, Prentis and Varley were ever dreamed of.

Because it probably had a certain bearing on my own professional career I must (quoting from *My Life and History* by Berta Szeps, published by Cassell, London, in 1938) recount another typical Berthold Frischauer anecdote: "Among the many remarkable people working on the *Neues Wiener Tagblatt* in those days," Frau Szeps writes, "the figure of Dr. Frischauer, the diplomatic correspondent, stands out. Already he was one of my father's most interesting pupils, and later became one of the great journalists of his time. He had an unequalled genius for striking and following up trials. His gift for piecing together the truth of some hidden political crisis from a few scattered indications, and for scenting the most important news long before anyone else, brought him into the front rank of European journalists. I remember his famous acrobatic masterpiece, when he climbed down the chimney of the fireplace at Skiernevize, where the three Emperors were having a secret interview. From a precarious hiding-place Dr. Frischauer overheard every word, and the *Neues Wiener Tagblatt* was the only paper to have a full and verbatim report of it."

Examining what little evidence there is, I have come to the conclusion (without prejudice to any alternative interpretation which any one or all of my brothers may prefer) that Berthold Frischauer deserves to be remembered as a reporter rather than as a rebel; his "friendship" with Rudolf was a tender plant nourished by the invaluable news which was bound to flow profusely from such a highly placed source. After the Mayerling tragedy, far from setting the world alight with the bundle of highly inflammable letters addressed to him in the Crown Prince's own hand and thus serving his late imperial friend's great liberal cause, Berthold took the Establishment's way out, requested an audience with the old Emperor and (while others garnered small fortunes from selling similar epistles in the political black market) handed the embarrassing correspondence over to him with a loyal citizen's compliments. As long as he lived, the imperial sun never set on Berthold Frischauer.

Berthold later joined the *Neue Freie Presse* (Austria's *Times*), became mentor to the owner's son, moved to Paris as the paper's correspondent and, an outstanding authority on troubled, bickering, corrupt southeast Europe, graduated to semidiplomatic status as head of a permanent Balkan arbitration commission with headquarters in Paris. He fell in love with France, amassed a great fortune (mostly invested in Paris real estate), returned to Vienna at the outbreak of the First World War, allowed his patriotic feelings to run away with him in the form of a signed anti-French article, regretted it bitterly (and had every reason to) when the French retaliated by sequestrating his property, which had so far remained immune, and even more so after the war when, while attending the Peace Conference in Saint-Germain, he was publicly pilloried as "Un Indésirable" in the caption under his picture which one day covered almost the whole front page of *Le Figaro*.

Back in Vienna, a broken man, he awaited death as serenely and comfortably as he knew how—a rapidly aging but still handsome dandy and *bon viveur* with a great eye for the ladies and an even greater love of both the best and the most vulgar food. He once paid the equivalent of a golden sovereign for a slice of *Quargel*, the world's most atrociously smelling cheese, which a coach-and-pair had been dispatched to collect for him while he was dining on the outskirts of Vienna in the exclusive Lusthaus restaurant, where ordinarily such low-type fare was neither demanded nor served.

Father's other brother, Dr. Emil Frischauer, was a very successful advocate whose claim to fame also rested, so to speak, on an imperial pillar. Among clients whom he advised on their financial affairs was Frau Katharina Schratt, Vienna's somewhat bourgeois Nell Gwyn, the old Emperor's *amante du coeur*. Frau Schratt, an actress by profession, was a typical and popular Vienna musical-comedy figure (of the sentimental, not the funny, variety), an indispensable ingredient of any stage representation of old imperial Vienna, who was in her lifetime impersonated on the stage more frequently than she had ever appeared in person. While the beautiful, restless Empress Elisabeth roamed Europe incognito rather than permit herself to be squeezed into the straitjacket of the Vienna court's near-Spanish etiquette, and more so after her tragic death by assassination on the shores of Lac Leman, the lonely Franz Josef whiled away at least two evenings a week playing *Tarrok*, an old Austro-Hungarian card game, with Frau Schratt—and Emil Frischauer.

Under the circumstances it will not come as a surprise that I, too, following faithfully in my uncle's footsteps, have, in my own time, established contact with the Habsburgs, though on a somewhat lower if no less impressive level. I was still a very small boy when, one day, I was told that our cook had taken unto herself a husband by the very appropriate name of Koch, but had graciously consented to continue to work for us. Herr Koch was a balding, middle-aged man with wide shoulders and enormous hands who delighted me by throwing me into the air and catching me safely in his firm grasp. His job remained a mystery to me for some time (I assumed that his wife was keeping him, since I frequently heard my mother complaining of the high wage Frau Koch demanded and received—yes, even in those days.)

One day, I cannot remember how, I found out that Herr Koch was Emperor Franz Josef's masseur. For the past twenty years, it appeared, he had attended the Emperor every morning at 4:00 A.M., pummeled the old gentleman's body mercilessly for half an hour, tweaked his neck, twisted his arms, and stretched his legs. Imagine! I learned that, in spite of this close association between Emperor and masseur, they had never—not once in twenty years—exchanged a single word. Herr Koch, in fact, had strict instructions not to greet Franz Josef on arrival, not to speak while performing his duties, and to take his leave in complete silence.

My admiration for Herr Koch was unbounded but also tinged with a dash of opportunism. Because neither of my uncles had ever shown the slightest inclination to introduce me or any of my brothers to their imperial acquaintance, Herr Koch appeared to me as the only tangible link between me and my monarch. Mother must have guessed my secret thoughts, because for several months before the great occasion of Franz Josef's birthday, which was celebrated by Trooping the Color in the courtyard of the Vienna Hofburg, the prospect that it might be arranged for me to see the ceremony was dangled before me as the only means of making me behave with tolerable courtesy to my elders, eat my spinach, go to bed without howling my head off, and put on my too tight new shiny black patent-leather sandals. Herr Koch, I was told, might be persuaded to take me to the imperial servants' quarters and let me watch the Emperor from his fourth-floor room in the Hofburg overlooking the courtyard.

As a boy, I was not easily fooled. I continued to be atrociously rude, did not eat my spinach, and screamed the house down when it was suggested that it was time for me to go to bed. I knew in my heart that the matter had been settled and that Herr Koch would take me anyway. My only concession was to wear the sandals without protest because they were my only footwear fit for the occasion. The weeks passed slowly, but at last the great day came. At the crack of dawn I was in my place, a goldilocked, excited little horror of a boy surrounded by the children of imperial coachmen, aging pantry girls, and some venerable figures who enjoyed the privilege of waiting on the Emperor's table on festive occasions.

Excitement mounted. The courtyard was crowded with impressive figures in multicolored uniforms and cock-feathered helmets; the trumpets issued their thunderous salute; the gallant knights stood to attention. Their eyes firmly fixed on the scene below, the people around me were solemnly silent and an irritable "Sh-h-h" was the only response to my many questions. In the event, it appeared that all the time my gaze had been following the wrong man and, when the whole hullabaloo was over, Herr Koch was tactless enough to tell me so. That is how I did not see the Emperor. It was the end of my friendship with Herr Koch.

But my family profited from Herr Koch's—or was it our uncles'?—connection with the House of Habsburg even after the death of Franz Josef and the collapse of the monarchy. By that time my brother Edi was an aspiring young lawyer, and Herr Koch asked him to represent his claim for a pension against the new Austrian Republic. Edi went to court—legal, not imperial—and succeeded. As a result, all the other ex-imperial servants entrusted him with their cases, which he also won. His fees were substantial. He bought me my first school tie, which I proudly wore on the day when my teacher told me it was about time I learned the new Republican national anthem. What did I mean by singing *"Gott erhalte, Gott beschütze—Unsern Kaiser, unser Land"?* "Are your people monarchists or something?" she asked.

Reconstructing the 1880's of which I have so impetuously raced ahead, we find Father truly burning the candle at both ends. He managed—I shall never know how—to hold down three jobs at once, rarely getting or needing, more than four hours' sleep. Apart from serving his apprenticeship in a solicitor's office, he worked in the judge advocate's department and went on duty every evening as a subeditor helping to make a daily newspaper ready for the presses. He still found opportunities for rather exciting private enterprises. Indeed, I recall hearing an authentic whisper to the effect that, at the time he met and fell in love with my mother, he was still desperately trying to cut himself loose from an embarrassing entanglement with a woman of the kind that is always described as "a woman."

Yet, according to all accounts—of which I found some confirmation in the years I grew to know and love him dearly—he was never an obvious target for a woman's infatuation. He was not only Bohemian in territorial origin but also in his mode of life. In contrast with his brothers, he was anything but a natty dresser. *Avant-garde* in many of his ideas, notions of modern hygiene were beyond his comprehension. A few years later a story was current in Vienna according to which my father, on holiday by the Adriatic, asked a friend to go swimming with him: "With you—in the same sea? Never!" was the reply. From early morning till late at night he was never without a cigar, which had a disastrous effect on his teeth: "By the time he was forty he had none left," Mother used to tell us, trying to persuade us to smoke less and holding him up as a ghastly example.

His attractions, I was later told, were those of a caveman, but with a fierce intelligence illuminating his unusual personality. He was harsh, unbending, bellicose except for the rare moments when—like the sun breaking through many layers of dark cloud—a gleam would momentarily light his clever eyes, and the affection which he harbored for his family like a guilty secret would erupt and manifest itself in some small gesture. Sometimes I found his brief moments of tenderness more disconcerting than his stony aloofness, which was more in character, much as if I had discovered a sign of weakness in one on whose strength I counted at all times for support.

Where his two elder brothers glided elegantly across the parquet floors of upper-class Vienna with the practiced ease of born socialites, and felt perfectly at home with the high and mighty, Father was likely to elbow his way unceremoniously through the same crowd, hardly disguising his contempt for them and their conventions, rudely spurning all attempts to involve him in their small talk. Although he eventually acquired a great deal of money, throughout his adult life he never owned more than one suit at a time, discarding it only when it was in tatters, and then reluctantly. The most violent quarrels between him and Mother invariably occurred on those mornings when he inadvertently awoke before she had carried out her weekly maneuver of changing his shirt, which involved the complicated transfer of his cuff links from one pair of starched buttonholes to the other.

Under the more orthodox influence of Mother, who never really became reconciled to Father's more eccentric habits—I suppose in those days a bride never got to know her groom well enough before marriage to find out about such things and, once married, it was too late—their five sons developed in some respects in the opposite direction, although not all of us went as far as Edi, whose daily morning toilette used to take up all of two hours. Father, at heart, was a Spartan; we grew up into Athenians—would-be Sybarites.

With tastes and habits so diametrically opposed, Father on the one hand and his two brothers on the other were bound to drift apart. This they did, which is why I saw little or nothing of my famous uncles. In the passage of time, Father too reached the top of his profession. But first he planned a little excursion. Unable to resist the lure of Rome, he interrupted his work in Vienna and spent a year in Italy earning a precarious living as a free-lance foreign correspondent. I suppose his notion was that one year's apprenticeship in journalism was an essential part of a young man's education for life, whatever the profession of his ultimate choice. All four of my brothers in turn worked as reporters for a year or so before moving on to more permanent professional pastures: economics, literature, the law. I alone never progressed beyond this preparatory stage

—which prepared me for nothing but journalism. In our age of specialization, a stint in journalism with its built-in proliferation of interests and its tendency toward superficiality is probably less useful than it once was. Father would have been shocked had he lived to see the deterioration in journalistic standards, and concurrently, in prestige.

But I suspect that he himself was not so lily-white as he exhorted us to be. In Rome he worked hard on his dispatches, which took many weeks, even months, to reach Vienna. Some of the people who figured in them were dead by the time their story got into print. To avoid such pitfalls—and no doubt to increase his earnings by making sure of regular appearances in the columns of his Vienna journal—Father invented (or so I was told) an Italian criminal organization under the name of "The Black Hand," his own private Mafia, as it were, whose hair-raising activities he described in weekly articles keeping readers on tenterhooks until the next installment. Fifty years later I raised the subject. He looked at me sternly and did not respond; he never admitted this journalistic escapade.

While in Rome he went to church every day—to a different church as often as possible—learning as much as he could about the Eternal City's Houses of God, their history, religious, and temporal significance, and the part they played in the lives of generations of worshipers. He never ceased trying to hand down some of his love for Italian churches, indeed, his deep religiosity, to his sons. In view of their varied temperaments, he met with varying success. On his return to Vienna he once more immersed himself in work on many fronts, with an emphasis on newspapers and the law. He figured in many famous trials, but what always amused me more than the accounts of his forensic triumphs were the anecdotes that accumulated around him.

One of these described him as pleading Not Guilty on behalf of a client accused of burglary but, impatient with the defendant's frequent interruptions of his eloquent plea, snorting angrily: "Will you stop interrupting me! I did not interrupt you during your burglaries, did I?" Another client was accused of two burglaries, both in aggravating circumstances because—in

the words of the prosecutor: "One was committed in broad daylight and with great audacity, the other, cunningly, stealthily, under the cover of night," to which Father, with a fine flourish
of rhetoric, is supposed to have made the following rejoinder:
"Members of the Jury, the prosecutor has described as aggravating circumstance my client's burglary by day; and as equally
aggravating his nighttime burglary. With due humility, may I
ask at what time my client is *supposed* to commit his burglaries?"

It was also said that Father once slept through the whole of
the proceedings in a "hopeless" case but woke up just in time
to plead and obtain an acquittal. All good, amusing stuff as far
as legal gossip goes but uncorroborated except in one or two
instances where the "hero" was obviously not Otto Frischauer
but another Viennese lawyer who practiced years after Father
had retired from the bar.

Be that as it may, by the time he met Mother he was already
a public figure—lawyer, writer, eccentric. Mother . . . I still
have a picture of her at the age of two, wearing a tiny crino-
line and with one pudgy hand holding onto the leg of the chair,
head up and looking into a grown-up world without self-con-
sciousness or inhibition. That is very much as she remained until I last saw her at the age of sixty-eight—quite beautiful, still
completely unselfconscious, a little childlike, pursing her lips
petulantly when things did not go as smoothly as they should
in a respectable, if somewhat naughty, bourgeoise lady's life
where everything—anyway, almost everything—was predestined,
well organized, and where any hitch was a reflection on her,
or worse, a sign of heavenly disfavor. With the help of a bevy
of servants, she organized her home extremely well. I am at a
loss to think how she could possibly have incurred heavenly
disfavor, yet, alas, so much went wrong in her life that in retrospect I often wish Fate could have spared her and selected me
for greater suffering, because I could always take it in stride
and I am sure she could not.

Ferdinand Klebinder, my mother's father, was a journalist
who had graduated from reporting communal affairs to the own-
ership of the small local newspaper which served the Leopoldstadt, Vienna's predominantly Jewish borough. He was a jovial,

rotund little man, bald but for a fringe of gray hair and with a characteristic round Viennese face, typical of the district where Jews and gentiles intermingled, intermarried, and lived in such close proximity that it was difficult to distinguish them by behavior or appearance—very much, come to think of it, like the pre-independence Jerusalem Palestinians. (During my visit to Palestine in 1946, I would innocently ask a Jewish taxi driver in Jerusalem to take me to an address in the Arab quarter, or vice versa, be refused and left uncomprehending until enlightened by an older Palestine hand.)

In my young life Grandfather Klebinder figured as a Very Important Person, and I remember him best—well, actually, it is the only thing about him I remember—holding me on his knee while I reverently fingered the golden chain he wore around his neck, symbolizing, unbeknownst to me, the peak of his career as the Leopoldstadt's mayor, a life office. As such, he was also a member of the Vienna City Council under the legendary Lord Mayor Dr. Karl Lueger, Vienna's Dick Whittington.

Yet another photograph that tells a story is of myself as a teen-ager, wearing the pants of my pajamas and no top, with a vacant expression on my face, rather stupidly flexing the muscles of my arms in a mirror on the wall of my parents' bedroom. Whenever I see the photograph, which makes me look like an infant all-in wrestler, I shudder, and I should probably have thrown it away long ago if it had not, quite incidentally, also caught the picture which adorned the wall next to the mirror—God only knows what happened to the original—presenting the whole venerable company of Vienna's city councilors in the first decade of the century. Hardly discernible now in the photograph of a photograph, but still strongly in my mind's eye, is Grandfather standing by the side of Dr. Lueger, and looking more like an amiable, carefree old suburban grocer than an astute and highly honored Viennese local government politician and a Jew, both of which he emphatically and proudly was.

In the spring of 1962, at the Hotel Sacher in Vienna, I met an elegant Austrian in his late fifties, Fritz Mandl, whom I first encountered when I was a young reporter in Vienna, when he was the center of a much publicized international incident known at the time as The Hirtenberg Affair. He was the owner of central Europe's biggest munition factory in Hirtenberg, near Vienna, which was said to have defied the 1918 Austrian Peace Treaty, and sponsored the importation of arms from Italy into Austria. It was a paradoxical situation. The arms were destined for the *Heimwehr* (Home Guard), an Austro-Fascist paramilitary organization with the help of which Mussolini, as yet jealously and contemptuously hostile to Hitler, intended to frustrate Nazi designs on Austria. Since in Austria's permanent civil-war atmosphere these arms threatened to strengthen the violently anti-Left Heimwehr against the Socialists, the illegal transaction was uncovered and denounced by the Socialist railwaymen, precipitating a government crisis and an international commotion.

We regarded Fritz Mandl as the power behind the throne of the handsome, youthful Prince Rüdiger von Starhemberg, the somewhat quixotic scion of one of Austria's oldest aristocratic families, erstwhile supporter of Hitler and founder of the Heimwehr, which eventually entered into a coalition with the Christian Social Government, Starhemberg becoming vice-chancellor of Austria. Mandl not only supplied most of the money that kept the Heimwehr going but also the brains which helped to turn Starhemberg into a "statesman."

As a reporter in the late twenties and early thirties, it was impossible to escape preoccupation with Fritz Mandl, who was wealthy, brilliant, high-living, industrially and politically active, and spectacular—in a wholly gentlemanly manner—the type of all-pervasive manipulator of power of whom one always hears but whom one can never quite definitely identify as the proverbial "man behind the scenes." Fritz Mandl kept me busy once more when—a social event in Vienna—he married a pretty Viennese girl called Hedy Kiesler, daughter of a local bank manager, who had acquired a flash-in-the-pan prominence as a *soi-disant* film star by appearing in the nude in a film called *Ecstasy*. I knew Hedy because her father had often visited our newspaper office, trying to get publicity for his daughter.

The marriage broke up as suddenly as it had been contracted.

Hedy went to Germany, thence to Hollywood. A New York newspaper reported the divorce under the heading "No Ecstasy for Pocket-Zaharoff"—the name of the late Sir Basil Zaharoff, "Merchant of Death," as he has often been called, being a synonym for an omnipotent arms dealer. The boss of Hirtenberg was married again not long afterward, and Hedy Kiesler-Mandl —long since better known as Hedy Lamarr—eventually chose an old friend of mine, the tall, handsome London actor John Loder, as her third partner in another short-lived marriage.

Fritz Mandl spent most of the last war in the Argentine, where he was as closely associated with Juan Perón as he had previously been with Prince Starhemberg (who died a few years ago). Now Mandl was back in Vienna, and I was face to face with him again, and, as he told me, Hirtenberg was bigger than ever. An amazing, impressive man whom I should probably dislike but for whom, as for many others of his kind, I could never—*malgré moi*—suppress a sneaking regard. Our encounter sent my mind back to the turn of the century, to Grandfather and Dr. Karl Lueger. Let me explain why.

In the 1890's Lueger was one of the newfangled Progressive Democrats who believed that the people and not the Emperor had a right to choose their leaders and, moreover, leaders who were prepared to *do* something for the people. Four times Dr. Lueger, founder of the Christian Social Party, presented himself for election as lord mayor of Vienna; four times Franz Josef, defying the popular choice, refused to confirm him in office. In a desperate attempt to achieve his ambition, Dr. Lueger launched out on a demagogic campaign, cynically and ruthlessly exploiting the deep and latent anti-Semitism of the Viennese. His nefarious political calculation paid off. On his fifth attempt the overwhelming support of the people of Vienna carried him into office as lord mayor and forced the Emperor's hand. Grudgingly, Franz Josef at long last accepted Dr. Lueger.

The new lord mayor turned out to be a most progressive and enlightened Father of Vienna. A close friendship linked him with Leopold Klebinder and another Jew—Fritz Mandl's father. What was more, he often sought them out publicly and showed himself in their company. "Damnable! Outrageous!" blustered Dr.

Lueger's anti-Semitic supporters. "Dr. Lueger associating with
Jews!" It was not long before this violent criticism reached Dr.
Lueger's ears. But, like a snake shedding its skin, Dr. Lueger had
abandoned his anti-Semitism as soon as it had served its purpose:
"It's for me to decide who is a Jew!" he said in a phrase which
has entered the history books but was later, quite falsely, at-
tributed to Goering, who jocularly repeated it only once (though
he certainly made "honorable Aryans" out of some useful Jews,
or half-Jews, like his Luftwaffe adviser Nazi Field Marshal
Erhard Milch).

   Grandmother Klebinder—Kati (Catherine), née Hahn—was
a sweet little old lady for whom I had a strong affection. She
was like a storybook granny, infinitely kind and loving and obviously genuinely concerned about every single one of her vast,
unruly, and not universally attractive brood of grandchildren, the
total of which, though I can no longer compute it, can be guessed
from the fact that she bore Grandfather thirteen children, ten of
whom survived adolescence, married, and proceeded to procreate
with the gay abandon of the period. As was the case with most
Jewish families, each Friday evening Mother, her brothers and
sisters and not a few in-laws gathered around old Granny with
as many of her grandchildren as could be coaxed along, which,
owing to the quality and the quantity of the food we were offered, was a substantial contingent. I cannot remember any ex-
plicit mention of the Sabbath on these occasions or the fast to
follow the feast, and I suspect that the family preferred to observe the more pleasurable rites of the Jewish religion rather than
obeying its injunctions to moderation and sacrifice.

   These weekly get-togethers took place in the old lady's flat
(Grandfather had died during the First World War) in the heart
of the Leopoldstadt into which she had moved on the day she
was married and in which she lived till the day she died, and
where Mother, her firstborn, saw the light of day in April, 1870.
Although as a boy I was not exactly a sentimentalist—what boy
is?—I could nevertheless never quite escape a vague and incomprehensible feeling of awe and wonder when rummaging through
the rooms where Mother was born and had spent her childhood.
   From the huge dining-cum-living room where my uncles and

aunts and their offspring were stuffing themselves on goose breasts, *ritschert* (a Jewish dish), and sweet gherkins, a babel of voices came through the high doors linking the present with the past as I examined, time after time, Grandfather's old rocking chair; the rickety old piano—one of my aunts used to play it, but Mother played no instrument and was tone deaf; the cupboards from which Granny, sometimes escaping the turmoil around her and tiptoeing behind me into the quaintly still rooms, would extract a few coins to supplement my pocket money (the amount she gave me was pathetically small because, in her old age, she did not realize how quickly money values had deteriorated); the old carpets worn down to the canvas; the big yellowish framed photographs on the wall . . . to me it was all a somber, strange, and at once familiar world which enveloped me with a curious feeling of security. I cannot imagine my grandson ever becoming similarly engrossed in contemplation of my own rather austere apartment.

As the eldest of a rapidly growing family, Anna Klebinder, my mother-to-be, shared her own mother's domestic burdens. Although by the time I came along she already presided over her own kitchen, cook, and kitchen maid in the manner of a Leonardo da Vinci putting the finishing touches to the work of his apprentices, she learned housekeeping the hard way, looking after ten or more younger brothers and sisters. A great cook who loved and understood good food, she brought up her five sons in her image. Watching her preparing a meal with the artistry—but also with the temperamental outbursts—of an *afficionado*, and observing a succession of cooks carrying out her most detailed instructions, has implanted in me a passion for cooking which came to full flower in later years and which I, in turn, being too indolent to persist in a hobby for any length of time, have done my level best to communicate to all the women with whom—to use an all-embracing term—I have kept house.

How times change. In my mother's early days it was the aesthetes, the artists, the intellectuals who were gourmets. Austria's big monasteries, for instance, were not only seats of learning but also housed exquisite wine cellars and sheltered some of the greatest masters of the culinary arts. (One can still eat re-

markably well in restaurants administered by monasteries.) Today intellectuals affect what they seem to regard as a kind of
monastic asceticism and indifference to civilized standards, some
of which they perversely exhibit by a demonstrative contempt
for food—people who never eat a square meal, regarding as
square all those who do. Why all this distinction between the
pleasures of the spirit and those of the flesh? Reciting poetry
gives me a physical thrill, and my generation all but swooned
when listening to Mozart's *The Magic Flute* at the Vienna Opera.
I cannot for the life of me see any difference between feasting
one's eye on a Braque or a Monet and indulging one's palate with
Backhendl (chicken fried in egg and breadcrumbs) and *Salz-
burger Nockerl* (Salzburg dumplings).

Though as thin as a weed until my mid-forties, I inevitably became a fat man, but not one, I might as well establish here and
now, hiding within him a thin man screaming to get out. If
Mother was responsible for my girth, she has nothing to reproach
herself for, wherever she is now. Neither can her early cooking
efforts, in the Leopoldstadt, to provide a dozen mouths or more
with breakfast, second breakfast, lunch, *Jause*—the Vienna afternoon coffee-and-cake meal—and dinner have done much damage
to her brothers and sisters. With one exception they were a
well-built, handsome lot, and the exception made up with intellect
and personality for his lack of physical presence.

Mother herself was—and not only in the view of a doting
son—by far the handsomest of the Klebinder clan. Finely chiseled
features, a straight nose, strong auburn hair whose tendency to
crinkle was the sole discernible evidence of her race, full sensual
lips and an even fuller figure which, by the time I came to notice
it, was already overfull, and legs (at most times hidden by a long
skirt) which Father in one of his rare unbending moods proudly
and appreciatively acclaimed as beautiful but which in my jargon
I must now irreverently describe (as it would never have occurred to me to do in her lifetime) as piano legs. She was temperamental in a very womanly way, easily moved to tears, demonstratively but genuinely affectionate, even though occasionally
she seemed to affect a certain upper-class restraint or appeared
worried lest her little boy's overenthusiastic embrace should dis-

turb her veil. But when, before she had reached the age of twenty, she and Father met and fell in love, she must have been truly delicious.

Although the Klebinders were liberal Jews, they were not enchanted with the prospect of their eldest daughter marrying a Roman Catholic (almost as if they could foresee that several of their sons and daughters would follow such an example). But Father's unorthodox, storming approach brushed their objections aside. Why should they worry? It was not their daughter who would be making a sacrifice but he, the devout Catholic. Franz Josef's Austria being a Catholic state, marriages of Catholics to non-Catholics were proscribed by a Concordat. Since there was no question of Mother changing her faith, there was nothing for Father to do but to leave the Church. Once he was no longer in the fold, he could marry Mother quite legally in a registry office. It all sounds perfectly simple, and I wish I could add that they lived happily ever after. But that was not so. In Father's eyes, leaving the Church was a grave sin which he had committed only after long and painful soul-searching—yet I am quite positive that, in taking this drastic way out of his dilemma, although probably never realizing it, he acquired a guilt complex of gigantic proportions. To my mind it was this guilt complex which shaped his aggressive attitudes and eventually materialized in the form of many setbacks, heartbreaks, and complications throughout his life. There is no question but that it accounts for his tragic end.

All my life I have been bothered by a question which Sigmund Freud, who in later years lived only a few doors away from us, could probably have answered for me—namely, whether there is such a phenomenon as a hereditary complex, like asthma, as a psychosomatic complaint coming down from father to son or daughter. From my view it often looked as if my brothers have, at one time or another, exhibited unmistakable symptoms of an inherited guilt complex which made them seemingly invite disaster on the brink of triumph very much as if Sir John Hunt were to twist his leg deliberately just before reaching the summit of the Himalayas. I, for one, have searched in vain—torturing myself with ruthless autoanalysis in all critical situations—for a rational explanation of my failures (under the sum total of which

I groan) other than a subconscious blockage that rises like the ugly Berlin Wall between me and fulfillment.

By this I do not mean that life has been one long succession of missed opportunities. Not at all. I have enjoyed long periods of happiness and have been elated about all manner of achievements which have received a measure of recognition. "Recognition" is the operative word, for, frankly, I have had little satisfaction from anything without the crowning glory of acclaim. Whether it fed a basic feeling of insecurity or a very old-fashioned inferiority complex I am not sure, but a seemingly insignificant incident in my boyhood has furnished me with a conception of happiness I have found rather difficult to live up to.

Every other week a rag-and-bone man used to knock at our door, a pathetic figure of an old man who tried to make a miserable living from paying a few pennies for old clothes and selling them for a few pennies plus. I used to watch him coming down the street, see doors being slammed in his face, observe him haggling over a pair of tattered old pants which an angry housewife would tear from his gnarled hands if he would not or could not pay the right price. As soon as he approached our house I would hurry inside and, invariably successfully, persuade our maid to produce an old jacket or some other garment discarded by one of my brothers. Then I would hand it over to the long-suffering old fellow, grandly refusing whatever puny payment he offered.

Nothing gave me greater pleasure than to see his face light up with joy, hear his sigh of relief that, at long last, he had struck a bargain. I shall never forget how happy he looked on these occasions. I was sure he was happy. But, in the passage of time, I began to look at his kind of happiness as something pitiable, almost contemptible. Already as a boy I said to myself that I never wanted to be happy the way this old man was. The notion has persisted. I always wanted to be *pleasantly* happy, and at every stage I knew exactly *what* happiness I craved. The harsh truth, I fear, is that, the way I look at it, there are class, cultural, even national differences in happiness. I have never envied other people their happiness, because in ninety-nine out of a hundred cases I was sure that their happiness was not for me. Similarly, I have often stubbornly refused to accept happiness of a kind that did not meet with my definite scales of value, however irrelevant they may seem to others.

But when I said I have had little satisfaction—that is, happiness—without acclaim, I did not mean that I have not done some good deeds secretly and stealthily; or that I have not, apparently selflessly, helped a number of people. But it was mostly done in the wholly unworthy spirit of a game that I played with myself and from which I emerged holier-than-I.

Perhaps this is one of the reasons why, in the final analysis, all my successes have carried within themselves the seed of ultimate frustration. Admitting to a certain weakness for English clichés—to be conversant with them has often reassured me about my command of colloquial English—I cannot, in this context, keep out of my mind the old saying that "all's well that ends well." It is not a sentiment I can honestly share. In my instance the opposite is true. Throughout my life all was well, but nothing has ever ended well. My parents, affairs of the heart, friendships, professional efforts, long-term plans were all intermittently going great guns. None has ended well.

It was often possible to diagnose my trouble as ambition outstripping ability, which is one of human nature's most soul-destroying, not to say murderous, weaknesses. Targets, set too high, became unattainable, and disillusionment temporarily corroded ambition, led to indifference, laziness, apathy, and lethargy (or alternatively to aggressiveness, bred by inadequacy). Moral and mental deterioration set in, and the temptation to look for "the easy way out" became irresistible. Lack of imagination (from which I have never suffered) in the absence of a strong character (of which I cannot boast) might have been a great help in steering a safe course between nondefeatist contentment with my "place in society" and the pitfalls of ambition.

Although naval metaphors do not come naturally to me, I have, after almost every defeat, thought of myself as a ship's captain prepared to go down with my hopes rather than try to *corriger la fortune,* as the French so charmingly circumscribe cheating. This has been my main struggle all through life, and I am sure that it is a problem I have inherited. Of course I have taken the easy way out on innumerable occasions; of course I have cheated in almost every department of life. The best that

I can say of myself is that I have tried not to. I am not now speaking of a guilty conscience—which I have also, in many respects—the primary penalty for lapses from the straight and narrow path, but a natural and healthy reaction, not to be confused with a psychological defect. But feelings of guilt can persist long after a sin has been truly expiated or a misdemeanor justly punished.

Father, in fact, having married Mother at a hurried, almost furtive registry-office ceremony, proceeded to do something about the sin he had committed. Having abandoned the Church but not lost his faith, he looked for guidance concerning the best way to resolve his painful state—outside the protective mantle of Grace. Redemption, he was advised, could lie in only one direction: if he truly repented, he could find forgiveness, which should lead him back to the Church. There was nothing Father wished more than to be readmitted. The penance imposed on him was a series of pilgrimages to Rome to visit seven churches in seven consecutive years. In retrospect it seems that he never really repented the sin of marrying when he did, nor was this particular penance anything but sheer pleasure in intallments. Thus he never, in his own stern judgment, absolved himself from guilt.

"Wer nie sein Brot mit Tränen ass,
Wer nie die kummervollen Nächte
An seinem Bette weinend sass,
Der kennt euch nicht, ihr himmlischen Mächte.

"Ihr ruft ins Leben ihn hinein,
Ihr lasst den Armen schuldig werden—
Dann überlasst ihr ihn der Pein.
Denn alle Schuld rächt sich auf Erden." *

    * Who never ate his bread in sorrow,
     Who never spent the darksome hours
     Weeping and watching for the morrow
     He knows ye not, ye heavenly Powers.

     You let him shoulder guilt within,
     To you the wretched owes his birth,
     You leave him to the pangs of sin,
     For all guilt is avenged on earth.
       —GOETHE: "Wilhelm Meister's Apprenticeship"

How often Father recited these lines in my presence! I could sense the deeper meaning they held for him; somehow he handed it down to me. Hard work drowned the pangs of his conscience. He advanced himself rapidly as an advocate, made money, fathered four sons, dutifully traveling to Rome summer after summer—seven times. His reward was readmission to the Catholic Church. Was he content? Happy, yes; content, no. No sooner had he attained his objective than he squared up to wresting a further concession from the ecclesiastical authorities. Why, he asked, could his marriage not be legitimized to the satisfaction of the Church? Why should he not be married for a second time in church, even to a woman of the Jewish faith? A long search through every nook and cranny of Canonic Law revealed precedents. The Church relented. Father received a special Papal dispensation to marry his wife in church. That is how my parents' unusual marriage, attended by their four sons, came to be solemnized in the Schottenkirche in Vienna.

2 | *1906 and All That*

*A*ntoine Casanova, an impressively moustachioed, practically bald, but very good-looking and endearing young Frenchman, Corsica-born and related to all the two hundred Casanovas in his native village, came to join the Frischauer household for a short visit in 1904 and stayed as Mother's confidant and the boys' teacher and friend for the next ten years.

On the late afternoon of September 8, 1906, a Catholic holiday commemorating the birth of Mary, "Casa," as the family called him, was asked to take the four young Frischauers to the circus—but quickly. For weeks they had been pestering him to take them. That evening none of them wanted to go, each for a different reason, but Father's instructions were firm, and they went. Years later, Casa told me how the turbulent four, noisily competing for attention with the clowns, had made a thorough nuisance of themselves. It was 10:00 P.M. before they were permitted to return home. By that time—at 8:45 P.M. to be exact—I had been born.

Not until I came to write these lines did it occur to me to investigate the kind of world into which I was thus cast. The result was disappointing. Because of the Liberal victory it was an exciting year for students of British politics. An earthquake and

24

fire almost completely destroyed the city of San Francisco. Disarmament was the topic of a conference in the Hague which was promptly wrecked by—who else?—the Germans. France was in the throes of a virulent nationalist revival—*plus ça change*. . . . Nearer home—nearer, that is, to where I was born—the Hungarian Liberal Party failed to win office; they had tried to win the election honestly, an unheard-of thing in these days. Vienna was concerned with the language problem, a permanent preoccupation in the multinational Habsburg monarchy.

Father took a lively interest in current affairs and was a voracious newspaper reader. All these subjects were bound to give rise to heated discussions, because the virtue of dispassionate objectivity of which the British are so proud was not practiced where I come from. Father's views, forcefully expressed, seemed to have been most anarchic. He was against the government—not the monarchy—against Germany, against the Hungarians, the Bohemians, and the Bosnians, the inhabitants of Bosnia and Herzegovina which Austria had annexed in 1908.

At the time, the family occupied a magnificent residence in the Renngasse, Vienna One, very upper-middle class, perhaps even a little above our station. It had two entrances, one of them "for servants and tradesmen only," which was rare for a Vienna apartment, and a four-window dining room, which Mother regarded as an indispensable prerequisite of gracious living. The twenty-two-room apartment covered the whole mezzanine of a rather stylish house just across the road from the Schottenkirche. The *palais* next door belonged to the Counts of Schönborn-Buchheim, an ancient Austro-Bohemian family.

The dining table for twelve was made of carved oak to a special design and, surprisingly, convertible into a full-size billiard table. As the feudal era passed and we upper bourgeois retreated from our old standards, the magnificent table, like a loyal retainer, accompanied us to our two next, progressively less grandiose, apartments. Today, fifty-odd years later, I still have the smell of the oak-and-leather chairs in my nostrils, and remember the proud and pleasurable first occasion on which I was allowed to join the grown-ups at the table and sit on one of the chairs.

In most of the rooms one's feet sank deeply into luscious and colorful Persian carpets of extraordinary size. (All Vienna knew Father had received them in lieu of payment for carrying out some legal transactions on behalf of the Turkish grand vizier— together with the hideous-decorative octagonal coffee table, an ebony-and-mother-of-pearl mosaic affair which was too precious to be exposed to coffee stains and was never used.) Of the im- maculately polished, dangerously slippery parquet floor, only a fringe was left visible. Once a month the carpets were cleaned; they were sprinkled with sauerkraut, several kilos of it, which, having mysteriously absorbed the dirt, was then vigorously brushed off. There were scores of huge deep easy chairs, each big enough to accommodate Father's heavy frame.

Unless you can keep it up all your life—and I could not— it is no great asset to be born into such a solid-oak, deep-pile- carpet, luxuriously comfortable environment as I was, after an interval of eight years, the fifth son of the strangely assorted but obviously happily double-married *Herr und Frau* Dr. Otto Frischauer. Apart from Mother, Father, the boys, and Casanova, the household included "Tante Kati," my father's maiden aunt, a source of constant irritation to everyone except me. Kati treated Mother, who gave her shelter, as an intruder into the Frischauer family, and Mother reproached Kati for, among other things, having taught me to play poker before I had reached the age of five. *Alte* Anna, tiny, withered, and toothless, had joined the menage as my eldest brother's nurse some fourteen years earlier, and dominated the domestics like a primitive but benevolent matriarch. Aline, a busty nurse of doubtful French antecedents and morals, taught my elder brothers—God knows what. Frau Koch, the cook with the "imperial" husband; two kitchen maids and a tolerably handsome parlor maid (a new one every other year); and Alfons, the chauffeur to go with an early Mercedes motorcar, an important status symbol, the first to be seen in the streets of Vienna, made up the balance of the inmates. Various domestics flitted across the scene, which from time to time was enlivened by Father's female secretary, in these days also a glamorous and exciting rarity of whose attractions Father and chauffeur seemed equally aware; and then there was a constantly changing population of my brothers' school friends, some of whom either did not have a home of their own, or, if they did, seemed to like ours better.

The room which served as my nursery was the one farthest removed from the quarters of the grown-ups. It overlooked the courtyard around which Vienna apartments were invariably built. In an otherwise nonconformist home Father shared the contemporary notion that children should be seen but not heard, and preferably not seen often, and he refused to take an interest in his boys before they had reached the walkie-talkie stage, after which he quickly made up for lost time. Not very successfully, I affected a similar lack of interest when my own child was born; by the time my grandchild appeared on the scene I tried but could no longer sustain the act.

Aline moved into the nursery and was a magnet which irresistibly attracted my elder brothers and their friends. The new baby gave them a pretext for hanging around the most accommodating female in the house. Too young to be eligible for such fun and games, my brother Paul's frequent visits, I gather, had a different purpose. He used great cunning and ingenuity to distract Aline's attention and find a direct, unimpeded approach to my bottom, which he pinched as hard as the protective armor of the cumbersome swaddling clothes permitted. Only Brother Fritz is said to have displayed genuine signs of affection for the new baby (and continued to do so, heartily reciprocated, throughout his life).

Arrangements for me to be christened at the Schottenkirche were made promptly to comply with Father's undertaking to bring up all the male issue of his marriage in the Roman Catholic faith. Compulsion was not really necessary; all my brothers had been christened at birth, long before Father's second wedding. The ceremony took place twelve days after my birth on September 20th—a date to remember. Refusing to submit, even by implication, to Hitler's race laws, I have always regarded myself as a Roman Catholic, and regretted every time I have—unthinkingly submitting after all—elaborated on my antecedents which have bequeathed me a Jewish countenance.

My godfather was the tall, dignified-looking elderly Count Friedrich Wilhelm Schönborn-Buchheim—alas, not the head of the house who occupied the *palais* next door, but an offbeat member of the distinguished clan who, with Father's professional help, had been feuding with his family in the courts for many years. Not having paid Father a penny for his legal advice, Count Schönborn-Buchheim "settled the account" by honoring me with his patronage. But he did give me the traditional monogrammed gilded-silver spoon, tumbler, and bell in a velvet case which I kept for years in a cupboard, among other knickknacks, until it disappeared from sight.

So did Count Friedrich Wilhelm Schönborn-Buchheim, whom I cannot remember ever having met again. As a young man I valued my association, fleeting but officially registered, with a member of the old Austrian aristocracy, although, as one of my brothers had previously been christened Friedrich (Fritz for short), I took my godfather's names in reverse: Wilhelm Friedrich. Except on official documents (birth-and-christening certificates, passport, and so on) these names have never figured in my life and have always sounded rather remote to me. From the first day to this I have been Willi.

Conscious memories of my childhood are few but vivid. None are of unhappiness, which I have sometimes been tempted to regret because so much seems to have been achieved by men who rose to greatness on the rough stepping-stones of early suffering. A touch of claustrophobia may be due to my having felt a little hemmed in in my baby cot with the sliding barrier. What displeasure I may have experienced the day Aline disappeared must have been compensated by the joy of being put in Fanny's charge. Ah, Fanny! Fanny was a Polish girl, well built, with a squat face, a white spotless skin, a broad smile revealing two rows of big, gleaming, even teeth, capable hands—I remember her firm safe grip—and a smell all of her own which must have been the *dernier cri* in eau-de-Cologne. Fanny was closer to me than Mother, whose sweet face, framed in a wide-brimmed, flower-decked hat, used to appear fleetingly on my horizon, shedding a warm glow. Father does not figure at all.

Fanny took me for long walks along the Danube Canal, and

on rare, exquisite occasions gave up her free Sundays—well, not quite—to take me along on her assignations with a certain Herr Salzer, a most impressive gentleman with a round, smooth piggy face, a small moustache, pudgy hands with innumerable rings, and a coat with a fur collar like Father's. He was a prosperous shopkeeper with lecherous eyes, and he blushed whenever they rested on Fanny's ample form. There was something about his approach which, in later years, I came to associate mistakenly with love until it dawned on me that this must have been the first occasion in my life when I came face to red face with sex. In the meantime, I took it that, for Herr Salzer, the road to Fanny's heart—at least on Sundays—led through the Prater, Vienna's Coney Island, where I had a marvelous and usefully distracting time. Mother told me that Herr Salzer had been anxious to marry Fanny but that she could not bear to leave me. Bless her! When she did leave me it was too late. By that time Herr Salzer was married. According to a less romantic version circulated by my brothers, Herr Salzer had already been married while playing fast-and-loose with Fanny who, when she found out, not only left Salzer, naturally, but also our employ, me, and Vienna.

There was an interregnum then, during which, by time-honored practice, *alte* Anna took over, helped to dress me and put me to bed, gave me my meals, and took me out for long afternoon walks in wintry Vienna during which she firmly rebuffed the daily commiseration (or, as the case may be, angry protest) from some passersby who frequently stopped us in the street to ask whether I was not feeling cold; for reasons which have remained obscure, Father insisted that I, like my brothers before me, should wear ankle socks even in winter when the temperature remained well below zero for months. I never did feel the cold in my legs and could not understand what the commotion was all about. Come to think of it, strangers must have taken an inordinate interest in me, because they also used to comment when they saw me talking—as I did every day—to the imposingly tall and bearded, uniformed and gold-braided doorman of the Rothschild bank, which faced our house in the Renngasse; "Clever boy" they used to say, or something to that effect, "you have chosen your parents well!" From my familiarity with the doorkeeper, whom I adored, they assumed that I was one of the Rothschild children.

For the summer months we moved to our villa in Pötzleins-dorf on the outskirts of Vienna, where my earliest companions were two gigantic, good-tempered and mild-mannered but tre-mendously powerful St. Bernard dogs, Moench and Hektor. On the rare occasions when I left the big garden to walk out into the road, the dogs positioned themselves so as to protect me on both sides—I assume against the traffic, except that there was not much traffic in Pötzleinsdorf in those days. It was from Pötzleins-dorf that I was first taken to school, a memorable day of crisis. The school, Schwarzwald's, was private and coeducational, and being a superior and self-assured young fellow, I cannot remem-ber any pangs of fear or apprehension the first day I was left alone there. But no sooner had I been received in the new com-munity than I felt that there was something distinctly strange about the establishment. I had come dressed as usual in a smart velvet dress, with a three-inch-wide patent-leather belt, which all but covered the very short, short velvet pants underneath. My thick, obstreperous reddish-golden hair which grew well below my ears was kept out of my eye by means of a biggish barrette.

"Aren't you a sweet little girl!" said the teacher, patting my hand, and pulling me fondly and reassuringly toward her. I thought the woman was odd, but said nothing. All morning it was "little girl" this and "little girl" that whenever anyone talked to me. Mother, with Alfons, the chauffeur, was there to meet me when I left school at 1:00 P.M. The car took us quickly back home where a gathering of family, friends, and servants was waiting to bombard me with questions. Had I been good on my first day at school? "Yes," I said a little tearfully, and added, so as to make my point quite clear, "Teacher said I was a very good little girl."

"A very good—what?"

I repeated truthfully what the teacher had said. Everyone thought it was very funny, but Alfons, who took me to school next morning and pointed out to the teacher that, good or bad, I was *not* a little girl.

Worse was to come. The curriculum that morning included an hour's religious instruction, and presently my group was divided into an overwhelming majority—Roman Catholics—and a small minority of Jews. They did not elicit any information from me, just looked me over carefully and put me among the Jews. An awe-inspiring instructor taught us to pray, handing little skullcaps to me and the other boys. I spent a busy hour and quite enjoyed myself. Back home, once more subjected to a cross-examination about the morning's proceedings, the story of the skullcap was extracted from me. It caused another explosion of laughter. Frankly, I have never taken school very seriously since. But there remained with me a vague feeling of some incongruity somewhere. I was a boy who looked like a girl, a Catholic who was taken for a Jew. Ambiguities like this, real or imagined, have dogged me most of my life.

Although I seem to recall an undertone of excitement when we first heard the news of Archduke Franz Ferdinand's assassination at Sarajevo, the First World War, as far as I was concerned, came in like a lamb. Casa disappeared, and the next I heard from him was a postcard with his picture—a big square beard accompanying the familiar moustache—which he sent me from a German camp where he was being held as a French prisoner of war. He had had a brief and singularly unsuccessful war, and returned to Vienna as soon as it was over, resplendent in a French officer's uniform, to stay on for some time as a member of the Allied Commission which was to draw the new frontier between Austria and Hungary. The war and the long separation had not altered our mutual affection. When, at the age of thirteen, I was confirmed in St. Stephen's Cathedral, Casa was by my side. Fortified by his French francs, I was one of the few boys in this arid postwar period able to afford the traditional confirmation fiacre ride to the Prater.

But back to the outbreak of war, which did not find the Frischauers as a family wholly unprepared. Brother Leo had already joined the k.-u.-k. (*kaiserlich-und-königliche*) Hoch-und-Deutschmeister Infantrie Regiment No. 4., the notoriously famous Vienna house regiment as a "one-year" national-service conscript (early school-leavers had to serve three years) a few

months before Sarajevo. My brother's company had a reputation
as a refuge for some of Vienna's worst malingerers and upper-
class goldbricks—a real imperial Sergeant Bilko outfit. Slouching
up the long garden path toward the villa in a uniform that was
too big for him, his belt loose, his bootlaces untied, Leo was the
most unmartial soldier I ever encountered. Yet I recall running
to meet him halfway and embracing him, intrigued by his strange
appearance but oblivious of his embarrassment, happy that a
brother of mine—even though a big brother who was fairly distant—should wear a uniform which, in my eyes, put him on a
par with my beloved Rothschild doorman.

Leo was soon commissioned (that went without saying for a
young gentleman of his background), transferred to the quarter-
master branch, and posted to a depot in Poland a couple of
hundred miles from the front line, where the Russian and Austrian armies faced each other. Every other month members of
his unit coming to Vienna on leave called at our home carrying
rucksacks full of lard, sides of smoked pork, sacks of flour, rice,
and mountains of other foodstuffs which were beginning to be
increasingly scarce at home. Among the men in my brother's
unit it was, I think, understood that the surest way to get leave
was to volunteer for such a back-breaking food-bearing mission.
On one occasion Leo accompanied two of his heavily laden emissaries. We were overjoyed to see him so unexpectedly. It turned
out that he had hastily retreated to Vienna because the Russians
had been shelling a position some 150 miles east of his depot. Leo
had decided that the war was getting too uncomfortably close
for a man of peace like him.

Soon it was Edi's turn to join the imperial colors—though
"joining" is, perhaps, not the best word in this context. Edi, a
brilliant student of law and mathematics, with a sharp and acute
brain, soon developed an aggressive antipathy against his superior
officers—idiots, in his view, who were entitled only by the accident of rank to order a man of his superior intelligence about.
His antipathy inevitably developed into insubordination. As a
boy, whenever I heard Edi's name mentioned, it was in connection with some military offense that had just earned him another
confinement to barracks, if not worse. Twice he missed his draft

to the front, then became seriously ill and underwent an operation. There was consternation at home when it was learned that Edi, barely recovering, had made a most forceful pass at his attractive nurse, who does not seem to have been entirely unresponsive. A high-ranking medical officer making an unexpected spot check of the military hospital had found Edi in bed—which was not surprising, so shortly after his operation—but with the nurse, which *was* rather unusual.

Fritz followed his two elder brothers into the army, became a brisk, efficient, even enthusiastic officer and soon found himself in action at the head of a company of his Hungarian regiment. On the Russian front his batman on one occasion saved his life in the nick of time when the deep trench in which they spent the night collapsed under Russian fire without Fritz waking up—he was always a heavy sleeper. Both were decorated. From the Italian front, to which he was transferred, Fritz returned with another medal earned for taking nearly a thousand prisoners single-handed; the Italians were hungry, and anxious to eat even at the price of captivity. Before his next combat assignment, and while nursing an injured leg, ever-dutiful Fritz insisted on doing a job, and was appointed temporary military commandant of a big army hospital in Vienna.

On taking up his new duty, Major Frischauer, hobbling with the aid of a stick, inspected his new domain, including the old wooden barracks which served as a detention center for military patients who had committed an offense. Pointing his torch at a miserable figure lounging on a bundle of straw in a dark corner of the detention barrack, Major Frischauer ordered the man to rise and stand to attention. Blinking into the glare of the flashlight, the ailing prisoner rapped out a few waspish words which left no doubt as to his identity: "It's me! Do you hear? Get me out of here at once or I'll box your ears! Understand?" The prisoner, Private Edi, was talking to his younger brother, Major Fritz.

It was but a minor episode in Edi's war. Eventually, Uncle Ernst Klebinder, Mother's brother, persuaded the army's chief medical officer in Vienna to help get Edi out of his misery. Edi was called before a medical board; but, although his discharge from the army was a carefully prearranged, foregone conclusion, he insulted his examiners in such outrageous fashion that they had no choice but to deal with him according to regulations— either to punish him severely (which would have meant military prison) or to declare him mentally unbalanced. Out of the kindness of their hearts—and to oblige Uncle—the board sent him to Steinhof, Vienna's famous mental hospital, where he spent the next few months happily studying for his graduation. He was soon released and was one of the first postwar students to graduate from Vienna University *summa cum laude*.

By the time he was sixteen, Paul, the youngest of my brothers, preferred the army to school or, perhaps, to the impending exams, and volunteered. He was quickly commissioned in a good artillery regiment and sent to the top of a mountain to watch out for approaching Italians who never came. As far as I remember, he returned to Vienna only to cadge money to supplement his meager pay. What he did with all this money on that mountain top has forever remained a mystery to me. Although his health was undermined by the rigors of conditions on the mountain, Paul did not take the war too seriously—I think. I was made to write to him "to the front," and dutifully put down my innermost thoughts: How nice it was that he could no longer lock me up in our dark attic, or for that matter smack my bottom at the slightest, or even without, provocation. He answered with a charming poem in which he explained that beatings were a good preparation for such hardships as he was exposed to now and that a dark attic was not half so bad as the deep, dark forest in which he had spent the previous night; in spite of the attic and the beatings, he said, he was deeply fond of me.

The first inconvenience the war caused me was due to an accident: I lost the five-kronen piece I had been given to buy a patriotic war badge. I never dared to tell Mother, and was, for many months, the only boy in school without the wretched thing pinned to my lapel. Teacher made no secret of her conviction that my father was a dangerous revolutionary who opposed the war and who deliberately refused to let his poor little boy have a badge. I was the Odd Man Out at school when —the war dragging on much longer than anybody had expected

—we gave up the car and the Renngasse and moved to Pötzleinsdorf, which became our only home. Transferred to a local school, I left Schwarzwald's without regrets. I had not made any friends and cannot remember any of my schoolmates except for one pretty little slip of a girl with whom, some fifteen years later, I renewed acquaintance in the shape of a wild one-night affair.

Our garden in Pötzleinsdorf was the biggest and, thanks to Herr Schitnik, the gardener, the best tended for miles around, even though we were soon forced to grow potatoes in what used to be beautiful big flowerbeds. The orchard behind the villa was a boy's paradise in which I and my retinue, the toughest kids in the district, were allowed to climb and ravage as many fruit trees—plums, apples, pears, peaches, apricots—as our hearts desired, with only the gentlest injunction to leave enough raspberries on the bushes for Father's daily ration.

Still, as evening fell, we went on raiding expeditions into our neighbors' much smaller and less fertile gardens to pick all the forbidden fruit we could lay our hands on. What made me take part in these exploits was, I think, mainly a subconscious urge to conquer fear—and I was terribly afraid. Inevitably we were caught and received a good hiding from one of our victims. Relieved that he did not tell our parents, we gave up the dangerous sport. What I had done, incidentally, was very much a case of the rich robbing the poor, a foretaste of the kind of society into which I grew up.

I did steal once again, but that was the only other criminal act I ever committed. When Uncle Ernst, at the time a high-ranking dollar-a-year kind of wartime civil servant at the Vienna Ministry of Food, launched an organization, sponsored by Emperor Charles, to aid undernourished children, I begged him to take two of my underprivileged schoolmates under his wing— my first attempt at influence peddling. Uncle included the boys in a party of thirty who were sent on a free four-week summer holiday to a farm in Aspern, near Vienna, where Austria's Archduke Charles had defeated Napoleon in 1809. But when I complained with childish logic that I would thus be parted from my two best friends during the long school holidays, Ernst

Klebinder arranged for me to join the party as the personal guest of the hospitable farmer.

Our days were spent gathering fruit, helping with the harvest and feeding the animals. I slept with my friends in the boys' dormitory and took my meals with all the other boys and girls, who regarded me as one of them. In the evenings we roamed over the estate, and a few of us soon discovered a big, apparently disused, barn which was stacked with packing cases. The combined efforts of half-a-dozen determined eleven-year-olds succeeded in forcing open one of the cases which, to our delight, we found to contain a veritable treasure trove of strange and wondrous things. Each of us selected what took his fancy. I chose a most attractive old Chinese parasol from which I immediately ripped off the spokes and the silk, retaining only the smooth, long stick with the ivory handle, and also a French cookery book, while others chose silk scarves, paperweights, finely carved inkstands, and other small *objets d'art*. Later it turned out that the cases were enemy property: the farmer was storing them for a Frenchman who had had to leave Austria hurriedly at the outbreak of war. All that the proceeds of my crime added up to was a bad conscience. I lost the stick but did not get rid of the sour conscience for a long time—or, I confess, of the French cookery book which, as time went by, I wrapped in an impenetrable web of lies. It accompanied me through life as an inseparable companion to which I was shackled by chains of guilt. It was a great relief when I lost it while moving house some years ago.

This adventure alone would have imprinted the summer of 1917 on my memory. But there was something else I am unlikely to forget. I fell in love. Now, I must admit to something of a sex life before I was eleven. Some time earlier at Pötzleinsdorf, a friend, three or four years older, had lured me into a practice of regular but most unwelcome and embarrassing wrestling matches in the nude which I later—many years later—diagnosed as having had strong sexual, or rather homosexual, connotations on his part. With him I had also furtively discussed such delicate matters as the pubic hair of a girl we had seen and which had intrigued us more than the notorious little difference between her and us. Finally, though less animalistically, during a winter holiday with Mother in the Austrian Alps when I was about eight, I had become attached to an older girl without any clear understanding of what drew me to her with such a painful, confusing compulsion, although my attentions were obviously unwelcome to her.

But among the girls in Aspern was a spindly, rather undistinguished little thing about twelve years of age, with long brown plaits, slightly protruding eyes, and thin legs, whose simple cotton dress had a pleasant solid smell of home laundering. I regarded her as the most wonderful and precious creature in the world. I loved her. I am positive I did. I said so. She was my first love. But I did not know what to do about it. I cannot imagine what attracted me to her (I often think back to that occasion when, now, observing infatuated couples, I ask myself what they see in each other), but it was certainly not sex.

On the contrary, I am quite certain it was sex that made me drift away from her, although I continued to see her when we returned to Vienna. I was going through a painful period in my puberty when—in the school which I joined as soon as the family moved from Pötzleinsdorf back to town—I became aware of the existence of a mysterious, bewildering, puzzling, indefinite and undefinable boy-and-girl activity of which I had not had a hint before. I could not fully fathom what it was all about, although, floating through the conversation of my new schoolmates, I discerned a word denoting—I did not know what. It has a vulgar ring; it made those who said it and those who heard it blush, as I remembered Fanny's Herr Salzer blushing. It tended to drive tears into my eyes because I was consumed with curiosity and yet afraid to ask—afraid, perhaps, of finding out and having a difficult, intractable dimension added to my life.

My perplexity was so apparent that Mother delegated Fritz, the brother who was closest to me, to tell me about the birds and the bees—except that nobody in my family thought of that simple way of getting round the awkward subject. Instead, Fritz, spent an hour or so dragging the embarrassing word from my lips before going on to explain the physical difference between boys and girls. Although I had been anatomically aware for some time, what he told me suddenly invested everything with meaning—and purpose.

Yes, purpose, for no sooner had the mist of uncertainty lifted from the subject than articulate physical desire replaced the indefinite yearnings of childhood. I felt as if I had grown up, and knew now what I wanted. I was not thirteen yet, but there was no longer any doubt in my mind about what I owed to my new status. I knew what I wanted in concrete terms—in the shape, in fact, of one or another of the girls whom I passed every morning on my way to school as they walked to their own school in the opposite direction. I joined forces with another boy in a similar predicament who, however, was taller, better looking, smoother in manner, and generally more suave than I. His name was Franz. He was slim, with fair wavy hair, and, I thought, very wise. Franz was also more forward than I, and, in the event, made the first tactical move toward our objective. He pin-pointed two girls whom we had observed passing the same spot at the same time every morning, at 7:50 A.M., ten minutes before the start of our first lesson. We rehearsed positioning ourselves in such a way as to obstruct the girls' path on The Day. Having long noticed our posturing and meaningful glances, the girls willingly fell in with our scheme; when they found us all but barring their way they stopped briefly, smiled provocatively, and brushed past us, coming deliberately close.

That morning, we reached school five minutes late, which schoolmates and teacher thought responsible for our red faces and panting confusion. With brief intervals, caused by bad timing and other inadvertencies, we repeated the maneuver on three or four more mornings, by which time we were on speaking terms with the girls, Elli and Geli, who turned out to be the two most precocious little bitches in the whole of Vienna. They were approaching fourteen and the end of their schooldays, and determined to enter adult life fully equipped with the sort of knowledge and experience that no school provided in those days. Came the summer when, most fortuitously, I was unable to join my family for the holidays because I had flunked my exams and was due to sit them again in September. I was left at home in the care of Gustav, our new young manservant; a grumpy cook, and a roly-poly student tutor who had been engaged to supervise my studies, but was in an embarrassing position because, unthinkingly, Mother had entrusted me with the money for his wages, which I paid him at the end of each week. I ruthlessly exploited my advantage as paymaster to ease my lot as pupil.

I promptly fell in love with Elli, the more attractive of the girls (I still have her photograph). But it was my young friend, *der schöne Franz*, who eventually conquered her affections, and I who was left to hold the hand of Geli, who also had her charms. I had confided my designs on Elli to my tutor, who, anxious to ingratiate himself with me, was still working on an acrostic embodying her name while I was laying siege to Geli. During these hot and humid summer days Gustav closed his eyes to my new paramour's almost daily visits to the apartment. The preliminaries, extending over several weeks, were exciting beyond my wildest fantasies. But consummation threatened me like Scylla and Charybdis; fear of a situation which I might find myself incapable of handling "like a man" competed with an urge which became less manageable every day.

I lived through hell and heaven every twenty-four hours of this torrid Vienna summer, pleading, fighting, shrinking back, advancing roughly, apologizing tenderly, wanting to—and wanting not to—making another clumsy attempt and giving up in despair until, one evening, after a brief, inconclusive skirmish, Geli ordered me out of the room and told me to wait until she called. Presently I heard my name faintly through the door. Responding, I found Geli lying on the couch, her head buried in her arms. I was half numb with apprehension. On the floor was a neat pair of white pants: I have always thought of it as Geli striking her flag. Ten minutes later—not without great tribulation and a pounding heart—I was a man.

After my baptism of sex, I reverted to preoccupations more congenial for a boy of my age. Two years must have elapsed before another girl made an impression on me or I on her. Her name was Gretchen, and our association soon moved toward a Faustian climax. Most of my free time was devoted to swimming and playing water polo, which I took very seriously, seeming to have a natural aptitude for the sport. Owing to my stamina and long hours of back-breaking training sessions, I had become one of Vienna's leading boy swimmers. Gretchen was our German trainer's niece, and she was drawn toward one of her uncle's most promising pupils. Our meetings, however, were furtive affairs because our kind of association, not being conducive to my prospects in the forthcoming competitions, would surely not be encouraged—least of all by Gretchen's uncle. Our hole-in-the-corner friendship, reduced to late night meetings under porches in dark streets, stoked passions which did not find release until, the following winter, we joined a small party of youngsters from the club for a week's skiing excursion at Mariazell.

Out of her uncle's reach, Gretchen's resistance collapsed, and the inevitable happened. And what happened produced the inevitable result. I was barely fifteen and about to become a father. I did not think of it in such solemn terms—I mean, it was not like real fatherhood which, when it came legitimately later in my life, made me reach for a cigar. At fifteen I was, on the contrary, calm, sophisticated, prematured by impressions gained on the fringe of the rather progressive adult talk and ideas in the circle of my family and their friends. My main thought was how to get rid of "it," but, although I was well aware that there was a way out, I did not know where and how to find it.

A way out . . . I had, in fact, always persuaded myself that there was a way out of every predicament, however desperate; that, to put it into much-quoted Austrian terms, a situation could be hopeless but still not be serious; that—to use a contemporary cliché—as one door closes another opens. My youthful philosophy, which the passage of years has since reinforced, was already clearly formulated. I was convinced that, in the event, nothing was ever so bad as I had feared, and nothing so good as I had hoped. There, then, I was saddled—as I felt, unkindly—with the problem of this girl's condition, and my reaction was not to extricate myself from the situation but to regard it as a challenge to be met. (I have long since discarded this expression and am suspicious of those who use it.)

Like most middle-class Viennese, though a little early in life, I had already acquired the coffeehouse habit. Every Viennese had two abodes, his home and his café, a social phenomenon which can be traced back to 1683 when, the Turkish siege of Vienna having been broken and Sultan Suleiman put to flight, a man by the name of Franz Georg Kolschitzky found a sack of coffee beans and a pot of still-steaming coffee in the sultan's tent, and, recognizing the potentialities of his strange spoils of war, opened the first coffeehouse and introduced the delights of caffein to Vienna, whence it quickly spread to the Western world. Vienna, in my time, was a city of coffeehouses—big ones, small ones, luxurious ones, shabby ones, coffeehouses for suburbanites and for city slickers, for artists and for phillistines, for lone wolves and for loving couples.

Coffee was and still is served in a dozen different ways, color and shade being judged by connoisseurs as art experts view old masters, and giving as much rise to disputes. Café waiters were friends, informants, confidants, and moneylenders; many of them transferred their patronage from father to son or from older to younger brother, as in my case (the amount of money I have at various times owed to a long line of splendid, generous, long-suffering waiters is prodigious). Stacks of daily newspapers were available to the clientele, stimulating political argument and perambulations from table to table but also creating angry exchanges between habitual horders and news-hungry customers waiting for a particular sheet. We ate, drank, read, played cards, chess, dominoes or took a nap in a café, where the atmosphere was that of a social club rather than of a commercial enterprise bent on making a profit.

One coffeehouse, for instance, had a customer who arrived at his regular table every afternoon at the stroke of two, gathered up a dozen newspapers which he read diligently until 4:00 P.M. when, leaning his chair against the table, he called the waiter and asked, as if it were the most natural request in the world: "Please keep my table for me—I am just going home for a cup of coffee." A Vienna café used to be a way of life and, in the twenties, if you wanted to do business with a Viennese you did not seek an appointment with him at his office but arranged to meet him in his *Stammkaffee*, his regular café where he would spend all his leisure and many of his working hours as well.

Many famous middle-European intellectuals chose the Café Central in the Herrengasse as their *Stammkaffee*. Within these somber, cheerless, high-ceilinged halls into which little daylight penetrated, Trotsky used to meet his Austrian Socialist comrades, and chess champions like S. G. Tartakower and Emanuel Lasker practiced the infinity of moves with which they dazzled their opponents. The Central was a home away from home for some of the moving spirits of the postwar social revolution which spread from the defeated Central Powers to infect the victors. At tables around me day after day I saw Franz Kafka, destined to die so soon (1924), Franz Werfel, and, at a lower level, Egon Erwin Kisch, the "raving reporter" who created a vogue for international descriptive reporting—these three being Prague's gift to German literature; there were Alfred Polgar, critic and essayist, who carved delicate gems out of the rocky language; Felix Salten, whose *Bambi*, setting out from Vienna, stalked daintily across the globe to reach the peak of "the book-of-the-film" fame; and Egon Friedell, wit, philosopher, and social critic who hurled his powerful body out of a window when the Nazis invaded Vienna in 1938. There were others: delightfully useless, amoral creatures like Anton Kuh, whose biting wit amused the rich men on whom he practiced it; a perennial scrounger (he once asked a wealthy man for a loan of a hundred, received fifty, did not bother to thank him but just asked: "I am not sure—who owes whom fifty now?") and another "Bohemian" who, seeing a fellow scrounger turn up in a pair of riding breeches, exclaimed, "I haven't got a horse either—but I have more of a horse than you."

Gathering in little groups at their regular tables, most mornings between noon and 1:30 P.M., accompanied by vapid but often quite beautiful women and a sprinkling of more formidable female intellectuals (some of whom, like my one-time sister-in-law, Gina Kaus, could also be very attractive), these writers and artists—actors had not as yet been admitted to the exclusive ranks—engaged in verbal combat, bombarding each other with epigrams, sipping their little cups of black coffee in an atmosphere of bad temper and acid, torn between fits of megalomania and bouts of self-deprecation. For better or worse, this little segment of literary life was an integral part of Vienna's charm which survived the collapse of the Habsburg monarchy.

It generated a spirit that quickly fused with progressive thought in the Western world. The strong Jewish element was the spice that flavored the native Austrian wit, and it is no accident that, apart from Alois Musil and, perhaps, Heimito von Doderer, few other contemporary Austrian names have burst their narrow national frontiers to take their place with Oskar Kokoschka's and Gustav Mahler's—but Vienna's contribution to music is a different and undisputed matter. As a way of life all this has now vanished, even though the spiritual progenies of the Viennese interwar intelligentsia have survived in small pockets in New York and Paris, manfully trying to keep, if not a tradition, at least the memory alive. To paraphrase the passage of Goethe from which I have taken my cue:

"The rest who held their music sweet and cherished,
Stray through the world dispersed, or they have perished."

The Frischauers to whose coattails I clung, although as yet without any claim to distinction, were part of this world. Being so young and, literally uneducated, I was not made welcome when I turned up after school and, without much ado, planted myself firmly at one of the three or four tables occupied by my older brothers. They were there every day, although it was only rarely that two of them would join the same party at the same time. The waiter, being on the side of the underdog, brought me a cup of white coffee with a huge dollop of whipped cream, without waiting for anyone to treat me, and charged it to one of my brothers. I just sat there in an intellectual quarantine, impervious to the unspoken rebuffs, my attention—like a spectator's at Wimbledon—following the talk which crossed the table with the speed of lightning, compounded of literary allusions, erotic insinuations, phsychological analyses, critical deprecation of political events at home and abroad, cruel vivisection of people in and out of the news, all with a leitmotiv of finance in relation to every subject.

Perhaps I was, after all, not quite so impervious to my isolation as I pretended, because I soon came to appreciate the most insignificant acknowledgment of my existence even if it were only someone passing me the bread basket. Anyone moving a chair so much as an inch to make it easier for me to squeeze in earned my silent gratitude. One of the intellectual viragoes, a woman twice my age, handsome rather than beautiful, performed such small kindnesses more frequently than any of the others, and I interpreted this as a sign of official recognition. I admired the way in which she deployed her erudition, her nimble wit and mental dexterity to hold her own in conversation, forcing the men to accept her as an equal and provoking them into violent retaliation which threatened to shatter her arguments, whereupon she took evasive action, twisting and turning while retreating behind the protective screen of her femininity and imperceptibly transforming an intellectual argument into a banter between the sexes. Intellect and sex were so closely intertwined —they all slept with one another—that my juvenile curiosity could not but be roused by the atmosphere of promiscuity. My sexual fantasies began to veer toward this woman, a most unlikely partner.

That was the stage I had reached when Gretchen's problem demanded my attention. One day at the Café Central—or was it the Café Herrenhof, which eventually took its place?—before I had consciously made up my mind I found myself for a matter of seconds standing next to this woman, somewhat aside from the main stream of our party, and heard myself saying, "You may be able to help me, and I need help badly." I must have sounded rather desperate, because she frowned and looked acutely concerned. "Come and tell me all about it," she said and, turning to her regular companion, a thin red-haired man, told him: "We have a little problem to discuss, Willi and I. I'll see you later."

Without any ado I told her all about Gretchen's condition. She seemed amused and delighted at the opportunity to help a minor in distress. She asked me to bring Gretchen to her flat the following evening, but as soon as we got there sent me away, telling me to leave the whole thing to her. I was relieved, and persuaded myself that, by establishing this contact, I had done my duty. Gretchen was introduced to one of the many doctors who provided this kind of medical service with the legal safe-guard of a second opinion which confirmed danger to the preg-nant girl's health. The operation was performed, and the whole incident was closed within a week. I never discussed the matter with either Gretchen or our guardian angel, who took all the trouble and paid all the bills.

My selfish reaction to the episode was to keep away from Gretchen. I had had a fright which made it impossible for me to resume where I had left off. Anyway, I was young and cal-lous; having had my fun I was impatient to move on. We saw less and less of each other; our friendship withered and, although my intensive training absorbed much of my energy, I was once more on the prowl. But not for long. I had taken to discussing my problems, such as they were, with my Café Central "angel" whom I adored, and if there was no current problem to discuss, I ingeniously made mountains out of molehills so as to sustain her interest in me.

"Angel" had spent a year in London and had a way of sprin-kling her conversation with English expressions. While French influence and fashion were commonplace in our parts, English was not, and I looked upon her as a rare, exclusive "Stone & Blyth" woman (Stone & Blyth being Vienna's English shop), an English cardigan-and-sweater, strong low-heeled-shoes type marooned on the incongruous island of a Vienna coffeehouse. She radiated a breath of the big world and seemed to look down on life as from a great height which made everybody else look small and ordinary.

Within a few weeks I realized that I, on the other hand, ap-pealed to her. A tallish, well-built boy of sixteen was bound to have his uses, and was certainly eligible for a little experiment. Once a week or so I went to see her at her flat where she re-ceived me lying in bed in a darkened room as if she had just awakened from her afternoon nap. She made me sit on the bed beside her, and listened with closed eyes to my ramblings as I tried to dredge one thing after another from the recesses of my bemused mind. Her body seemed to exude a current which kept me aglow. All I could hear was her gentle "hmm, hmm," which sounded like encouragement to keep on talking. I could sense her command to do something . . . but I honestly did not know what. Her leg protruding from below the light coverlet solved the problem, and I touched it, stroked it, moved further afield before drawing back. I had never dared to hope for that, not consciously. It seemed inconceivable! Me and this rare creature, this English lady, this goddess!

For the first time in my life I was deeply unhappy. It was not unrequited love—rather the contrary. For a precocious adolescent like me it was an unusual situation. I consulted Fritz, who was quite firm with his advice. It was: "Be a man, and all your troubles will vanish." With his words in mind I decided to pull my goddess from her pedestal. I gave up my reticence and, the next time that opportunity presented itself, went boldly to the attack. How right Fritz had been! It was a splendid adventure unlike anything I could possibly have anticipated. I was thrilled and grateful. But the spell was broken. What remained, however, was an inclination toward all things English which she implanted in me and which developed into a lifelong love affair with England. That was something else to be grateful to her for.

It may well be that writing without the aid of a diary at my time of life accounts for the memories of my amorous adventures pushing themselves into the foreground. They have remained remarkably clear, although I have failed to rescue many other more important facets of my early life from the fog of oblivion. The end of the war and the revolution that transformed the multinational Habsburg monarchy into a rabble of self-important but economically unviable and politically unstable small states with little to commend themselves except their rabid nationalism did not make a great impression on me at the time. Father took me for a walk along the Ringstrasse to see "history in the making," and we were soon engulfed by a dense crowd of people converging on Parliament, shouting slogans and waving red flags. Father explained that Kaiser Karl had left the country; but, having been an intense Franz Josef fan, my boyish imagination had not caught up with his successor, whose departure did not strike me as a personal loss, as Franz Josef's death had done two years earlier.

Defeat in the war, the upheaval and the collapse of our way of life, came as a great blow to Father. In spite of his contrariness, his whole thinking was wedded to the idea of empire—the Habsburg Empire. It was bound to take years of readjustment before people like him could accept the harsh reality of Austria as a small country of barely six million inhabitants whose views counted for little in international councils. Although I have always regarded myself as much a citizen of the world as a Viennese, I have inherited this sense of loss, and often grappled with the problem of striking a balance between tradition and culture and the inescapable contingencies of *Realpolitik*. It was an ironic twist of fate that I should encounter a similar mood in Britain nearly half a century later.

Necessity lured Father from his orthodox legal practice into the kind of commercial enterprises for which previously he had had nothing but contempt. Among other sidelines he administered a gasworks in Carinthia, which meant that we were separated for many months at a time. I missed our walks through the woods in Pötzleinsdorf, when we would march together to the rhythm of his favorite student songs, his *gaudeamus igitur* ringing out like an atonal fanfare by Schönberg. We recited Schiller's *Glocke*, many of Goethe's poems, classical monologues, Ovid—I owe it to him that there are few situations for which I have not a suitable tag from the classics to toss off. He taught me to love Shakespeare in German, and I have never taken to the English original. He never lectured me about right and wrong in so many words, but told me what he would do—which was always the decent thing—and what he would not do, which, I fear, was often what I did. I went to church with him every Sunday, but chiefly because I knew that after mass he would treat me at one of the many exquisite patisseries near the Stefanskirche where we worshiped.

Had Father been a gypsy I could not have been to many more schools. I was constantly on the move because, come the end of term and examinations, I was restless, obstreperous, insufferable, the *consilium abeundi* constantly hanging over my head.

Although reluctant to give in to my understandable desire to get away, Father usually exploited the teaching staff's determination to get rid of me and bartered my passage into the next grade for a promise to remove me to another school. Yet I do not look back on my schooldays with any strong revulsion. From a private school in Grinzing where the new wine grows, I moved to Mariahilf, switched to a Catholic *Gymnasium*, after a particularly sticky patch was exiled to a provincial boarding school (the exception rather than the rule in Austria), and returned to Mariahilf, where at long last I settled down to a tolerable existence and reasonable relations with my teachers (except for a professor of geography who, in the interest of peace, let me read my sports paper in class on condition that I allow him to lecture undisturbed).

For a brief year, like so many Viennese youngsters, I fell under the spell of the Opera, queuing for tickets for the *Steh-parterre*, the standing room behind the stalls, on five days a week from 2:00 P.M. till the beginning of the performance. Before I knew what it involved, I was enrolled in the claque and became an innocent associate of a gang whose leaders manipulated applause according to the amounts they were paid by the players and members of the orchestra. It was plain blackmail. The gang's recruiting technique would have done credit to Al Capone. We youngsters could not hope to survive in the queue without the protection of the gang, and in exchange for their patronage were required to applaud—not when our enthusiasm carried us away but when they gave the signal.

Sometimes we were forced to keep silent after a truly great aria beautifully rendered. On other occasions our applause was timed so as to put the most practiced performer off his stride. It made me uneasy but, like other boys in the same predicament, I had no clear idea of the evil design to which I was lending myself. The situation was getting increasingly oppressive, and I had been pondering for some time how to extricate myself when, one evening, defying my brother Fritz's strict injunction, instead of doing my homework I went to hear *Rigoletto*—for the thirteenth time. I found myself at the back of the standing enclosure and, in order to see the stage, pulled myself onto the high rail along the wall.

Before the lights were dimmed and the overture began, I saw to my horror that Fritz and a girl friend were occupying seats in the stalls no more than a few feet from where I was precariously perched. I could not possibly remain undiscovered for long. The worry spoiled my enjoyment. For once *Rigoletto* seemed to drag on and on. By the time Gilda intoned "Caro nome" I was so uncomfortable that I tried to wriggle out, but the rail snapped under my weight and I crashed to the floor. On that day, I knew, Gilda had been rather generous with the leader of the claque, who had consequently prepared a rousing ovation for her. Instead, here was a barbarous interruption of her tender aria by a member of his own gang! I felt as if all eyes were on me, which was technically impossible because I was on the floor and flat on my back. Worming my way through a forest of legs, I crawled toward the door, got to my feet, and ran for dear life. I never went back to the *Stehparterre*. A few months later the scandal of the claque was exposed, and three of the leaders were indicted and sent to prison for blackmail. I was well out of it. Another phase of my life had come to an end.

Had I, as a boy, analyzed myself as diligently as I did in later years, I would have come to the conclusion sooner that I was unclubbable. I made one desultory attempt to join the Boy Scouts but did not find the company congenial, and drifted away without ever donning their uniform. I put my name down for the Socialist Youth Movement and genuinely tried to be sociable and Socialist during the two or three Sunday outings on which I went with my group, but my political education was further advanced than theirs, and their primitive political jargon pained me almost physically. When, much against my will, I was induced to take part in a protest march against something or other, my face was as red as my new tie, and I felt a complete fool carrying a big painted sign like a sandwich man. My aversion to street demonstrations dates from these days. I have never been in another—not, at least, as a participant.

Only when I was bitten by the sport bug did I learn to subordinate my undisciplined individuality to a common cause. I joined a swimming club, Vienna S.C., but when I told Mother she looked at me uncomprehendingly, and Father shook his head in quiet despair. My people regarded sport—with the exception of tennis—as a plebeian hobby and a waste of time. They talked about *mens sana in corpore sano*, but the idea of a Frischauer wallowing up and down a long pool for hours to perfect his crawl or treading water while practicing ball control seemed utterly ridiculous. At school, teachers showed little more understanding and forcefully expressed their view that, if I had so much time to spare, I had better improve my intellectual capacities, such as they were.

Undeterred by all this opposition, I trained hard and made rapid progress. Had I entered the sports arena in the television age, I would have become a national figure. Even so, whatever was said at home or in school, so many people cheered me as I streaked through the water or bulldozed my way through the opposition in a water-polo game, that I was caught in the trap of my own vanity, and responded with ever greater efforts. I soon made the first team. What I lacked in finesse I made up for in stamina and brute strength. If I did not shine in the first half of a match, I invariably dominated its closing stages, when most of the others were exhausted and I sailed on as strongly as ever.

Before I was sixteen I traveled to Czechoslovakia to play against the famous "Slavia" team; but, as representatives of the Czechs' erstwhile oppressors, we Austrians were not welcome in post-1918 Prague, and were pelted with apples and other missiles until the police came to our rescue. But we won the match. Surprisingly, we also won against "Hellas," Magdeburg, Europe's finest water-polo team—only to be badly beaten in the return match. Johnny Weissmuller, before he became better known as Hollywood's original Tarzan, visited Vienna and played against us. My strength was matched against his speed, and it was a draw. I was already a seasoned campaigner but well aware that a thousand eyes were on me whenever we played. Although, like my teammates, I tried to practice abstinence in the interest of physical fitness, I was ever mindful of the club's girl swimmers who were our most enthusiastic fans and spurred us on to greater glory.

At eighteen I earned my first cap. It should have been a joyous occasion, but instead it created complications. It so happened that Edi, already a successful young lawyer, had been briefed as one of the defense counsel in a big lawsuit with international implications—the Wöllersdorf case involving rackets in obsolescent war material. The case was scheduled to come before the court the very week I was selected to represent my country against the Hungarian national team. My position was that of a fullback. "Two Brothers as International Defenders" announced a newspaper in a caption over our pictures which revealed an unmistakable family resemblance between Edi's grown-up, dignified stare and my own exuberant boyish grin. Father reproached me for having grievously harmed Edi's reputation. Such close relationship with a water-polo player could only damage him in the eyes of both his client and the court, and I was begged to give up this silly infatuation with sport. My teammates were none too happy, either, to see my picture in a newspaper which had hitherto treated our most glorious exploits with contemptuous silence.

In the circumstances it would not have been surprising if, by the time we entered the water for the fateful match, I had lost my nerve. I did not. Instead, as soon as I had my first brush with one of my opponents, I lost my suit. The effect was instantaneous and dramatic. Officially I was never forgiven. The customers enjoyed the incident, but I was held responsible for the publicity which was said to have damaged the reputation of the game.

At this period Vienna—indeed, the whole of Austria and Germany—was in the toils of inflation, but it is only with the wisdom of hindsight that I look back in horror on what was, at the time, a completely novel economic phenomenon. My spontaneous recollection, I am afraid, does not conjure up a picture of unmitigated woe, and I must confess that when I first came face to face with inflation I soon found myself on the wrong side of the catastrophe. I was not yet seventeen when I was already an *Inflationsgewinner*—a profiteer. To be truthful, I did not even know what inflation meant when it was already upon

me. It appeared in the shape of a new young cook (not a bad
shape at all) whom I remember sauntering down our long corridor, hips swinging and wrapped in a fur coat which she had
just bought with the proceeds of her first stock-exchange transaction. The following week she sold the coat at treble the price
and invested the money in even more promising stock which
presently yielded her a small villa not far from our own.

Mother, whose traditional affection for her servants was as
yet untempered by the somewhat harsher postrevolutionary climate, was nevertheless embarrassed when her cook became, so
to speak, her neighbor. It was just as well that the girl soon
gave her notice. But there was no escaping the all-pervading
embarras de richesse. My elder brothers abandoned their legal
careers, obtained a lease on a well-known café (cafés went down
like tenpins), redecorated and reopened it as a bank with a shiny
brass plate. Trade was roaring, and customers crowded the
thickly carpeted *comptoir* waiting for news of foreign exchange
and local share raids.

Like the impoverished Austrian aristocrats who, after the
collapse of the monarchy, had discovered a novel way of making money—buying motorcars on credit and selling them for
cash—Viennese bankers in those days sold with gay abandon,
shares which they did not own, and bought shares which nobody
could supply. A small army of bookkeepers, frayed cuffs framing
spidery fingers, worked overtime (unpaid) recording the rapidly
changing but constantly mounting fortunes. It was a breath-
taking paper chase. On my first visit to the bank I observed the
commissionaire turning up his nose at a 1,000,000-kronen note
with which a naïve stranger tried to tip him. The youthful bankers (my brothers) were lounging in deep armchairs, smoking
big cigars, manipulating several telephones at the same time,
calculating with lightning speed the profits from a sale of lire
against sterling which were quickly exchanged for Swiss francs
to be invested in French shares with instructions to sell at the
end of the week—that is, tomorrow. Not a single Austrian krone,
nor any other currency or share certificates, changed hands, but
within a few days the miraculous profit had materialized—*must*
have materialized, or how could each of my brothers have af-

forded to keep two cars and three expensive girl friends? Which, incidentally, was exactly what Father wanted to know. But the financial fever chart rose ever more rapidly, and he received no answer.

We lived in a world the contemporary English equivalent of which would be a small town where half the inhabitants had won top dividends in the football pools and decided to spend the lot while the other half—well, we'll see about them presently. The turnover of currency and the rise in prices were astronomic. Though I myself never saw the legendary lavatory which was supposed to have been papered with 10,000,000-kronen (or mark) notes, it was not unusual to see people carrying little suitcases crammed with paper money representing their monthly salary, or men whose monthly salary, paid on a Friday, was insufficient to buy a single loaf of bread on the following Monday.

The occasion of my call at the bank was an impending expedition to Göteborg which I was to visit as a member of the Austrian water-polo team. Miraculously, under the circumstances, my banker brothers had obtained some Swedish currency which they had promised to give me as pocket money for the trip. Gratefully, if a little absentmindedly, I stuffed the notes into my pocket, went on the trip, played one game in Magdeburg (and lost), another in Leipzig (and won), crossed from Sassnitz to Trelleborg on the train ferry, quickly settled down among my fellow competitors from all over Europe, came nowhere in the water-polo tournament, and, a few weeks later, sunburned and pleasantly exhausted, returned to Vienna and our inflation. The Swedish currency was still untouched in my pocket.

This is how I became a financial wizard at an age at which the Midas touch had not as yet revealed itself in a Clore or an Onassis. My brothers pounced on my Swedish currency like benevolent vultures and waved their magic wand which transformed it first into millions of kronen, then into securities—or what was described as securities at the time, although nothing was really secure. Their value and my credit rose so quickly that I was able to collect a wad of notes from the bank every afternoon (at my own level the old notion of exchanging money for goods or services still persisted) and I was given the repeated assurance that no matter what amounts I withdrew, my account, like my shadow, would never grow less. The proof of this strange proposition was in the money I drew and spent. It enabled me to press a few million kronen on my current girl friend, whom I accompanied on her daily shopping round in the local market where the rocketing prices of vegetables and meat—an unattainable luxury for ordinary people—drove her to despair. However reluctantly she accepted my help at first, by the second week I had become the sole support of her whole family: father, a minor civil servant, mother, and two brothers.

The money did not soil our young love. No courting couple who ever held hands in a flower garden could have abandoned themselves to romance so completely as we did, walking arm in arm among the cabbages, cauliflowers and kohlrabies, the green salads and the red radishes, or, at the other end of the market, looking longingly into a butcher's shop window until I pulled my love inside to buy her a calf's head very much as a young cavalier might coax his fiancée into Cartier's to buy her a tiara. We spent our weekends traveling on local trains to villages in Lower Austria where I exchanged big bank notes for sets of *Notgeld*, emergency money, such as every council began to issue in most attractive sets.

It was good to be rich. But my new mode of life as a successful speculator, though it impressed my school friends, interfered with my training, and I was dropped from the water-polo team. I decided to try to forget my sorrow with the help of an extra large amount—say, a hundred million—from my account, and called at the bank but was unexpectedly asked by the cashier to "wait a moment." He went backstage, presumably to consult his books, and returned with an expression on his face that was horribly self-explanatory. My brothers were out; they did not seem to attend to their business as enthusiastically as before. The murmur of the waiting crowd had a different inflection—sullen grumbling tones replacing the previous roar of excitement. Hints of deflation and a currency reform began to penetrate even my thick skull.

Father sent me on an unscheduled midterm holiday. As I had no money and no valid explanation to offer her, I welcomed this enforced separation from my girl friend. The long holiday was spent in a village not far from Vienna, yet a million noninflated miles from the kind of self-supporting life I had been leading. There were plenty of fresh vegetables, as much butter and meat as the heart desired, and a gaggle of pretty girls whose strong hands had never touched a bank note. By the time I returned to Vienna, my brothers, rather subdued and without cigars, motorcars, or girl friends, had once more resumed their legal careers. Their noses were deep in their briefs—Father's condition for arranging and financing a settlement with their creditors. Cook, minus fur coat and villa, had asked for, and got, her job back. The bank was closed, to be turned into a café once more. I never drew another million in my life.

3 | *Women All the Way*

On the day I settled down to write these lines, the *Manchester Guardian* carried a letter from a writer called Alan Dent asking readers with out-of-the-way recollections of Alice Delysia to write to him, as he was about to collaborate with that delightful artist in the preparation of her memoirs. "She is exceedingly well and happy," Dent added, "and is now the wife of the French Consul in the Canary Islands."

The last time I saw Alice Delysia was in 1926. No, that is not strictly correct, because I had a fleeting glimpse of her in Le Touquet ten years later but no occasion to renew our acquaintance. I have kept a photograph of her in an old box: rosebud lips, sensuous nostrils, languid eyes, one hand on her hip, the other behind her head in the artistic pose of the twenties. How lively the old picture looks in the frame of a disturbing period in my life! On the back of the photograph—it is all almost too novelette-ish to be true—she had written: "It would really give me a great pleasure to thank you *de vive voix* for your lovely flowers. Would you care to come in my dressing-room after the show?"

When, all but forty years ago, Delysia wrote those words in her bold handwriting she was *the* toast of the town, London's very symbol of Gay Paree, C. B. Cochran's star of stars. She was the hit of the London Pavilion, saucy, temperamental, talented— the tops. Eligible bachelors, and not a few husbands, queued to take her out. But, though many sent her flowers, she rarely responded with an invitation like this. It was eagerly accepted. For her, I suppose, it was the beginning of an episode. The end— which was what really concerned me—came a few months later, in July, 1926, in her Paris flat when she handed me a small paper-wrapped parcel and saw me to the door, nervously, hurriedly, before tears completely misted up those beautiful eyes of hers. It was only with great difficulty that I kept back my own tears. The small parcel weighed me down. It seared my hands as I carried it down the street. Near the Arc de Triomphe I cast it away in the first dark portico I passed. . . .

How I came to meet Delysia on that day is a story that began while I was still in Vienna and about to pass from the purgatory of school through ordeal by matriculation into the heaven of adult life. As chief subject for matriculation (a minimum of two passes required) I had chosen Greek, although I was not particularly good at it, and mathematics, although my mental store of formulas was woefully meager. In the event, my Greek essay on "The Life and Work of the Sophists in Athens" contained not a single Greek word (my device for disguising a basic weakness) and caused learned arguments among the examiners but was finally accepted as a clever little piece which proved that I had devoted some thought—if no Greek syntax or vocables—to a significant period. My math effort was equally rewarding because I was able to demonstrate that I had grasped some of the basic principles. At the oral examination I arrived at correct solutions without the help of any formulas whatsoever. It wasted much of the examiners' time, but they acknowledged that my individualistic approach had led to the same result as the traditional method of mental automation. The ink was not dry on my certificate when I raced to the university to enroll, paid the fee, and received an Index, as it was called, but had no thought of attending lectures, which were, anyway, not obligatory.

If, at the end of my schooldays, I had looked back—which I am sure I did not—I would have freely admitted that life in

Vienna had, on the whole, been good to me, although these were unsettling days. It was the time of hunger riots, incipient violence, a steep decline in morals. An ugly political mood reflected the impoverishment and reduction of a once great nation which found readjustment to the new circumstances well-nigh impossible. As if whistling up their courage, people still thought and talked in imperial terms, but grandiose ideas and brilliant schemes evaporated in a vacuum labeled "No Opportunity." Everything had grown smaller; even minds had shrunk. I remember Vienna's Socialist city administration trying to instill a sense of urgency into the people. The first big economy drive affected the expensive street clearance in the snowy, slushy winter: "Let the bourgeois get their feet wet," said Hugo Breitner, Vienna's able finance expert. Like so many economists, he was sadly lacking in *Fingerspitzengefühl*, or intuition. The bourgeois kept their feet dry; they traveled by car or taxi. But the working class, whose interests were so close to Breitner's heart, had no alternative but to wallow ankle deep in the icy mire. It cost Labor as much sympathy as it gained with their grandiose municipal building program for working-class apartments, the finest in the world and the first instance also, I think, of priming the pump of a sagging economy by massive public spending.

Though well informed about day-to-day politics, I was strangely unaffected, as if these matters did not concern me at all. Our reduced circumstances caused me no hardship, but Father was anxious for me to be removed from the unstable, unhealthy atmosphere while my mind was still a political blank. His suggestion that I spend a year in London struck an immediate chord, although I had only the most rudimentary knowledge of English, and that only as a result of my brief English-oriented affair. Father's decision was prompt and, as usual, unfussy: "Make your own arrangements. I'll give you £4 a week, double for the first month, the fare and enough to spend two days in Paris en route!"

So it was. With eight crackling white £5 notes in my pocket, I joined the Paris coach of the Orient Express—a bland, unimpressionable, fun-seeking but otherwise indeterminate young Viennese of average appearance, pleasant manners, no views (ex-

cept on sport), but a formidable armory of diverse, if superficial, knowledge acquired at home, much as a *Hausfrau* today
might get to know the current hit tunes by daily exposure to the
soft background music at her local supermarket.

I had not been in Paris long when I had occasion to readjust
my self-evaluation. After a day's orthodox sight-seeing—Notre-
Dame, the Louvre, the Eiffel Tower—and a first quiet, footsore
evening at a small pension not far from the Opéra, I set out confidently the next morning to seek the kind of adventure a young
man traditionally seeks in Paris. It is a brief, sad tale. After hours
of wearying search I found two girls. Though they looked typically Parisian, in the sober light of hindsight I discovered some
evidence to suggest that their origin was in Romania. They accepted my invitation to a modest dinner; they took me with them
to their modest apartment, and, having reinforced my view that
adult life, particularly in Paris, was, indeed, heaven, went so far
as to take me back to my pension. My head was still so much up
in the clouds that it never even occurred to me to take a note
of their address. There were fond farewells; I was off to London
at the crack of dawn and would never see them again. I went to
bed pleasantly exhausted and woke up to find that my first
month's allowance—thirty irreplaceable pounds sterling—had
vanished. I have taken a jaundiced view of Paris ever since.

Poor Casanova! My loyal old friend, that is; I am not asking
sympathy for myself. . . . I had not even bothered to call on
him. But I knew he was married to an old Viennese flame and
was well established as a newspaper executive. He had quite a
shock when, having pushed my way past a bulldoggy concierge,
I knocked at the door of his flat in the rue Saint-Placide: *"Mon
petit . . ."* he said, completely bewildered. I was nearly a foot
taller than he.

"I am on my way to London," I blurted out, as if there were
nothing unusual about my dropping in on him in Paris at 7:30
A.M., and went on without giving him much time to think: "My
train leaves in three-quarters of an hour. I have lost all my money.
Can't pay the bill at the pension. Please help!" I hustled the poor
man, nearly tore the hesitatingly proffered notes from his hand,
was off and down the stairs before he could ask me any embar-

rassing questions. Dear Casa! I was to see him once more a year later, and again. . . .

Had I had more than a few shillings in my pocket with which to start a new life in a strange, overpowering city, and to survive for four weeks, until the arrival of my next monthly allowance; had I been able to persuade myself that I could expect help from Father in this desperate situation if I just plucked up the courage to write and confess; had I not been (and remained) the kind of person who worries in advance so as to meet any situation prepared, if only with a subterfuge . . . then I could now wax lyrical about my thoughts, emotions, and observations as I crossed the Channel and set foot on the soil of Britain for the first time. But preoccupation with my problem blanketed all new impressions. I have only the haziest recollection of sitting among the steaming teapots in the train from Dover and nearly getting lost in the maze of Victoria Station. With a sheaf of elaborate instructions clutched in my hot hand, I made my way by bus to Kensington High Street. I had no ear for the noise of the London traffic, which soothed me in later years until it became a roar that robbed me of my sleep; no eyes for the kaleidoscopic view of London seen from the top of a bus. Like the man who (in Leo Perutz's novel *Between Nine and Nine*), jumping to his death from a high roof, sees the film of his whole life unrolling in the brief seconds before he hits the ground, I made a heap of all my experiences to get me over this big hurdle.

Standing outside a charming old house in Lexham Gardens, I heard the bell ringing without being aware of having pulled the knob. The door opened, and I was greeted by a huge smile and a row of very white teeth. I noticed the flat, Slav nose in an open face with a peaches-and-cream complexion, surveyed the figure—tall, slim, sporty—and tried to guess the age: solid, mature forty (being so young, I did the lady an injustice; she was nearer thirty-five). If I say I was welcomed with open arms, I am literally truthful but anticipating the next few days—or nights. "I am Stella," she said, and proceeded to attack me with a fusillade of English verbiage which, though only a few odd shots struck home, left the imprint of her good intentions on her target.

Behind the maid who carried my suitcase upstairs, Stella, gripping me firmly by the arm, led me to my room—a friendly, pleasant little chamber much more comfortable than I had expected. Giving me no time to change, she marched me downstairs to introduce me into the little world of her boarding house. I felt like a puppet, with Stella manipulating the strings and speaking on my behalf in the kind of pidgin English some people adopt in the presence of children or foreigners: "Willi . . . from Vienna . . . here for a year . . . very happy!" I was not sure whether she meant me or herself. In the sitting room a middle-aged couple, roused from months of monotony, eyed me greedily, and four hands reached out like the tentacles of a dear old octopus. They avidly tried in a most un-English manner to gather as much information about me as could limp across the shaky bridge of our language difficulty. Two young men—one round-faced, flaxen-haired, ebullient (pint-of-bitter-in-a-country-pub), the other bespectacled, clerkish, quiet (cups-of-tea-at-Lyons)—completed my new little world.

Stella and I liked each other. She was aggressive in her attitude toward me. Because of my lack of English I must for once have appeared hesitant and timid. A helpless stranger like me was bound to grasp the first hand offered, and she made quite sure that it was hers. She came to my room unexpectedly and at times that were not strictly suitable, glossing over her friendly intrusions with impromptu lessons in English: "Knock . . . at . . . the . . . door" she would repeat over and over again, demonstrating from the inside what she had failed to do from the outside. I swear she felt instinctively that I was harboring some guilty secret concerning her but—whether tactfully or cunningly, I shall never know—prevented me from ever broaching it. Came Friday, when I could not possibly overlook the procession of my fellow lodgers paying their weekly bill. The time had come to make a clean breast of my trouble, and, when the others had finished their business, I strode into Stella's office, determined—English or no English—to dominate the situation. Before I could open my mouth she put her arm round my shoulder and said quietly: "Leave everything to me—we'll talk tonight."

Burying myself in my new English grammar to escape the

daily after-dinner cross-examination (Octopus already knew all about me), I could not concentrate, and the ridiculous, meaningless hat-cat-mat rhymes danced a Charleston in my head. When I tried to gather my thoughts in German, they somehow did not fit the English circumstances. Every attempt to work out an English sentence foundered on the rock of how to say it. Although as yet not fully aware of the two-way reflex relations between words and actions, I already firmly believed that language was of great importance because, to quote Confucius loosely, "If what is said is not what is meant, confusion and chaos follow." How was I to know that we were entering upon the age of double-talk when "what was said" was no longer "what was meant" and that, all my life, I would be forced to grope through a fog of universal hypocrisy. "Outspoken," which in my book means "honest," became synonymous with "tactless," "undisciplined," "rude." In politics as in private life the currency of truth was debased until—superb evasion—it has become "relative."

How little need there was for me to say anything on that evening in Lexham Gardens became clear when the old clock in the lounge struck eleven. To be honest, I must have known what to expect or I would not have instinctively and crudely prepared for it, undressing slowly and deliberately while keeping an eye on the door. It opened when I was about to put on my dressing gown. Instead, she took hers off.

Armed with a Baedeker and two English phrase books, I crisscrossed London on buses for hours every day, conquering the sprawling city by stages, getting to know it. But it was years before I learned to appreciate it. London's dimensions cut me down to size. London taught me her first lessons. Everybody was so polite and restrained, my bumptiousness began to grate on me. The English kept their voices so low that mine sounded noisy and boorish. In Vienna, Prague, and Budapest I had been pushed in buses, trams, railways, cinema and opera queues, in shops, cafés, restaurants, even on beaches, and had pushed back for all I was worth, with apologies neither received nor expected. During my first weeks in London, in and out of buses, museums, underground stations, Selfridges, not a single person touched me, yet the word I most frequently heard was "Sorry"—I never knew what for.

A lifetime in Britain has polished my rough edges. How well, I realized only decades after those early perplexing excursions. Whenever, in the 1950's, I walked to my plane at London Airport, I took deceptively slow but very long strides so as to get ahead of my fellow passengers without appearing to hurry—a good example of how to win without actually cheating, and an exemplary compromise between my native impatience and cultivated British restraint. It always worked; I was always the first to board the plane. When I tried the same technique at Tempelhof Airport in Berlin, I was left virtually standing. Pushing past me, the German passengers rushed toward the plane without any inhibition. I was the last to get in. By 1962 I was left as far behind at London Airport as in Berlin. It was when the British were trying to join the Common Market. The wheel had turned full circle. My English reticence was out of date. The British were anxious to show that they truly belonged to Europe.

Paul Frischauer once wrote an O. Henry-type short story about a man who, crossing the street, veered slightly to the right and met somebody who, eventually, affected the course of his whole life. In the story Paul showed that, had the man turned only a few degrees to the left, he would have run into someone else whose influence would have given his career an entirely different direction. I forget the details, but the idea impressed me deeply. For decades I have almost obsessively kept my eye fixed on such critical moments, trying to recognize them for what they are. That is what happened one day when I went sightseeing.

He was tall, stately, the type of man who, one feels instinctively, looks older than his age. In spite of his uniform—dark overcoat, highly polished boots, shiny top hat—he did not really look like an English city gentleman because his complexion was swarthy, his features South European: they might have been Marseillaise, Neapolitan, Catalan, or just Slovene. He was, in fact, Viennese; and, though once seen it was impossible to forget his face, I could not place him when, almost larger than life, he infiltrated between me and the view of the Old Lady of Threadneedle Street I was contemplating on this October morning of 1925.

"Willi . . . Willi Frischauer!" he said. "You are Paul's little brother, aren't you?" Little!

It came back to me in a flash. He had been one of the young men whom my brothers had entertained at our home in Vienna. Of course I knew him, but did not know him well because, like all of them, he belonged to the grown-up generation while I was still very much the little brother. Yes, of course I remembered; he was a friend of Paul's. In the family history—well, at least in the family album—he figured in a photograph which showed him staring grimly into space. By his side, boyish, equally serious, and wearing an incongruous uniform, stood Paul, on whose other flank Mother had posted herself: *"Paul s'en va-t-en guerre . . ."* The photograph was taken just before Paul left for the front— his mountain. Meeting his friend so unexpectedly after so many years, although I recognized him, I still had to grope for his name. Awkward. But I thought it was terribly *savoir faire, homme du monde* and all that (schoolboy French often surfaced when I dipped into my mind for the right English expression; it's the other way round now) when he rescued me by saying casually: "I'm Heinz Dank. How do you do?"

It was weeks since I had heard a word of German. Vienna was thousands of miles away. Mother's letters were but a slender link with the life I had left behind. I had not matured all that fast. Beneath a tough facade I felt a soft center of homesickness melting into near tears. I could have thrown my arms round this man's neck and shouted "Thank God for a friend from Vienna!" Something of this spontaneous emotional combustion must have communicated itself to Heinz Dank, because he asked me whether I would like to dine with him. Yes, please, let's go right away, I wanted to say, but answered instead with a politely controlled *"Gerne."* It was four-thirty, and already getting dark. Heinz Dank stopped a taxi. No, I did not have to go home first, I said, and surprised myself with the sigh of relief that accompanied my words.

Looking back, I can easily recognize our meeting as a break with my past and the beginning of a new era. No, not only in retrospect; I knew it there and then. As the taxi carried us—I did not know where—I cut the slender roots I had struck at Lexham Gardens, and burned my boats. I never wanted to see Stella again. I had all but paid back what I owed her, and the strength of my subconscious resentment against the chains of sex and money by which she held me was stronger than I cared to admit to myself. I was equally anxious to escape from the Octopus—such nice people, but they were grinding me down with the steamroller of their monotony.

It was a laughable reaction because all that had happened was that I had accepted a dinner invitation from an old family friend —I guess he was ten years older than I—and my dream world, which had got no further than the demolition of the old site on which to build something new, nearly evaporated when I noticed the cab taking us along Kensington High Street. A feeling of doom overcame me. Was it, after all, only a dream, and was I going back to Lexham Gardens? I had been talking brightly while all this went through my mind and, barely hiding my disappointment, I turned to Heinz and said, "That's where I live— Lexham Gardens—on the left." He laughed. "So we are neighbors." It sounded a little condescending, but the cab did not turn left; it turned right and into Camden Hill, and stopped outside a big house in Airlie Gardens. For Heinz Dank, Earl's Court was Earl's Court and Airlie Gardens was Airlie Gardens. They may be less than half-a-mile apart, but never the twain shall meet.

Heinz deposited his top hat and cane on the big polished table in the hall. The butler took my hat and coat. The affluence! Thick red carpets. White-and-gilt furniture. Damask curtains. Scents of cigar smoke and perfume. Upstairs, a huge drawing room, the light from half a dozen lamps barely penetrating the mysterious gloom. Silver trays. Exquisite glass. "Sit down." I sank deep into the soft couch. I told Heinz the story of my current life, leaving out the bit about Stella—not that there was much else that mattered. What I said betrayed a sense of frustration and fear that it might go on and on and on like this without end. Heinz Dank listened and smiled. I knew he understood.

If that man molded me in the pattern of his own unsatisfactory existence, I can testify in mitigation that he could not
have had a more docile or apt disciple. We were birds of a
feather, both polished but empty shells, operating on the pleasure
principle. I was showing strong symptoms of deprivation, like
an addict subjected to a cure by boredom. He must have wanted
me to fulfill some need in his life—for a companion, a toy, a
sparring partner—I never knew. Almost surreptitiously I moved
my things from Stella's place the next day, avoiding farewells. A
taxi, symbol of my new status, carried me to the other side of
Kensington High Street. I never went back to Lexham Gardens
—not until recently, that is, when I discovered that the old house
had vanished, like so much of my past. A new block of flats now
stands in its place.

Heinz was full of ideas for me. I was to enroll at London
University to improve my English. I was to take a short course
at Pitman's to acquaint myself with the rudiments of the commercial career which he had all mapped out for me. I was to join
his firm at the lowest rung until fit to qualify as his personal
private secretary. (He made it sound like joining the government.) I did all three things at once, a most impracticable proposition, and ended up as an office boy pro tem. The job to which
Heinz Dank devoted some grudging attention between 11:00 A.M.
and 4:00 P.M. was the management of a big German metal firm's
London branch. His partner was an able, serious-minded Englishman who did all the work; but, as is so often the case, it was the
more spectacular and less worthy Heinz who had the confidence
of the home office.

My position was ambiguous. I was the chief's house guest and,
traveling with him by taxi or hire car from Kensington to the
City every morning, arrived at the office in Draper's Gardens
over an hour after the rest of the staff. On the first floor he
turned left to step straight from the landing into his elegantly
furnished, secluded room, while I turned right to take my humble
place at a rough table in a dingy all-purpose office that served,
among other things, as a mail room and a telephone exchange.
Still, I had my uses. My knowledge of German came to the rescue of the telephone girl whenever she failed to communicate

with people in Germany, few of whom knew English. When she left I took over as telephone operator. Before long I had arrogated to myself another function, the encoding and decoding of business telegrams. "We offer you fifty tons of copper c.o.d. at £36.12.6." was the kind of message I translated into "LMDBK" or something like it—I can neither remember the code nor the price of copper, but I have never ceased to marvel at the amount of information I was able to compress into ten letters.

No promotion, but nevertheless enjoyable, was playing private postman—distributing inter-City letters by hand. For an hour every day I lost myself in the Casbah of the dark, mysterious passages through and under buildings, up and down stairs, past and over backyards, each shortcut a conventional route, and known to City workers only. Hitler's blitz carved big slices out of the old City I loved so well, and destroyed most of these rabbit warrens which held as much romance for me as the proverbial *toits de Paris*. I enjoyed my work, menial and inconsequential as it was. If only I could have gone on like this. But one day when, walking up the stairs to our office a few steps ahead of Heinz, I waited politely for him to catch up with me, he directed me toward his own office and motioned me to take off my coat and hang it in his cupboard. It was my informal appointment as his private secretary. I never did another stroke of honest work in that office.

"You answer!" Heinz ordered when the telephone rang. It was the home office in Germany, I told him; but, with a frantic gesture of his hand, he made me say he was not in. After picking out one or two letters from his mail, all of which he apparently had given instructions to be put on his desk unopened, he told me to skim through the others and to distribute them among the staff whose job it was to deal with them. The telephone kept ringing, and it did not take me long to separate the private calls that he would take from the business calls that he would not. When there was a knock at the door I had to answer it, and to say that he was busy and would attend to the person and his problem later. Later never came. I booked theater tickets and made reservations for him at nightclubs. I fixed appointments with a number of ladies, with his tailor, his shoemaker, and

Locke's—he was most meticulous about his hats—and arranged for special delicacies to be sent over from Fortnum and Mason. Ours was a spacious office, but as time went on it seemed to enclose me as tightly as a telephone booth. It was like a Kafka-esque beleaguered fortress. To escape from a feeling of claustrophobia, I stepped outside more frequently than nature demanded, only to be confronted by his desperate expression which implored me not to leave him, not even for a minute. What he said was, in contrast, sardonic, harsh, offensive: "What, again?"

But no sooner were we on our way home in the evening than Heinz underwent a complete transformation, reverting to his type, which was that of a composed, superior man of the world in full command of himself and his environment. He talked lightly—never really gaily—about a thousand-and-one subjects, current events, the theater, literature—and women; women always came into it. We often dined alone at Airlie Gardens before he changed to go out. "What have you been doing with yourself in the evenings?" he asked me—it was some months after I had moved into his house. I told him, truthfully, that I had made friends with the girl telephone operator on the international exchange who always put my calls through to Germany. One lunchtime we had met in the usual way—she worked at the Moorgate Exchange. With her Danish boy friend, a wonderful linguist and jack-of-all-trades, she lived in a couple of rooms near Notting Hill Gate, where I spent many evenings with them almost in a *ménage à trois* except that my new girl friend went far but never the entire distance. It was not a very satisfactory arrangement, but it did provide a brief escape from the increasingly oppressive association with my benefactor.

"That's no life," Heinz said after listening to my story, and proceeded to change it. "Put on your tails and meet me at the Kit-Kat at eleven-thirty." He was going to the theater with two young women I had never seen but who were more than names to me because he had often bemused me by describing their charms in graphic detail. Well, well. Considering how naturally it came to me only a few weeks later, it is difficult to explain why it should have taken me—perspiring profusely at that—fully two hours to cope with a stiff shirt, elusive studs, and a recalcitrant white tie. But the result of my efforts, when I surveyed myself in the mirror, appealed to me. I liked what I saw. What I liked even better was to see a dozen or more young men in the same uniform as soon as I emerged from the Tube in Piccadilly Circus, strangers all—yet I felt one of them.

The Kit-Kat in the Haymarket, café society's most popular nightclub, sucked me in like a whirlpool. Losing sight of the outside world, I was pleasantly numbed by the aroma and immediately attracted to this paradise of crackling brocade, jewels flashing in the half-darkness, horsy laughs and twittering women's voices. The liveried footmen, the smooth waiters—of a kind they make no more—the highly polished parquet floor . . . delightful! I was led to the table occupied by Mr. Dank and his two ladies. Ladies! When he rose to greet me they rose too, and I instantly recognized them as a couple of mediocre chorus girls dressed to the nines and overanxious to please. But however inadequate their manner, in every other respect they left nothing to be desired.

The rest of that evening is lost in a haze of champagne and brandy which was not conducive to the further proceedings when we all transferred to Airlie Gardens. At least not so far as I was concerned. But I had ample opportunity to restore my prestige, for our excursion was only the first of many, until I went in and out of London's nightclubs with the assurance of an habitué. The brocade and the jewels, the nonchalance and horselaughs and the twitter became part of my life. Subtly, Dank taught me to manage the kind of girl to whom he had introduced me. I learned fast. He impressed on me that it was bad form to discuss my night life with anybody. However madly enjoyable I found Paul Whiteman's band or Jack Hylton's orchestra— better not to talk about it. I might have roared with delight at Sophie Tucker belting her incomparable songs from the platform, or seeing the Prince of Wales lolling in his chair at the next table, bored to tears, taking his party home, to return an hour later with another party and enjoy himself like an undergraduate up West for the first time—but none of this was a subject for subsequent discussion. Neither were the goings-on in our bedrooms which invariably concluded the evening.

Another month or so and Heinz Dank was beginning to make himself scarce, leaving me in charge of the evening—and the girls. No liquor worth mentioning had passed my lips before I came to London, but in these last few weeks I had developed into a seasoned champagne-and-brandy-Charlie (I'm still loyal to brandy, but gave up champagne years ago), signed checks with aplomb, but never noticed that the letters from the Club, together with those from the tailors, the florists, the car-hire firm, which arrived on Dank's desk in the office, were the first ones to disappear into his pocket. We had an unending supply of girls, and Dank insisted there should always be two in case he decided to join us after all.

What, I wondered, was keeping him away? Oh, well, as long as he let me go on, why should I worry? We still dined together, still picked up our white camelias or red carnations from the table in the hall, but, once outside the house, went our separate ways. At last he told me what I had suspected all along—that he had found a woman. Or, rather, that he was laying siege to a woman who was the most wonderful, most desirable, most sensational creature in the world. He never wanted to have another woman again. He was determined to devote his life to this one. He was desperate to marry her. He was prepared for any sacrifice that might be necessary. It probably meant that he would have to move to Paris, or to travel, or—he was not at all sure what it would mean. Her name—I must not breathe a word, must tell nobody, absolutely nobody, ever! (He did not wait for my promise; he had reached the stage when he had to talk.) Her name was—Alice Delysia.

A few weeks earlier, he said, he had made a bold approach which had been rewarded. He showed me Delysia's photograph with the invitation to her dressing room. Whether he had got any further than escorting her to dinner—no mean triumph in the world in which we moved—it is impossible to say. Suddenly, Dank was the soul of discretion, but there was no doubt that he was utterly serious about the glamorous and, by all accounts, witty and intelligent French diva. As if reluctant to contaminate her with his humdrum, even sordid daily life, he did not introduce me to her, and when, on one of my nightly meanderings through the jazzy jungle of parties and clubs, I ran into them by accident Dank greeted me with the repressive kind of wave that keeps a friend at a distance.

Presently they were both gone. Delysia went back to Paris, and Dank, who had been reluctant to miss a single tortuous day at the office (lest the bubble of accumulating difficulties be pricked in his absence) was off to Paris, too. "Keep my mail for me—unopened!" was his only instruction. That first morning alone in his big office confronted me with the truth. Nothing in particular happened, but my eyes were suddenly opened. What I had tried to hide from myself now stared me in the face and demanded recognition. For months I had drowned all doubts and fears, blinding myself to the evidence that all was not well with Dank, with the firm, or with me, who was hopelessly entangled. With him to back me up I had stood up to the pressure, but without the support of his physical presence I felt inadequate to cope with the undefined danger. Those unopened letters—every one of them concealed a menace; the sound of the telephone bell startled me like a siren. Then it all broke around my head: embittered business associates, impatient creditors, jilted and unrewarded girl friends, they all bombarded me with their anger. And then came the blockbuster from Germany—the call to which I responded with an inexplicable gaucherie for which I have never forgiven myself.

The call was from headquarters and, instead of saying casually that the chief was not in and would call back later, I blurted out excitedly that "Mr. Dank is in Paris," for no reason except that my bad conscience had me confused. The German brought the conversation to a quick end, leaving me suspended in a daze of guilt and apprehension. I called the number in Paris that Heinz had left me—on strict orders not to pass it on to anybody else—but when "Madame Delysia's residence" answered, I was told in a curt French voice that "Monsieur Dank n'est pas là," I, too, put the receiver down hastily, relieved that, for the time being at least, I did not have to bear the evil tidings. I toyed with the idea of trying again the next morning, but when I arrived at the office and went into my—into Dank's—room, his desk was occupied by a German gentleman who was blithely going through

Dank's mail with an expression on his face which gradually changed from the pursed lips of an astonished whistle to undiluted horror.

He greeted me with a suspiciously friendly smile. Yes, he knew all about me; we had talked on the telephone; surely I remembered. . . . Talking a pleasant German, with a voice and manner modulated by international contacts, he was so suave and definite at the same time that it did not occur to me to protest when I saw him stuffing Dank's letters into his pocket. Before leaving the office to talk to the rest of the staff, he suggested that we might have dinner, he and I. And I, like a fool, taking "dinner" as a password to my very own London after dark, promptly offered to fix it, and fixed the Ritz. This, coming from the juvenile secretary of a man who was suspected of grave irregularities, if not defalcations, was not the best way to reassure an emissary from the head office in charge of the investigation!

That evening I was, as usual, perfectly at home in the elegant atmosphere of the Ritz; at the same time my poise only confirmed the German's suspicions about our mode of living. When, to cap it all, I insisted on signing the bill, "p.p. Heinz Dank," and the waiter, after a brief consultation with the manager, came back and wondered, with due deference, whether it would not be more convenient for me to settle such a small amount in cash—and I did not have enough cash on me—and was forced to let my guest pay—our fate—Heinz Dank's and mine—was sealed.

Dank called me from Paris the following morning, and I told him frankly exactly what had happened. He groaned. He implored me to stall the man, to tell him that he, Dank, was indisposed but would be back in a day or so. After a terrible day, I came home to Airlie Gardens at five-thirty, dying for a drink. Before I had time to gulp it down there was a call from Paris.

"Come at once!" a Frenchwoman's voice said, and gave me an address.

"How is Heinz?" I managed to ask. I felt like choking.

"Il est mort!"

I went upstairs and started packing. Some sixteen months earlier I had arrived in London with one suitcase; now it took three (of Dank's) to accommodate my wardrobe. From a small frame on his bedside table I took Delysia's photograph to impress her features on my mind. Within half an hour of the telephone conversation I was on my way to Victoria Station. The news of Dank's death had come as a shock, but also as a shameful relief. With a spectacular, if not very honorable, feat of psychological acrobatics I had propelled myself over the painful situation to land on both feet in a new dimension.

The trip to Paris no longer appeared to me as a frightening rendezvous with death; the loss of a friend did not really perturb me. What it signaled was something that had lurked submerged in my subconscious mind—a reunion with my old girl friend and her Danish beau who had since married and settled in Paris. The shock of Dank's death having liberated me from the hypnotic shackles of London's night life, I reached out for this prospect of a *Wiedersehen* with the only real friends I had left after my London debacle. The thrill of sailing into an unknown future with an underlying, if misguided, sense of Sophoclean tragedy in which I saw myself as a participant accompanied me on this night trip across the Channel. Such mixed feelings of anticipation were balanced by pangs of distress at leaving—a heart-gripping sensation that affects me every time I take my leave, however temporary, from the shores of Britain. Ovid's lines, as on so many later occasions, assumed a personal meaning for me:

"Cum subit illius tristissima noctis imago
Qua mihi supremum tempus in urbe fuit
Cum repeto noctem qua tot mihi cara reliqui
Labitur ex oculis nunc quoque gutta meis. . . ."

It took me all day to sum up enough courage to face the facts of—death. At her elegant apartment in Paris, Delysia received me in a highly emotional state. Speaking in French too fast for me to take in all the details, she explained that Dank had taken his own life. Maybe she thought he had taken his life because (as I assumed) she refused to marry him. But I knew he had other, perhaps even weightier, motives. I had no inclination to linger and theorize on the tragedy, however. Saying that Dank had left a few personal belongings with her, Delysia thrust a small parcel at me. From its shape and size I assumed it contained a pair of slippers and a dressing gown, but my imagination may have carried me away, and I was probably wrong. For an instant. in my mind's eye, I could see him in his dressing gown with the black-and-red slippers—and a bullet hole in the head. I shuddered, and fled. Getting rid of the parcel a few minutes later was my crude way of dissociating myself from the whole oppressive episode.

It took some time for the proprietor of the small Left Bank hotel to reconcile the voluminous and luxurious baggage of his new lodger with the tiny third-floor room, the only one available at the price I felt able to pay. But although it was barely half the size of the bathroom in Airlie Gardens, it seemed, after the hectic harassment of my London life, a haven of peace. The problem was how to pay the price of peace. I had no thought of working. I had no clear idea of the future, and a shortage of money confronted me as soon as I had spent the few pounds I had brought with me from London.

First to go were the boiled shirts and the two dinner jackets. These paid for three weeks' lodging, breakfast and dinner. It was not long before I was nibbling away at my tails. Piece by piece the outward trappings of a lordly way of life were dismantled; but, even while living in this clothes-to-mouth fashion, I was still not averse to an idle afternoon spent at the Café Marignan or at Fouquet's in the Champs-Elysées watching the girls go by, and an evening or two a week at a cinema with one of them. I took a present whenever I went to dinner with my Anglo-Danish friends, which was frequently. At long last I consummated my affair with the English half of the duo. In the process a sheet of music of a current hit song got crumpled up—"I Wonder Where My Baby Is Tonight?"—which burdened my conscience and came home to roost in later life. Whenever I was consumed by jealousy, the flippant little tune warbled itself into my consciousness. The sacrifice of the first of my six lounge suits was a danger signal I could hardly overlook, but when the silk shirts had to go—superficial, vain young fellow that I was—that really hurt.

Without any clear idea of what might save me at this late hour, I devoured the newspapers of half a dozen countries and, from the vantage point of a table at a café, scanned the horizon of the Champs-Elysées for help, hoping against hope for some *deus ex machina* to reveal himself among the perambulating crowd. Who was I waiting for? Another Heinz Dank? God forbid! And if I could wait no longer, what else could I do? Never having experienced it, I was not afraid of hunger, nor was it the prospect of having to leave my hotel room that terrified me. Grim as the future looked, I could not quite visualize myself in such dire straits. Yet I was helpless and afraid.

The same paralytic helplessness that pinned me down in Paris in 1926 descended on me on many occasions in later life. I tried to comfort myself—as I did many times thereafter—with the old Till Owlglass philosophy: you know, the wandering German apprentice whistling gaily when walking uphill, and deeply despondent when descending into the valley because, during the downhill walk, he already anticipated the inevitable uphill stretch soon to come—and vice versa. Alas, I did suffer from depression whenever things went well, paying for my luck with apprehension about hard times that would surely follow. But whenever, during long and enervating bad patches, I caught myself inadvertently succumbing to the Till Owlglass hope for the easy times ahead, weighty Goethe words stopped me from abandoning myself to such optimism:

"Du hast gehofft, Dein Lohn is abgetragen
Dein Glaube war Dein zugewognes Glück . . ."

Which means that hope is its own reward, a substitute for fulfillment:

"Nur was Du abweist mag Dir wiederkommen,
Was Du verschmähst naht ewig schmeicheld sich . . ."

a simple English version of which is the popular warning against trying too hard. In short, no escape from despair for me, not even the consolation of trust in God looking after his own, although He had always done so in His own tortuous way. There is a hint of fatalism in this attitude which has always disturbed me because, for a basically indolent person like myself, fatalism is—well, fatal.

The trouble with me in Paris was that, at the age of twenty, I had few intellectual and virtually no spiritual resources to guide me out of the cul-de-sac into which I had stumbled. But, as usual, things did not turn out so badly as I had every reason to fear. Casa came once more to my aid. When I girded myself to go to see him, I did not have a stitch of clothing left except what I was wearing, no money, and had had no breakfast. No, I was not hungry, but a most sensitive part of my system—snobbism camouflaged as self-respect—was injured by this descent to the bottom of the barrel. Casa's kindness helped to bring me to my senses. He was not angry, did not reproach me. He was simply anxious to help. There was no question of my repeating the London performance in Paris. I had to go—the sooner, the better. What he said sounded so definite that I made no attempt to resist; I was ready to admit defeat. I was ready to go anywhere—anywhere but Vienna.

Casa must have dispatched quite a few telegrams behind my back, for within forty-eight hours he turned up with a plan. My brother Paul, he informed me, was in Berlin and anxious for me to join him and his young wife. Casa showed me the train tickets, but he was not prepared to hand them to me until he saw me safely to the station. He bought me a small suitcase with a few pairs of socks, underwear, and a shirt or two. "You are having dinner with me," he announced firmly. "Your train for Berlin leaves at 10:00 P.M." I shall never forget him waving to me vigorously with a big white handkerchief while I looked out of the departing train's window. There he stood, the dear little man, waving, waving, getting smaller as the train carried me away, until his bald head was but a tiny speck in the distant crowd. It was the last I ever saw of him. Two years later he was dead.

I should have gone home to Vienna at once. The ensuing weeks in Berlin only prolonged my agony. Paul, a writer of promise with a first biography (of Madame Du Barry) on the stocks, could not easily support another hungry mouth, and his wife was not anxious to add to her burden of domestic chores. Left to my own devices, I wasted my days. As soon as dusk fell

I gravitated toward the fringe of Berlin's night life. Paris had nothing so degrading and demoralizing as Berlin to tempt an unstable young man. The only satisfaction I have rescued from the experience of getting to know it at firsthand is that I came away from it in one piece.

But a vivid memory of the startling scene with its freakish cast of a rotten, amoral society has remained with me, and, like evil shadows from the past, hovers in the background of all my later impressions of Berlin—the boyish, flat-chested girls (some, like Anita Berber, the dancer, were very beautiful) whose stock-in-trade was studied wickedness and who pandered to the perversion and ambivalence of men and women; the more mature masculine high priestesses of Germany's national vice, sado-masochism, equipped with the twin symbols of their bestiality, high boots and whips—the spiritual ancestors of Irme Grese and Ilse Koch and the legions of minor Nazi women who were let loose on the helpless inmates of Buchenwald, Dachau, and Ravensbrück fifteen years later, high boots, whips, and all. . . . The cavalcade of vice—noisy, quarreling, drunken male and female prostitutes were so commonplace they attracted little attention—populated the Kurfürstendamm, which is now in West Berlin, as well as the Friedrichstrasse, which the division of Berlin has left inside the Communist half of the city.

Brighter than Broadway thirty years later, these nights-into-day fascinated and repelled me at the same time. Whispering their bargain-basement prices in my ears—supply far outstripped demand—women lured with novel, unheard-of gimmicks. One used to take her glass eye out in a horribly suggestive gesture. I seemed to be fair game for the male hunters who flashed big bank notes before my eyes. There was not a vice I could not have bought or sold. The small packets of diluted cocaine on offer were among the more harmless devices for titivation. Half sick, half stunned, and in a strange state of intoxication (neither drug- nor liquor-induced), I gaped at this amazing public peep-show and felt as if the whole circus somehow revolved around me. That I kept my feet, that I was not swept away and drowned in the murky waves, I owe to a miracle—or to a healthy instinct which has often saved me at the edge of the abyss. Like a child, I played with fire, returning to the scene of temptation night after night, simply to test my power of resistance.

"Sanitation," which the *Oxford English Dictionary* interprets as improvement of unhealthy, dirty, infectious conditions, is the literal and rightly suggestive English translation of the German word by which we referred to the rescue of Austria's tottering economy in the aftermath of inflation. "Sanitation of the currency." "Cleansing of the Aegean stables" would have been as descriptive, because we encountered inflation not only as an economic problem but also as the inevitable deterioration of morals, business as well as sexual, and the loss of self-respect and confidence that always goes with it. Having stabilized the currency, Monsignore Ignaz Seipel, the Catholic statesman-priest and Chancellor of Austria who was as concerned about the moral as he was about the financial health of the people, preached the urgent need for a sanitation of the soul . . . sanitation as a requisite for salvation.

Both were a long time coming. Vienna in 1926, when I returned from my peregrinations, was no Sunday school. But I was just as much in need of sanitation as my native city. Self-respect at a low ebb, bruised by the futility of my expedition into the wide world, a stranger in my own country, not rating very highly in Father's estimation either—but still lovingly welcomed by Mother—I merged ideally into the overall picture of an unstable society. "The fine days of Aranjuez are over now," are the first much-quoted words of Schiller's Don Carlos. "We have been here in vain." They perfectly suited my mood. Like a Boy Scout setting out on a hike in a dinner jacket, I wore the phoney polish of a young man of the world, which was all I had salvaged from my excursion. But (reversing the predicament of the emperor without his clothes) the camouflage deceived everybody except myself. How gullible people are!

Mother's worried world of luxury was disintegrating. She did not take easily to the need to budget and to economize, and tried to close her eyes to the political and social changes affecting our lives. We were "reduced" to two servants. Three of my brothers—all except Fritz—were married and installed in homes of their own with problems of their own. The atmosphere was oppressive; difficulties and hardships were everywhere. The healthy Viennese capacity for sober self-appreciation deteriorated into a habit of universal self-pity, engendering a defensive aggressiveness which transformed the proverbial old *Wiener Gemütlichkeit* into bitter, wounding quarrels whenever more than two or three gathered to talk. What is the opposite of togetherness? Whatever it is, that was the prevailing mood.

Still desperately trying to avoid involvement, I resumed my studies halfheartedly but reverted almost imperceptibly to the life of a useless loafer. Too proud to accept more than a morning's cup of coffee from a household to which I could make no contribution, I frequented my favorite coffeehouses. At the Café Central I had breakfast on the cuff, read newspapers, gambled for a couple of hours—there were always several écarté schools going on simultaneously in the half-light of the Café Central's glass-covered arcades where I could back the player of my choice. It was a useful source of income. And then there were, of course, women. Always women.

It has been suggested that I should preface this chapter with the frank admission (also a strong selling point) that all I seem to remember between the ages of eight and twenty is women. Well, it's true. But my record in this respect is not so edifying as to justify a great deal of crowing, and I return to the subject only to throw a light on the social conditions in these years. The poverty of the professional classes weakened the backbone of the country. Their anxiety to keep up appearances created confusing social repercussions. Out for an afternoon's amusement with a couple of wealthy friends, we would make a smart five-o'clock *thé dansant* our starting point. For a small *pourbois* the head-waiter, surveying the crowded dance floor, would invariably offer advice.

"Nothing much here this afternoon," was his routine response. Shaking his head gravely, he would consult his address book which contained the names, telephone numbers, and prices of a large number of available ladies—amateur tarts from respectable families who supplemented their small housekeeping and pin money by private enterprise in the afternoons while their husbands were at their unrewarding work. At the age of twenty-one it seemed reasonable to sleep with as many of these women as one could afford (they charged only half the price of professional streetwalkers). Today the memory depresses me.

Nor was there any shortage of genuine lady amateurs, who loved to love, and did for pleasure what provided their less fortunate sisters with an income. We eligible young men were passed from bed to bed, our respective reputations for physical prowess preceding us and determining the number and elegance of open bedroom doors. Husbands who had their own mistresses closed their eyes to their wives' promiscuity, many going so far as to encourage their inclinations by financing parties at their homes or in Vienna's many bars. We danced, we drank, we slept far into the day. When I first tried to recapture the nightmarish existence of these days I called the book *Twilight in Vienna*.

A rude awakening was in store for us.

4 | *Age of Violence*

A continuous row of stationary two-car red trams encircled the Ringstrasse like a bloody ribbon. Traffic was at a standstill. It was either a citywide electricity failure or a riot. Meeting me, as I tried to cross the wide avenue, were the bare, sun-tanned, glistening bodies of powerful men in their blue denim working trousers marching ten deep in the middle of the road between the trams. Muscular arms swung iron bars and heavy tools which reflected the light of the sun and invested the sinister spectacle with an eerie theatricalism.

The men marched to a background music of angry rumbling voices rising like the tide, ebbing away and cascading into loud belligerent shouts whenever they mingled with a new wave. I had just enough time to mount one of the trams and take a seat at a window. From this grandstand the demonstration looked like a procession of Roman gladiators marching into the arena. Presently, even before I could properly hear it, I could sense the approach of the rival forces; then came the clatter of clanging hoofs on the cobblestones, the silvery rattle of horses' reins, the savage swish of sabers being drawn from their scabbards, the clipped commands sounding like Tally ho!—and they were upon

81

us with the explosive burst of a cavalry charge which would have done honor to the Light Brigade.

Central Europeans of my generation have grown accustomed to the noise of riots, street fighting, head-on collisions between people and police. I had seen riots before and was to see many more in later years—the sound of heads crunching under the blows of the Paris police's wooden staffs in the 1934 February riots is still with me. Although I am no pacifist and no weakling (nor do I know physical fear but, never having been in a war, I cannot say how I would have reacted on the battlefield), a sick feeling overcomes me when man hits out at man. Few things are more revolting than physical violence—the ugliness of wounds, the spilling of blood, the faces distorted by hate and pain, the foaming mouths, the perversion and brutality of a mob. . . .

The cavalcade of mounted police cut into the marching column not far from my observation post. Within seconds whinnying horses, excited by the noise and the dust, sweating as profusely as the riders, caught the demonstrators in a trap, pushing them against the trams facing me on the other side of the road, and the cornered men retaliated by hurling their weapons at the enemy. Within seconds one of these metal chunks, missing its target, crashed through the window in front of me and hit a fellow onlooker on the ear. He collapsed in a pool of blood, but was quickly surrounded by ready helpers. His blood spattered me as I dived for safety. By the time I got out into the street, the crowd outside had closed in again behind the police squadron which went on galloping down the Ring. If I still had a will of my own, I was no longer able to exert it. Engulfed in a militant section of the demonstrators, I was carried away toward the ancient and beautiful Palace of Justice.

At this stage I had no idea what the riot was about. Snatches of conversation, some of the shouted slogans, curt replies to my questions helped fill in the puzzle in the next half-hour, in which I had no option but to abandon myself to the surge of the crowd. On the previous day a provincial court had acquitted a group of Right-wingers accused of killing two Socialists in a political skirmish. Socialist suspicion of political bias in the rural community was strong—and probably justified. The workers in Austria's

"Red capital" were ordered to come out and demonstrate against the "class verdict." Workers in the power stations and other municipal enterprises were the first to down tools. By midmorning Vienna's factories were idle, and demonstrators were converging on the Palace of Justice.

Smoke was pouring from the windows of the old building. Although I did not know it at the time, some of the demonstrators had forced their way in and were setting fire to the draperies, papers, and furniture. Approaching from the distance was the sound of the fire brigade's trumpets. Impossible to say what came first—the red of the fire engines or the big flames leaping through the smoke which shrouded the Palace. Forcing their way inch by inch through the crowd, the fire engines came close to where I was wedged in a group of six husky men who never so much as glanced down at the impeccably dressed but slightly disheveled young man in their midst. The fire engines did not get very far. No sooner had the firemen unwound their hoses than a hundred knives lunged forward to cut the rubber into shreds. The crowd swept me some distance away when yet another fire engine approached. Next to the driver stood Karl Seitz, the venerable Socialist mayor of Vienna, his handsome face framed in a white beard. So much did he resemble the Habsburgs in stature and bearing that his party colleagues called him "Archduke Karl." Seitz and his engine did not get through, either.

From the direction of the Rathaus the sound of shots could be heard, and a message was passed from mouth to mouth that the police, besieged in their station by the raving crowd, were trying to shoot their way out. The mob had lit a fire in the narrow station entrance to smoke them out. The shots were the signal for a new wave of fearful mayhem. Many of the policemen belonging to that station were killed; some of them were virtually torn apart. Only a few who managed to disguise themselves with oddments of civilian clothing escaped through a door inside the building and found shelter in upstairs flats.

Fighting spread throughout the city. Some military types interpreted the sound of *rat-tat-tat* as an indication that the police had been issued rifles—a rare emergency measure. It was late evening before I extricated myself from the dense, exhausted, aimless, milling crowd, and returned home, but I was up at the crack of dawn to return to the fray. Sporadic fighting was still— or again—going on. I made my way past the heavily guarded, still-smoldering Palace of Justice to the University, where the kettle of political excitement was always boiling. The young descendants of the freedom fighters of 1848 were leaning toward the Right. I was no rabid revolutionary, but the undercurrent of reaction which ran through the heated discussions was shocking. It sounded as if the students were chanting under their breath, "Down with Freedom!"

With one of the students' groups surging down the Ringstrasse, I was approaching the Burgtheater when a few hundred men came running from the opposite direction, stopping us in our tracks and sweeping us on with them. I surprised myself by taking to my heels so promptly simply because so many others were running, although I had no idea what had put us to flight. We came to a halt and turned in the open space between the Burgtheater and the high railings of the Volksgarten. We were now at the head of the crowd, and there was considerable pushing and shoving from behind. Before I could turn and give the impatient mob a piece of my mind, two thinly but strategically spread-out lines of police, rifles at the ready, moved in our direction from the Rathausplatz.

It went very quickly. The crowd was pushing from behind; the rifles were approaching fast. I wanted to run, but that was impossible. Cold sweat stood on my forehead—the menace of those rifles was like nothing I had ever faced before. From behind me angry curses were hurled at the police as they closed in.

"Stop provoking the police! It'll be me who'll get it in the guts!" I am not sure whether I spoke aloud or not, but that is what I was thinking. I did not turn my head because I did not dare to take my eyes off those muzzles. . . . Now rifle butts were being slammed against shoulders, and there was a staccato burst of shots fired over our heads. I was flat on the ground when the next salvo crashed against the wall of human bodies all around me. A few heels dug into my side, a kick grazed my temple, policeman's boots rushed by at eye level, kicking dust into my nostrils. Then the crowd, with the police in hot pursuit, was disappearing down the street. I lay where I was and took stock. I was one of a dozen or so bodies lying about. Except for one other man, I was the only one uninjured. Helpers materialized from all sides. I brushed away their hands and, a little dazed, went my way. *Feuertaufe*, I mumbled dramatically to myself under my breath: Baptism of Fire.

Recalling the incident in the light of later journalistic experience, what struck me most was how deeply one can become involved in events without knowing much about their larger context. Until, a few days later, things returned to normal (though in a way they never really did) I never guessed that the authorities had reason to fear an attack on Metternich's famous old chancellery in the Ballhausplatz in which Monsignore Ignaz Seipel resided as chancellor. The police had attacked us so ferociously precisely because they assumed that that was where we were heading. At the Ballhausplatz at that moment the chancellor was conferring with Otto Bauer, Austria's Aneurin Bevan, and with Police President Dr. Johann Schober who, incidentally, later sponsored an abortive attempt to establish an Austro-German Customs Union (*Anschluss* by the Tradesmen's Entrance).

One hundred people were killed in the two days of rioting— July 15 and 16, 1927. Their deaths gave birth to the armed semi-Fascist Heimwehr under the leadership of Prince Rüdiger von Starhemburg. The stage was set for a permanent civil war situation in which the Heimwehr and the Socialists' paramilitary *Schutzbund* (Protective Association) clashed regularly each weekend—and sometimes in mid-week too—as each of these two fully-armed party formations insisted on parading exactly where the other had scheduled a meeting.

This was indeed an era of violence. If I can remember little but women in my life between the ages of eight and twenty, in the years that followed it is violence that has displaced much of what was probably worthier of recall. Violence was all around me, difficult to avoid. Worse, it came crowding in on me at unexpected moments. One day I accompanied my brother Edi and a client of his to the district courthouse of a Vienna suburb where a judge in chambers was to hear their case. The client was Bruno Wolf, a well-known newspaperman who earned a little extra money by doing a stint on our family weekly, *Die Wiener Sonn-und-Montags-Zeitung*, and who was deeply involved in protracted litigation with an advertising man. The issues and counterissues were confused, and the subject with which this particular court was concerned was defamation of character. Both men were extremely bitter, each intent on hurting the other. Bruno Wolf was a Jew, and his adversary was a self-professed anti-Semite with strong leanings toward the Austrian Nazi Party.

The judge occupied a chair on a small raised dais in the tiny courtroom, the two contestants and their lawyers sitting behind little tables, facing each other across the room. The only member of the press present, I occupied one of the four chairs along the wall facing the judge—all the accommodation available for press and public. As soon as the proceedings began, Edi rose to make a legal point, but Wolf appeared anxious to speak for himself. Anyway, that is how it appeared to me. Edi was listening to him, and while the whispered conversation between lawyer and client on my left held my attention two detonations in rapid succession nearly made me jump out of my skin. Although I must have closed my eyes instinctively, I was aware of a flash on my right which seemed to dissolve in a thousand tiny stars behind my lids. When my eyes blinked open, Bruno Wolf was slumped over his little table, and a thin plume of smoke rose lazily from a small hole in Edi's briefcase. Looking paler than ever, Edi was on his feet, and his opposite number was wresting a revolver from the grip of his client, whose horrific expression has ever since remained imprinted on my mind: hate, triumph, madness, and fear mingling in an ugly mask of murder.

Seconds later the room was filled with officials. From all over the building people rushed to squeeze themselves into the presence of death. Paradoxically, at the same time, Wolf himself seemed to have been forgotten. Fully ten minutes went by while the murderer waited patiently for a policeman to arrive and take him into custody. A charge of murder against him was eventually reduced to one of manslaughter. His counsel claimed that he had been provoked beyond endurance by his litigious adversary, and the fact was taken into consideration as a mitigating circumstance. He got off lightly. There was much argument about the political inclinations of some of the jurors. Judicial Austria was accused of being blind to the violent death of a Jew. Those times were upon us. . . .

The little red sports car I was driving was stuttering along Kärnstnerstrasse toward the Ringstrasse. Either I was out of gas or the battery was low or the carburetor choked up or the old thing was simply in the process of disintegrating. Out of the corner of my eye, I noticed a commotion near the Opera. The car refused to take me any nearer the trouble spot. It was quicker to get out and run, anyway. Two groups were involved in separate scuffles. Each, it turned out, surrounded one man, grappling with him, hitting him with umbrellas, canes, fists, and handbags on the part of the ladies. Uniformed police busied themselves with the passengers of a big black limousine. The crowd grew bigger and bigger; shouts of "Murder! Murder!" rose up and alternated with cries of "Kill them!" Before I could reach the hub of the excitement, the big limousine drove off, followed by an ambulance. A police wagon pulled up and a gaggle of police, having wrested them from the clawing crowd, hoisted two men into the back as if they were sides of beef. Returning to my car which I had left immobolized in the middle of Vienna's busiest street, I found police and crowd as incensed about me as that other crowd had been about . . . about what?

It took an hour to sort out the trouble with my car and the police, which made me late for an appointment. After another hour I was still unaware that I had witnessed the attempt of two revolutionaries to kill Ahmed Zog, the ruler of Albania. The assassins had ambushed his limousine and fired several shots into the car, killing Zog's adjutant, but the Albanian chief had escaped unharmed. This kind of internecine Balkan warfare was nothing new to Vienna. A beautiful woman assassinated a Bulgarian premier in the middle of a Burgtheater performance. . . . I had sucked up such tales of political mayhem with my mother's milk. But the murderous incident in the long, involved history of

Balkan violence I had witnessed struck a personal chord. What connection could there possibly be . . . ? Of course! That was it!

The variegated fauna of my relations included a gentleman whose Serbo-Croat origin manifested itself in his intense and informed interest in the affairs of his native country's turbulent neighbor. A fine ex-Serb officer of the old imperial army, the dissolution of the Austro-Hungarian Empire and the uneasy peace that followed had left him on the slag heap of an ill-paid, inadequate civilian job. He was no friend of Ahmed Zog, of that I was sure. As far as I could remember his discourses on Balkan affairs, what bothered the old warrior most was Zog's dependence on Fascist Italy. The friends of Albanian democracy, on the other hand, enjoyed the support of the Serbo-Croats who, in turn, were hanging onto the democratic coattails of France. As a result of a rapid equation I came to the conclusion that, if my dear relative was against Zog, he was bound to be in the camp of the assassins—not necessarily, I hasten to suggest, in favor of violence and assassination as means to a political end, but nevertheless at one with the Albanian revolution, anti-Zog, anti-Italy movement.

Zog had long removed himself from the dangerous soil of Vienna when I received strong if circumstantial confirmation of my suspicions. Apparently out of the blue, Edi was entrusted with the defense of the two Albanian assassins—beg pardon: freedom fighters. His brief came from Yugoslav sources, but it was obviously not absurd to suggest that he would not have been chosen from among hundreds of able and willing Viennese lawyers had not certain family connections operated cautiously, tactfully, and discreetly behind the scenes. For the defense, then: Dr. Eduard Frischauer. Holding a watching brief on behalf of Ahmed Zog: Dr. Marcus Preminger, a distinguished veteran of the Austrian bar and former state prosecutor whose son Otto forsook the profession to win fame and fortune on Broadway and in Hollywood.

The threat of another band of terrorists invading Vienna to anticipate the course of justice and execute their own judgment before the courts could pronounce a verdict on the two ac-

cused men was so real that it was decided to transfer the trial
to Ried, a remote, compact small provincial town. As a young
reporter closely associated with the counsel for the Defense,
what was more natural than that I should be assigned to cover
the trial? But my own interest in the political acrobatics of the
Balkans was not so deep as to compensate me for the long absence from Vienna.

The trial nevertheless was a stirring experience. There were
fine clashes between the dignified Dr. Preminger, whose beautifully balanced orations, issued in a sonorous voice, pleaded the
case for Zog and Italy. They contrasted strongly with Edi's
much sharper, less decorous, but more pointed barks at judge,
jury, opposing camp—and even clients. The Austrian court was
obviously displeased because it had to grapple with the political
preoccupations of these violent foreigners, the old monarchy's
stepchildren barely a dozen years removed from Vienna's tute-
lage. "You've left the Austrian family," one could almost hear
them arguing. "Why did you not take your bloody quarrels
with you and fight them out at home?"

My interest was not really roused until the next to last day
of the trial, when my brother rose to plead on behalf of his
clients. He was most eloquent, moderate in tone for once, and
very persuasive. His arguments were clearly impressing the jury.
The judge leaned forward so as not to miss a word. Edi spoke
of the terror of Zog's rule, of the hardships he imposed on his
simple, hard-working people who were as proud and wild as
the mountains of the country from which they scratched a miserable living, refusing to be any man's slaves. He talked of Zog's
cruelty, of the corruption of his regime, his avarice and his greed
for the best land at the expense of the indigent peasants: "He has
imported Fascism from the land of his protectors across the
Adriatic Sea," Edi said in an unfashionable attack on Mussolini.
Those who fought Ahmed Zog were defending not only their
natural heritage against the pawn of a foreign power but also,
and perhaps even more important, democracy against the en-
croachment of Fascism.

About halfway through Edi's plea—he had been speaking for
over two hours—the judge adjourned the hearing until that after-

noon. Joining Edi for lunch at the local hotel across the square, I asked, "What's the verdict going to be?" Before he could answer a messenger arrived from the court: "Your clients wish to speak to you urgently." Edi put down his knife and fork, saying to me as he went, "I'll be back in a few minutes." He was. With a wide grin he settled down again to his meal. All eyes in the small dining room were on us. Edi had difficulty in keeping a straight face. "Incredible," he kept saying. When I pressed him to let me in on his secret, he told me what had happened.

It was indeed unusual. In spite of their imperfect knowledge of German, his Albanian charges had correctly gauged the impact their counsel's plea was making on judge and jury. They could sense the whiff of acquittal in the air. Were they jubilant? Had they called their attorney to ask him not to fail in the concluding stages of his speech? No! As Edi related it to me, he had no sooner entered the detention room belowstairs when both his clients sank to their knees and implored him to forego all further arguments in their favor and to persuade the court to bring in a verdict of guilty and hand down a long-term prison sentence for both. If you succeed in getting us off, they said in effect, our lives will not be worth a farthing; avengers will be out to get us wherever we go and hunt us down wherever we hide.

Their only hope of survival lay in prison, where they were content to wait until time had eroded their opponents' resolve to punish them for their attempt on Zog. However flattering his clients' confidence in his forensic ability, when Edi resumed his plea, it was, of course, incumbent on him to present their case to the best of his ability, but the fire was gone. Next morning the jury brought in a verdict of guilty. Each of the two men was sentenced to three and a half years' imprisonment. They were inexpressively relieved, and grateful to Edi.

Ernst Klebinder at fifty—which seemed to be his age throughout the decade I was most closely associated with him—was a shriveled-up little man, with a pince-nez on his hawk nose and an incongruously imperial mien, who somehow managed to look down on men two feet taller than he. Such was his magnetism that even people who hated him—and many did—could not resist his fascination. He was ingratiating and arrogant at the same time, offering favors and demanding them in the same breath, motivated by generosity and avarice in a perplexing combination of contradictions. Although parochial in many ways, his political acumen was uncanny, his business sense highly developed, and his influence on men of position astonishing to those who do not know how many high offices of state are occupied by small fry—a weakness in public life that he exploited to the full. Klebinder was incredibly agile and in perpetual motion, impatient to be everywhere at the same time. He had a habit of looking in at parties, including his own, and disappearing within a few minutes. Even for one whose life largely consisted of "getting around" (places and people), he was surprisingly well equipped with gossip, political rather than social, dropping a hint here, another there, without waiting for its significance to sink in. People used to run after him for elucidation which he allowed them to extract from him after a mock resistance. Even his most mundane anecdotes had a built-in point which put across exactly what he intended to convey.

In the political jungle of Austria in the late twenties and early thirties, he was the champion of his species, employing a chameleon's camouflage to adapt himself to all manner of surroundings. Though he was sniped at from many sides, he blended so perfectly into the confused background of these years that he was virtually invulnerable. In an atmosphere of political violence his favorite weapon was friendship—with everybody. He was indiscriminate in the choice of his companions—as long as they were at the top of their particular tree. Until, years later, hardly trusting my eyes, I observed Winston Churchill and Willie Gallagher walking arm in arm in the lobby of the House of Commons, king's man and Communist, I thought Klebinder was the only man to achieve a similarly remarkable political alchemy. Indeed, if I had not seen it myself, I should never have believed that Dr. Walter Riehl, founder of Austria's Nazi Party, a pre-Hitler Nazi (for which Hitler never forgave him) would walk arm in arm with a Jew in public. But then who was Riehl to rebuff a man like Klebinder?

Klebinder's fertile brain mass-produced ammunition for the political battles but suffered from overproduction; and, threatening to suffocate in the glut, one of his great weaknesses was that when it came into his head, he could not suppress a wounding *bon mot*. It did not matter whether it hurt friend or foe. Once he thought of a political maneuver he was like a child playing with fire; he realized he might burn his fingers but he could not resist the lure. Ernst Klebinder, my mother's younger brother, luxuriated in the splendid title of *Regierungsrat* (governmental councilor), which he had acquired during a brief First World War spell as a higher civil servant. Austria had thousands of *Regierungsräte*—but in any high-level conversation when people mentioned the *Herr Regierungsrat* they meant Ernst Klebinder. Everybody was on his lips; he was on everybody's lips. I was still a boy when one of my young cousins asked Klebinder what kind of newspaper the *Sonn-und-Montags-Zeitung* was. Klebinder was the sole owner of the popular Vienna weekly. "The *Sonn-und-Montags-Zeitung*, my boy" he replied with a fine flourish, "is a very exclusive paper; only very few people read it."

Whether it was a first night for which he had not bothered to get a ticket or a function at which one would have thought he had no business or the pleasant swimming pool in Baden, near Vienna, which had the "House Full" sign up on a Sunday, the little man with the great personality would arrive and dazzle the ushers, footmen, or ticket collectors with a reassuring gesture. "Klebinder," he would murmer, and add with emphasis: "*Regierungsrat* Klebinder," and, though these people had no idea who he was, he impressed them as somebody they could deny access only at the risk of their jobs. Some naïve people were firmly convinced that "Klebinder" was a sort of magic formula, an open sesame to the good things in life.

Long before telephonitis became a common disease, telephone wires, like an umbilical cord, linked Klebinder with Mother Earth. He called cabinet ministers from their bath, industrialists from their beds—or their mistresses' beds, for he knew when and where men slept out. Neither bank presidents nor politicians were safe from his telephonic pursuit. (The magic of the tele-

phone came to full flower the day Hitler ordered the *Anschluss,*
and Goering, in charge of the pseudodiplomatic operations, virtually conquered Austria by telephone.) The ease with which
Klebinder, by a sleight of hand, reversed the positions of men
of greater status never ceased to astonish me: "Herr Regierungsrat," I have heard an Austrian vice-chancellor addressing him,
and Klebinder replying condescendingly: "Yes, Karl—what is it
you want?" That Klebinder was at that time transacting some
major—if not quite savory—business on behalf of the vice-
chancellor was only part of the explanation. That man to whom
everybody else kowtowed was simply awed by Klebinder's personality.

Like many other Viennese newspaper proprietors, Klebinder
combined journalism and business in a manner that would never
be condoned in Fleet Street or Rockefeller Center but which,
in the interwar years, was commonplace not only in Austria and
all points East but also in the French press. Corruption was
perfected to a fine art. Advance payments for advertisements
that were never required to appear, subsidies from banks and
insurance companies, secret government funds, and the campaign
coffers of political parties were (in every sense of the word) accepted sources of income for newspaper proprietors and lesser
journalistic entrepreneurs.

The practice did not stop at Austrian sources. A charming,
most erudite but bashful old chap, a fine writer with a profound
understanding of international affairs who worked for us, was
no sooner appointed press attaché of the Polish Embassy in
Vienna than he drew me into a corner: he had something important to tell me. With signs of great embarrassment he took
an envelope from his pocket and handed it to me. It contained
the equivalent of £5 in notes. "You see," he said hesitatingly,
"I have been given some money to distribute among Viennese
journalists. But you are the only one whom I know well enough
to approach." He looked at me like an old dog begging for his
dinner. I tried not to laugh. Even if I had considered accepting
a bribe, the amount was hardly enough to tempt an office boy.
Instead I told him that I knew of one or two elderly colleagues
who, I was certain, would not be averse to a small addition to

their meager legitimate income. The old man toddled off disconsolately. I doubt whether he ever managed to get rid of his bribes. He was, of course, not the only foreign agent going around pressing money on people, but it was a comparatively harmless practice because, far from allowing themselves to be corrupted, the recipients simply put the money in their pockets and never did a thing in exchange.

Klebinder's career had been quite spectacular. Father, when he controlled a leading Vienna newspaper on behalf of a client, gave him his first job and helped him to climb the social ladder —not easy for a Jew in those days. But Ernst, a brilliant young journalist, quickly worked his way up to become general manager of one of Vienna's biggest publishing houses, which controlled four newspapers. It was when he severed his connection with this firm that, by way of a golden handshake, control of the *Wiener Sonn-und-Montags-Zeitung* was transferred to him. This was an old-established weekly newspaper which appeared on Monday morning when, because of the absolute Sunday restrictions, no daily papers were published in Vienna. Much of what Father advanced Ernst as working capital Ernst paid him back later—by paying me a salary.

In due course Klebinder, to please Father, made me a junior partner on condition that this personal arrangement was not divulged to outsiders—a typical, completely meaningless Klebinder formula. I had to fight for my share of the profits which, anyway, melted away in involved bookkeeping arrangements; and when my bills in Vienna's nightclubs began to mount and their owners, in retaliation, refused to pay for their advertisements in our paper, Klebinder decided to liquidate my assets by squaring what the advertisers owed him and what I owed them. In this way my assets became liquid in the form of champagne for the dancing girls of Vienna.

The *Wiener Sonn-und-Montags-Zeitung* had offices in the Berggasse, a few blocks from the apartment in which I had spent most of my childhood. Business was conducted in the conspiratorial manner of an ancient family firm, which accounts for some of the appalling nonsense which has been written about us. The paper's finances were inextricably intertwined with Klebinder's private and other business interests, which was the key to his otherwise inexplicable swift switches from almost irresponsible extravagance to beggarly economies. Often they went hand in hand. One day when Klebinder had brought off a relatively big coup he bought each of his seven sisters a fur coat, none below the Persian-lamb grade. On other occasions salaries—including mine—were paid like reluctant handouts, and often the only way to get expenses was for reporters to borrow the approximate amount from the charming girl cashier who, with her hand in the till, was in an ideal position to recoup the money.

Investing me with the title of assistant editor long before my abilities could possibly justify such rapid advance, Klebinder sometimes regarded me fondly as his dear young nephew, but on other occasions looked on me as an overambitious young rival who was scheming to step into his shoes; or, again, he treated me like an office boy. I was already virtually running the paper when he still sent me out for cigarettes. But though we employed writers of great standing, by dint of constant presence (particularly during Klebinder's frequent and prolonged absences when his health began to fail) the conduct of affairs on the spot soon devolved entirely on me. For a boy in his early twenties it was a heady position.

It was during one of these periods while I was in charge that some of the peculiarities of newspaper publishing in Vienna's difficult interwar period confronted me like a distorting mirror in which politics, people, and events appeared in disconcertingly freakish shapes. The telephone rang one Sunday morning—our busiest day—and the caller at the other end introduced himself in a soft voice as "Bosel." That, in the Vienna of the late twenties, was equivalent to taking a call in 1963 from Rothschild, Krupp, Rockefeller, and Onassis rolled into one—except that, in the case of Bosel, mystery was added as a further intriguing compound to the glamour of great wealth.

Each country and each epoch has its men who wield power behind the scenes by virtue of their wealth, inherited or acquired. What fascinated me most about Sigmund Bosel was the web of influence with which he covered wide sectors of public life long after his extraordinary wealth had evaporated or diminished to commonplace proportions. He was a fabulous character. I hate to call him, as everybody else did, an *Inflationsgewinner*, a profiteer from inflation, because it does not do the man justice, although it is true that, while still a minor merchant, he grasped the potentialities of the German and Austrian runaway inflations and amassed a great fortune; his transactions on the London Stock Exchange were in the neighborhood of £1,000,000 a day. Bosel acquired control of innumerable businesses and much property in Austria and abroad and, beginning with his own family, drew a wide circle of generous benefactions around an ever-increasing area of—as things stood in Austria in those days—important but impecunious people. (He also owned what was reported to be the finest collection of pornographic antiques which, if I am not mistaken, he later sold to King Farouk.) In Austria, where his name was as much a household word as Clore's and Cotton's in England forty years later, he was believed to be locked in constant rivalry with a rival named Camillo Castiglione, each projecting his views on things—the theater, politics, commerce—by means of one or more newspapers on which they exerted an enormous influence.

One daily newspaper, for instance, which was close to Bosel, ran an unusual serial which fictionalized the day's events. Readers scrutinized every installment for hints of economic developments, and interest mounted to red-hot excitement when the narrative moved toward a big party at which Bosel expected to meet his great antagonist, Castiglione. Did this mean that a reconciliation was at hand? And was a reconciliation not bound to lead to financial cooperation between, if not to an amalgamation of, the two vast empires? What effect was the creation of such a combine likely to have on the stock market? On the economy of the country? On future economic policy and prices and employment? The circulation of the paper rose by leaps and bounds. Even men of standing studied the daily clues with great concern.

The story was moving to a climax. The setting of the party had already been described in glowing terms. Bosel was in his place, ready to receive Castiglione, to whom the writer devoted some wildly flattering paragraphs. Anticipation could not have been greater if this had been Stanley meeting Dr. Livingstone. The day's installment ended with the pregnant sentence: "Castiglione stepped into the room and walked slowly toward Bosel, who held out his hand. . . ." That night some people I know could find no sleep. Next morning thousands were waiting on their doorstep for the morning paper to arrive. Disregarding the news pages, they turned to the absorbing serial. Alas, they could hardly have guessed that Sigmund Bosel, who had been preparing the way for financial talks with Castiglione, had suddenly changed his mind and sent word accordingly to the editor. The new chapter began: "Bosel shook Castiglione by the hand: 'I am glad to meet you,' Castiglione said, 'but sorry to be unable to stay.' Upon which he turned and left. . . ." That day fortunes were lost. Shares tumbled on the Vienna stock exchange. It was a long time before they recovered.

Stories like this had molded the popular image of Bosel. I helped Max Reinhardt acquire Leopoldskron Castle as a residence while directing the Salzburg Festival. The story went that when the world's greatest theatrical producer positioned a hundred liveried torchbearers along the drive of Leopoldskron at the ceremonial castle-warming party, his benefactor Castiglione commiserated with him: "What a pity the electricity supply should fail on such a night. . . ." He liked pomp and circumstance and led an active social life. But I had never set eyes on Sigmund Bosel—few had, for that matter—until he asked me to come and see him on that Sunday morning. It was more than professional interest that made me drop everything and be on my way at once.

As I might have expected, the entrance to his main office was an unobtrusively small door in a tiny side street. On the first floor was a long corridor (a corridor of power and corruption) with several side doors leading to small, comfortably furnished rooms—half offices, half drawing rooms. A servant quickly conducted me into one of these rooms as if anxious that I should not linger in the corridor. Presently a tiny man, dressed in a black suit, slid noiselessly into the room: black hair, black tie, penetrating eyes exuding a friendly magnetism not unlike Klebinder's but not at all aggressive. His voice was so low as to

be almost inaudible. Telling me how glad he was to meet me—
Klebinder had told him how excellently I managed the paper
—he promptly let me into a secret: "Regierungsrat Klebinder
and I have become partners," he said, suggesting in the friendliest possible manner that he was now my associate chief. "I
want us to start off in a pleasant way," he added, and handed
me a bulging envelope. "Take it. Take it. It's quite all right. I
have discussed the matter with Klebinder!"

There was not the slightest doubt that the envelope contained money, and by the feel of it, a great deal of money.
Greed fought with prudence in my breast. At this time I had,
of course, no idea that Bosel was handing out money regularly
to all manner of people in these little rooms—journalists, police
presidents, members of Parliament. Was he trying to bribe me?
If I refused to accept, how would Klebinder react? Perhaps
Klebinder had left it to Bosel to tell me of the new arrangement.
If that was the case—my salary was long overdue—I was not
doing any wrong. Bosel gave me no time to think, less to argue.
Had this doubtful transaction been the only purpose of his invitation? Gently but firmly he bundled me out of the room where
the servant again took over. Traffic was whirling all around me
in the street before I could collect my thoughts.

The wad of notes was formidable, the equivalent of three
months' salary. Back in the office I telephoned Klebinder, who
was in a sanatorium at the Semmering mountain resort, two
hours' journey from Vienna. When I had taken all the obstacles
—operators, nurses, doctors, one of his inevitable sisters in attendance—and got Klebinder on the telephone, I told him what
had happened. He sounded surprised. I could hear him breath-
ing heavily. I could also hear him thinking: "So Bosel has come
out into the open and tried to recruit Willi as an ally against me
—or at least as a dependable second string in case I fail him." But
Klebinder said nothing of the sort. After only the briefest pause
his voice came over the wire, easily, casually: "That's quite all
right; keep the money. We shall adjust your salary accordingly.
You will get a raise, of course, but you can't expect to have
it both ways, can you?" It was obvious he intended to rescue a

financial advantage even from so embarrassing a situation as Bosel had put him in.

All Bosel expected in exchange for the huge amounts he paid out was goodwill against future contingencies, and, in the case of journalists, that his name be kept out of the news. In that— no doubt owing to the huge handouts which, as in the case of Klebinder, sometimes brought him a partnership—he succeeded to a remarkable degree. In the end he acquired control of Austria's best-established daily newspaper, *Die Neue Freie Presse*. The wartime head of the British Ministry of Information's Soviet Section first came to London as a correspondent of *Die Neue Freie Presse*, appointed by Bosel.

During my visits to the Bosel office I made good use of the time I was kept waiting by watching the corridor through a slit in the door that I kept open surreptitiously. Had I circulated a list of the men I saw passing through that corridor, I could have brought down the government, decapitated the police, convulsed industry and big business, and caused havoc in all political parties, including the Nazi Party, which at that time already had several representatives on the Vienna City Council. One sample of the extraordinary fabric of intrigue and collusion among partners in political character assassination by grapevine confounded all accepted patterns. Soon after Austria's pocket-sized Chancellor Dr. Engelbert Dollfuss came to power, a Socialist leader told Klebinder jokingly how ridiculous it was that so small a man as Dollfuss should require a huge new limousine just because he had become chancellor. Klebinder passed that story on to Bosel; Bosel, in the privacy of his office, confided it to a top-ranking police official who, in turn, amused some of his Nazi friends with it. At the next public meeting of the Vienna City Council, a Nazi member made the story the central theme of his attack on the Dollfuss administration.

One of the *Sonn-und-Montags-Zeitung*'s leader writers was Walter Tschuppick, a Bohemian (in the literal and extended sense of the meaning), a highly respected historian who occupied a permanent suite at the exclusive Hotel Bristol but spent most of his days and nights at one of the small, obscure, and secluded

Heurigen, the new-wine gardens at the foot hills of the Vienna Woods. It was one of my early duties to try to extract copy from him. Sometimes when, at long last, I found him in a happy frame of mind, wineglass in hand, holding forth to all who cared to listen, I made him write his lead article on the spot. Whatever the quantity of wine he had consumed, it was written in a subtle, lucid, and admirably incisive style.

We were producing an entertaining paper, anticipating the magazine character which television forced many dailies to adopt decades later, but Klebinder's main preoccupation was politics and, above all, the Nazis. Loyal to his Jewish heritage but appreciating, earlier than most, the worldwide threat of Nazism, he joined forces with Vienna's Franciscan Order, some of whose members wrote the most impressive anti-Nazi articles I ever read. In exchange Klebinder freely contributed to the Franciscan funds. To see little Klebinder with the big telltale nose promenading down the Kärntnerstrasse in deep conversation with a Franciscan friar in his dark-brown habit was a sight to behold. Our Franciscans were not only brilliant historical scholars wielding a sharp polemical pen but also delightfully amusing and earthy companions with a fund of unprintable stories of their experiences.

In his incessant endeavor to harass the Nazis, Klebinder attacked many sacred cows that had become fixtures in our political landscape. When, one day, I told him of the increase in pan-German and anti-Semitic activity at the University, our conversation turned to the Numerus Clausus by which the academic authorities rationed the number of Jews to be admitted to the University. Klebinder seized on the Numerus Clausus to launch a furious attack on the rector, who retaliated with an action for libel. Edi Frischauer, defending Klebinder, pleaded that the attack was not a personal one but was directed against the Numerus Clausus; the rector was simply the man who represented this arbitrary and unconstitutional discrimination against one section of the community. Before judgment could be passed on the alleged defamation, Edi argued before the court, it was necessary to examine the legality, or otherwise, of the Numerus Clausus. The matter was duly referred to the Constitutional

Court, which ruled that the Numerus Clausus violated the Constitution. The rector's action against Klebinder was dismissed. It was a famous victory for democracy. It enraged the Nazis, who swore that they would "get Klebinder."

Long before Nazi pressure became a public menace, the country was already dangerously divided into Left and Right, with the Social Democratic Schutzbund locked in permanent battle with the Fascist Heimwehr which, however, unlike the Nazis who looked to Germany and Hitler, emphasized the Austrian character. In Vienna the Heimwehr was supported by many wealthy anti-Socialist Jews. Small sections of provincial Heimwehr cadres, however, were permeated with ineradicable anti-Semitism. Modeled on Mussolini's Blackshirts, the Heimwehr was determined to transform Austria's political structure.

Of the Heimwehr leaders, the good-looking, pleasant Prince Starhemberg had been with Hitler in the 1923 Munich beerhouse putsch which, alas, did not strike us as such a historic date at the time. Passing through Munich in November, 1923, a few days after Hitler's first attempt to seize power, my brother Fritz and I never even knew there had been a putsch. While Prince Starhemberg himself had switched his allegiance from Hitler to Fritz Mandl and Mussolini, some of his Heimwehr lieutenants still leaned toward the Nazi movement. One Sunday in 1931, I was in the air over Styria in a small German two-seater Klemm aircraft piloted by the German designer who was demonstrating the machine to me to get publicity for his Austrian sales campaign, when, from our precarious and flimsy but fast-moving observation post, we noticed a commotion on the ground—firing of shots, much running to and fro of uniformed men who dispersed in terror when we swooped down low over their heads.

It looked as if Austria were in the throes of a revolution. "Get me to Vienna as quickly as possible," I demanded. But train and car eventually got me back more quickly than the little Klemm could have done. Next morning the *Sonn-und-Montags-Zeitung* published my report of what turned out to have been a local Heimwehr uprising under the by-line "From Our Correspondent, Specially Flown to the Trouble Spot." It was the first time an Austrian reporter had been flown anywhere.

Not many months later I was invited to join the first flight of the *Graf Zeppelin* to Austria. Arrangements were made for Dr. Hugo Eckener's giant airship to leave its base in the German city of Friedrichshafen, by the shores of Lake Constance, one Saturday on the stroke of midnight, to reach the Vienna airport at Aspern at 8:00 A.M. on Sunday, take members of the Austrian government on an eight-hour cruise over Austria during the day, and leave for the return flight to Friedrichshafen at midnight.

As the *Graf Zeppelin* was due to arrive in Vienna on Sunday (our press day), it seemed a good idea for me to cover the Friedrichshafen-Vienna flight, which would give me ample time to write for publication on Monday morning. Leaving Vienna on the Friday-night train to Bregenz and Lindau, I was looking for my compartment when I spotted the small official Austrian party traveling to Friedrichshafen to represent the government on the first stage of the flight.

Three gentlemen who had obviously refreshed themselves before joining the train hailed me and asked me to join them: the diminutive Minister of Agriculture Dr. Engelbert Dollfuss, a cheerful Lower Austrian of peasant stock; Dr. -Ingenieur Fritz Neubacher, who was associated with Austrian aviation; and a General Schiebel of the Defense Ministry. It was a convivial party, and we had a most animated talk spiced with political allusions and indiscretions: "Don't you dare to write a word of this, please!" Dollfuss impressed on me in the friendliest manner time and again. Within an hour the conversation had yielded enough political dynamite to fill ten columns, but I kept my promise of silence.

Except for the sedate general (what utter bores most generals are!) none of us bothered to take advantage of our sleeper that night. The dining-car waiter produced a few bottles of excellent Gumpoldskirckner, meaty Austrian sausages and strong Hammer's peasant bread with the compliments of the management. Occasionally we burst into song for the sheer joy of it. Surprising how close people get on such jaunts. Dollfuss, Neubacher, and I were an incongruous trio, but when we emerged at Lindau station at the crack of dawn we were firm friends. (Because Dr. Neubacher played no further part in my life, let me just mention that he was already an illegal Nazi leader at the time, became Nazi Lord Mayor of Vienna after the *Anschluss,* and later *Gauleiter* (area commander) of Nazi-occupied Yugoslavia. He survived the war and a term of imprisonment. I never saw him again.)

An official German welcome awaited us. To greet a friendly cabinet minister the German authorities could not resist trotting out a company of *Reichswehr* troops. Dollfuss, Neubacher, and General Schiebel were invited to inspect the men who stood rigidly to attention. Dollfuss pulled me with him, and the four of us completed the ceremonial with as much dignity as we could muster after our lively night. It was the first and last time I was paid such military honor by a German—or any other—army. At Friedrichshafen, a little the worse for wear, we toured the big hangars—the *Hindenburg,* which came to a tragic end over Lakehurst, New Jersey, a few years later, was still a-building—and admired the *Graf Zeppelin,* which was to take us back to Vienna that night.

Of the mixed crowd which took part in this night flight, apart from my immediate companions I can remember only a young American honeymoon couple; they had been married that day in Friedrichshafen. The two youngsters were terribly thrilled, but they had a most unusual wedding night. Their imagination fired by what they assumed to be going on in the lofty nuptial bed, some of our fellow passengers organized a game that chiefly consisted of maneuvering people into such a position that they leaned against the honeymooners' lockless cabin door, whereupon they would be pushed into the presence of the embarrassed youngsters. Dollfuss engineered at least half-a-dozen such intrusions.

It was a glorious flight. The takeoff was so smooth and silent it was a purely visual sensation. One could neither hear the engines nor feel their throb. At the crack of dawn we were over the heart of Austria, much nearer Vienna than scheduled. Dr. Eckener, assisted by Captain Schiller, steered the airship toward the Vienna Woods. We saw the people below looking up in wonder at the strange silvery apparition that hedgehopped majestically and almost silently over the trees and rooftops.

At the stroke of 8:00 A.M. we were over Aspern airport with a company of soldiers ready to pull the *Graf Zeppelin* down. Dollfuss told me he was anxious to get away immediately after the official reception—he was due to make a speech in Lower Austria—and asked me to take his travel case to his secretary and to make sure his car was ready for a hurried departure. Running from the airship as soon as it touched down, I located car and secretary, and gave him the briefcase and message before turning back to watch the ceremonial welcome.

In the intervening seconds a police cordon had been thrown around the *Graf Zeppelin* and the reception party, which included the entire Cabinet. The police would not let me pass. Pleading with them, I explained that I had just arrived on the airship. I might as well have insisted that I was the Queen of Sheba. When I got angry—and, well, yes, insulting, they arrested me and handed me over to a couple of mounted policemen who half-carried me away between their horses, galloping off at great pace, only the tips of my toes touching the ground.

God knows how far they would have dragged me in this infelicitous manner had they not been forced to halt and let an official motorcar pass from which—mouth literally sagging in astonishment—Dr. Dollfuss stared at me and my escort. The car stopped and Dollfuss jumped out. The Viennese mounties straightened out, standing to attention, or whatever a mounted policeman does. As they saluted they let go of me, and before they could grab me again I was in the car with Dollfuss and racing away. The incident cemented our friendship.

Klebinder was not a man to pick a fight. Confronted with an armed robber, he would, I think, have tried instinctively to con the miserable wretch out of his spare cash—and probably have got away with it. In the early days it often seemed as if, far from worrying about what the Nazis might do to the Jews, he was thinking of ways and means of converting the Nazis to Judaism. But once he realized that not even his genius for compromise could blunt the edge of Nazi fanaticism, he declared war. Though less conscious of any threat to our own safety than he was, I became his loyal lieutenant. Hitler and Naziism—with emphasis on the Austrian Nazis—became our chief target. Night and day we thought of little except how to combat the menace.

Curiously, the thought that we could lose the struggle never occurred to us. Occasionally we discussed our friend Hugo Bettauer's little book *Town Without Jews* (Bettauer wrote another one, *The Joyless Street,* which was filmed with a beautiful young Swedish newcomer in the cast, Greta Garbo). *Town Without Jews* fictionally anticipated Hitler's "Make Vienna *judenrein*" order of 1942 but ended on a hopeful note: the Jews were invited to return. We mourned Bettauer, who had been murdered by a premature Nazi, but we did not draw any conclusions—yet.

Though we had lived with Naziism since 1926, frankly, we had no idea what a Nazi victory would mean to a community like Vienna which included half a million Jews and half-Jews. It just could not happen! They were a damned nuisance, these ridiculously noisy, uniformed youngsters with their red-and-black swastika armlets, marching up and down the streets, singing songs and shouting *"Juda verrecke! Deutschland erwache!"* Rowdies! Political gangsters! Their fanaticism was an alien element in the still-*gemütliche* mental makeup of our good old Danube city. Needed their bottoms smacked, we thought.

They struck first. In the assembly hall of the University I heard someone calling out my name. I turned, but the next minute I was surrounded. Looking for an escape, I made toward the entrance and, dragging my attackers with me down the stairs, warded off blows and tried to hit back. They were shouting "Jewish swine!" and instinct nearly made me reply: "No, I'm a Catholic!" but the words never left my lips. I was not afraid. Even a dozen men could not pull me down. For one thing, only three or four at a time could get at me and I could cope with those—I thought. Then something hit my chin. It must have been a knuckle-duster, because I could feel the skin splitting and a sharp pain shooting through my brain. With the strength of despair and anger I shook off the cluster of hands clinging to me and rushed down the stairs and into the arms of three policemen who had been watching the fight from the pavement (they were not allowed to enter the extraterritorial grounds of the University). Trying to grab some of my assailants, the police were confronted by a solid phalanx of students lining the steps but safely out of their reach. The four of us—the three policemen supporting me—accompanied by jeers and insults, made a rather undignified retreat.

The contact I had established with Minister of Agriculture Dr. Dollfuss was too good not to be nurtured and exploited; besides, I liked the little man. Dollfuss had a fine sense of humor and, contrary to the general impression he created later, no sense at all of his own importance. His peasant wit was astonishingly sophisticated. Writing about him, people who had never met him handed down a completely false picture of him as a primitive, pompous little ass. He was nothing of the sort. I often visited him early in the morning in his flat in the Stallburggasse, the heart of Vienna. On one occasion we talked while Frau Dollfuss hung curtains quite unconcernedly. At another time, his little boy insisted on being given a ride on father's knee. Dollfuss was as naturally uninhibited when spending an evening at the *Heurigen* with his political cronies. (The car which took them back from one such excursion overturned and Dollfuss's lip was split; the wound broke in death and gave rise to the rumors that the Nazi assassins had ill-treated the chancellor before shooting him down.)

Coincidence had, for once, forged an association between me and a "coming man" before Klebinder had spotted him, and I still remember Klebinder's condescendingly approving reaction when I suggested that he let me invite Dollfuss to one of his parties. Although at that time Klebinder seemed to have little use for a minister of agriculture, he asked Dollfuss to dinner and worked his usual charm. It was a providential idea.

Now, I have firmly resolved that there is one subject with which I shall deal as briefly as its importance warrants in retrospect, although I have, of course, frequently mentioned it in my life as "another feather in my political cap." I refer to the so-called Schicklgruber story. Acknowledging my proprietary right to Dollfuss (an "I-saw-him-first" sort of thing), Klebinder asked me to join the dinner party. One of Klebinder's sisters was also present. The conversation was a clash of two diametrically different types of humor—rapier versus cutlass—spiced with anecdotes about many political personalities. Inevitably, it turned to the Nazis.

The Hitler threat in Germany was very real. In two successive elections the Nazis had considerably increased their vote. Their success reverberated across the border and enhanced the prospects of our own Nazis. I ought to mention here what neither Klebinder nor I knew at the time, that Dr. Dollfuss had achieved high office in Austria against the fearful odds of what, in a Catholic country, was an almost unforgivable social handicap: he was born out of wedlock. Like so many people who, suffering from a defect, are anxious to expose that same defect in others (the psychological opposite of the old injunction to those residing in glass houses not to throw stones), Dollfuss laughingly and in a mock-conspiratorial whisper told Klebinder: "You know, of course, that, strictly speaking, Hitler is illegitimate. His father was, anyway. . . ."

Before I could burst out with an enthusiastic acknowledgment of this sensational disclosure, a stern glance from Klebinder bade me to keep quiet. Not a muscle in his face betrayed his own reaction to the news, but his swift-moving, flickering eyes indicated an important train of thought forming in his mind. Within a second he had steered the conversation away from the subject. Late that night in the car—we had taken Dollfuss home—Klebinder bared his thoughts: "We'll have to investigate this. It is quite sensational. I am glad, Willi, you kept quiet. If Dollfuss had realized the political significance of his remark, he would have told the *Reichspost*" (the organ of his party). "We must get everybody to work on this tomorrow. Not a moment to be lost!"

The result of our investigations proved that Hitler's father was an illegitimate child whose original name of Schicklgruber he changed to Hitler. The story was published in a special edition of the *Wiener Sonn-und-Montags-Zeitung* under the banner headline: HEIL SCHICKLGRUBER! Now, when it first became obligatory for people to have registered names, officials of the old Austro-Hungarian monarchy saddled many Jews in Austrian

Poland deliberately with ridiculous and impossible names which they were naturally anxious to change once they had migrated. One of Hitler's demagogically anti-Semitic demands was that Jews should be obliged to revert to their original names. If the Jews, why not Hitler? Let him revert to his family's original name, the *Sonn-und-Montags-Zeitung* demanded. If the Germans were compelled to shout "Heil Schicklgruber!" rather than "Heil Hitler!" the Nazi movement would sink in a sea of ridicule; such was Klebinder's argument. Another election was impending in Germany. Our sensational story, Klebinder persuaded himself, might turn the tables against Hitler. We know now that he slightly overestimated the effect of our special edition, and the Schicklgruber story, seen in perspective, was little more than an amusing stunt without any real significance.

Since 1940 the Schicklgruber story has been associated with Quentin Reynolds who, as a correspondent in London during the 1940 blitz, in one of his excellent broadcasts to the United States addressed himself rhetorically to "Herr Schicklgruber," telling him that "London can take it!"

If our revelation failed to hinder Hitler's advance toward total political victory, it enraged the Austrian Nazis. Two of them retaliated the only way they knew how: they attacked the small and fragile Klebinder with whips while he was peacefully sipping his coffee at the Café Rebhuhn, a journalists' haunt in the center of Vienna. Because all manner of threats against Klebinder were thereafter made, hundreds of Jewish boys gathered to provide a bodyguard when he went to testify at the trial of his assailants. The presence of so many strong and determined young Jews provoked a Nazi counterdemonstration during which shots were fired. A Jewish youngster was injured in the arm. Vienna of the early thirties . . .

Apart from carrying out my duties at the *Sonn-und-Montags-Zeitung*, I worked as chief reporter of an evening paper (two editions a day, *Mittags-Zeitung, Allgemeine Zeitung*), a job I especially enjoyed except for having to start work at 8:00 A.M., a little early for a young man who rarely went to bed before the small hours. For a few hectic months I produced the "Story of the Day" four times a week. One day, for instance, Elisabeth

Bergner arrived, and I was instructed to interview her. I telephoned her hotel, asked the operator to put me through to her room, spoke to the maid, was passed on to a secretary who, in turn, called Herr Czinner, Bergner's husband, who handed the receiver to one of Bergner's lady friends. At each of these junctions in my slow progress I was cross-examined about the questions I proposed to ask the great actress. This had been going on for over half an hour until everybody seemed at long last satisfied and I was told sweetly: "You will be put through now," to which—on a sudden impulse—I replied: "No, thank you, I've lost the desire," whereupon I wrote my piece under the title *"No* Interview with Elisabeth Bergner." I have not taken kindly to interviews with actors or actresses since, nor to Elisabeth Bergner. The "No-Interview" was reprinted in forty German papers, and netted me a tidy sum.

A fair amount of police reporting came my way and it thrilled me, as whom would it not? All my life I have never been able to resist the glamor of a detective (a uniformed man will do at a pinch), a reflection, I think, of a deep-seated criminal instinct and fear of punishment. ("See, I can associate with a policeman without going to prison!") One evening an informant called me from the nearby Franz-Josef Railway Station and suggested I send a reporter to the station cloakroom. I sent myself and arrived to find a small crowd of railway employees examining a gruesome piece of left luggage, a brown paper parcel leaking blood. It contained part of a human limb. I obtained as much information as possible from everyone concerned and was just about to return to the office when Hofrat Wahl, the grumpy, uncommunicative chief of the Vienna Criminal Investigation Department, arrived to initiate the police inquiries. To his consternation it turned out that the people I had interviewed—the key witnesses of the find—had assumed I was a policeman and, having told me what they knew, gone home. It was years before the little *Hofrat* forgave me.

On another occasion I—again ahead of him (we paid well for prompt information)—hurried to a dingy suburban room where a prostitute had been found murdered. Forty-five knife wounds disfigured her naked body, yet as it lay there lifeless on the floor, face down, the hair-thin incisions hardly noticeable, it was a strangely unreal, beautiful sight, even the pool of blood around the body forming an artistic pattern. (By a strange coincidence, only a few weeks later I was at the Vienna Concert Hall where, laid out on the cold stone floor of the foyer, was the body of a young Egyptian princess who had been shot dead by her frustrated lover. This body, too, looked like an exquisite marble figure rather than a corpse.)

The economic crisis was upon us. Arriving at the office one morning, I was told that—hard to believe—the Creditanstalt, pride of Vienna's banks (its president was Baron Rothschild) had closed its doors. There was pandemonium. Warrants were issued for the arrests of Baron Rothschild and his co-directors, among them the redoubtable Herr Ehrenfest, a financial genius who had disappeared. (I later discovered him in Lisbon and scooped the pool by interviewing him over the telephone.)

"Go and see what's happening inside the closed bank," I was instructed by the editor.

Without much difficulty I bypassed people who were banging at the bank's closed doors. As I had anticipated, I found a back entrance open. Inside, an usher willingly conducted me to the managerial offices on the first floor. "Which is Ehrenfest's office?" I asked. It was an impressive room with dark oak paneling, magnificent chandeliers, mahogany furniture, a vast desk. Probing a panel in the wall, I stumbled into the washroom. Beyond that was the lavatory, clinically tiled, with a most opulent seat. By the side of the seat—what do you think?—a telephone!

No need for me to investigate any further. I went back to the office and wrote my story: "So busy have these gentlemen been, squandering the money of their "investors," I wrote, "that they could not even afford to relax from their labors while sitting on the lavatory! So swift were the developments in the world's economic markets on which the survival of little Austria depended that the managers of the Creditanstalt had to keep in touch with events even while etc. . . ."

Frankly, I was not very well versed in economic affairs and had no means of knowing whether or not the failure of the bank was the fault of the management or the inevitable result of the economic crisis which had found the world unprepared. But this story was too good to miss. It was printed and became the talk of Vienna. "Every time my banker goes to the bathroom I tremble for my investments," a comic said from the stage of a Vienna cabaret.

It was a marvelously hectic life. Each day was filled with twenty hours' worth of distance run, unadulterated excitement, professional and personal, the only relaxation from hard work being hard play. Traversing Vienna in my tattered little red Italian sports car, I tried to emulate Klebinder and be in several places at once. Rather than waiting for news at the office, I established myself in the big lounge of the Grand Hotel, where the news was—economic, social, political, foreign—together with the people who knew or made the news. The Princes of Hyderabad arrived; I met them socially in the lounge and interviewed them long before other reporters knew they were anywhere around. Next door, at the Bristol Hotel, I talked to Jimmy Walker, New York's legendary mayor, but I had to go out of my way—a couple of hours' journey—to get a beat on Charlie Chaplin by boarding the train that brought the great man on his first visit to Vienna. We had a stumbling conversation. How could a young Viennese gadabout possibly establish contact with the sensitive little man who was at the peak of his fame, lionized all over the world, triumphant wherever he went? He showed little interest in my running commentary on the Austrian landscape which we watched from the window of his compartment until I pointed out Stein Prison, where Austria's most dangerous criminals were confined. He asked questions about the Austrian penal system, about which I knew only what I had been told by family friends of the postinflation and early currency-control era who had had an involuntary opportunity to study it at close quarters. Inevitably, I played up this part of our conversation in my reportage, which gave Vienna the impression that Chaplin was rather an odd chap, which, in a way, he was. To me, anyway, during those two uneasy hours I spent with him, he seemed distinctly odd.

Of the lounge of the Grand Hotel, as of the Café de la Paix in Paris, it could be said that if you sat there long enough, you were bound to meet everybody who was anybody. A regular inhabitant—of the lounge, not the hotel—was Johnny Soyka, a Czech-born Berlin film agent whose most successful client used to be Marlene Dietrich. Her popular record, "*Johnny, wenn Du Geburtstag hast, bin ich bei Dir zu Gast, die ganze Nacht . . .*" (Johnny, when it's your birthday I'll be your guest the whole night), was written and composed for the occasion and sung by Marlene as a birthday surprise. Johnny was an amusing, big, corpulent man with a little dark moustache in a small round piggy face. His roving eyes kept the hotel lounge under constant surveillance, and rumor had it that he was able to tell at a distance of fifty paces whether any two men talking in the lounge were just about to conclude a successful business deal, in which case he would join them, whether he knew them or not, asking them with disarming directness, "How about cutting me in for a small percentage?" If they did not comply—and why should they?—some of them, it was said, at least rewarded his good-humored intrusion with a stock-exchange tip or some other profitable business advice. One way or another, Johnny made a fair amount of money.

Mady Soyka, his wife, was a very beautiful, Teutonically blond, graceful and elegant *dame du monde*—well, at least *demi-monde*—whose arms were almost covered with rows of diamond bracelets, more than I have ever seen on any other woman. Mady was a reporter's dream acquaintance, flirtatious, well connected, gossipy and informative. I spent much time in her company, but it was several years before my professional interest in her was rewarded with a sensational story—a succession of stories. By that time (1936) I had settled in London. My Vienna past and most people who figured in it were all but obscured by a willful amnesia. Mady Soyka was the last person I expected to hear from when my telephone rang and a woman's German voice playfully told me to "guess who." Even when she revealed herself as "Mady," her English name, so popular on the Continent, did not immediately suggest Frau Soyka from Vienna. We met, and she told me that she had come to see her old friend Marlene Dietrich, and, "on instructions from the highest authority," persuade her to return to Germany.

This was too good to miss. What a fool, that woman, to tell me, of all people! "I'll call Denham Studios for you," I volunteered (Mady's English was not so good). "And I'll drive you to Denham in my car." She was always good at letting a man take care of the expenses. The rendezvous was quickly arranged, and when we arrived at Denham the following morning we were conducted to Marlene's dressing room. The two women embraced like the old friends they were, and Mady greeted Rudolf Sieber, Marlene's husband, with a kiss. Slowly, deliberately, she explained the purpose of her mission. "Confidentially," she admitted, "Goebbels himself has given instructions to bring you back to Germany. You can have anything you want. Anything!"

Marlene looked startled. "This comes as a great surprise," she said, speaking very slowly. Only a few weeks earlier the Nazi press had used the threat of the United States Internal Revenue authorities to impound her jewelry if she did not pay a staggering amount of income tax as a pretext to attack the German film star viciously. Because Marlene had decided to take out American citizenship papers, the Nazis accused her of abandoning the Fatherland and selling herself to the Jews of America.

As if she knew what was going through Marlene's mind, Mady stepped up the pressure: "There will be an immediate reversal of the press campaign against you. The German public will be suitably prepared for your return. You can choose story, director, co-star of any film you consent to make in Germany, and you will be paid £50,000 per picture in any currency you like!" That, in those days, was big money. The promise to pay it in any foreign currency ran counter to Nazi Germany's autarkic financial policy.

The political implication of this encounter between Marlene and Mady was considerable. Goebbels, who had made a spectacular attempt to use the Olympic Games to win friends and influence people, had decided to continue his campaign on another level. He wanted Marlene Dietrich to help boost his country's dwindling prestige. Mady Soyka's task was to lure the prodigal daughter back to Germany. But Marlene was not having any. "Darling," she said sweetly, "how nice of you to bring me this marvelous offer. What a pity I cannot accept it at the moment."

Quick glances passed between Marlene and Rudi Sieber. "You
see, I am under contract for the next two years—which takes us
to the end of 1938. I am committed to do a play on Broadway
in 1939 and I hope it'll run for a year at least. I shall be taking
a few months' holiday after that. . . . Why not return to the
idea, let's say, in 1940 or 1941?"

Mady's pretty jaw dropped. She recognized Marlene's evasive
reply as a brush-off. Her mission had failed. We had tea with
the Siebers and, at my insistence, had our picture taken by the
studio photographer. I knew what I had to do. With great self-
restraint I disguised my disgust with the woman who had clearly
become a Nazi agent—if she had not been one in Vienna already—and drove her back to town. You bloody bitch, I kept
thinking, almost saying it aloud. You dirty Nazi agent! What
about your husband, Johnny, who is a Jew? And you doing the
Nazis' dirty work!

Mady knew what I was thinking. I dumped her outside her
hotel and drove off without saying goodbye. A few minutes later
I was on the telephone to the *Evening Standard*. Next morning
the story appeared in a couple of brisk, impressive paragraphs in
the "Londoner's Diary," which presents important exclusive news
in the invariably sedate frame of the fascinating column, making
it doubly effective. As often happens with the "Londoner's"
paragraphs, the news of Marlene turning down Goebbels's invitation was reprinted in the world press. It was a public smack
in the face for the propaganda chief. I was pleased with myself
for having administered it.

Although I never exchanged another word with Mady, it was
not the end of my journalistic association with her. I warned as
many of my anti-Nazi friends as possible to beware of the attractive snake, but it appeared that, as soon as the Nazis invaded
Austria, she transferred her activities to Paris, where she spied on
the German and Austrian Jewish refugees. She was lost from my
sight when the war broke out and I had no idea what had become
of her when, in 1943, we received the news that the French
Maquis had murdered the German-born manageress of the Café
Marignan in Paris—"name of Soyka"—and appropriated her
jewelry. Once more I wrote a Mady Soyka story; again it was

reprinted all over the world. After the war I met Johnny Soyka in Paris once or twice, a shadow of his former self. We did not discuss his wife. I think he spent the war years in the United States. Since then, Johnny has disappeared from view.

Another of my Vienna haunts was the Femina, a nightclub that combined West European sophistication with the moral standards of a Balkan brothel. Vienna's Four Thousand (so many people included themselves among the upper crust there was virtually nobody underneath) were its most loyal customers. It does not at all surprise me in retrospect that the Femina should have exercised an irresistible pull on me. The proximity of so many beautiful (and willing) girls . . . For a young Viennese the Femina represented the acme of high living. Champagne, a bar cunningly placed so as to enable visitors to mingle with the performers in the intervals between their acts—it was Vienna's Folies-Bergère plus. Although they rubbed shoulders with many customers, only a few privileged young men (I was included because I occasionally published their pictures—it was said I paid them in lead instead of gold) and the most generous Champagne Charlies were allowed to offer them a drink or take the matter a step further.

The proprietor, who traveled far to recruit these beauties, managed the place with extraordinary skill and tact, guarding standards of *public* behavior (of both girls and customers) so jealously that a dowager's drawing-room rules could not have improved upon them. No visiting celebrity missed an evening at the Femina. On one of my last visits, the table next to mine was occupied by the King of England and his party. I shall never forget his enviously appreciative glance at the pretty girl who happened to embrace me playfully at the moment he passed by.

5 | *Never a Tear for This*

*T*he Femina was an excellent source of information, social, political, and industrial. There was no shortage of politicians and industrialists among the regulars or of newsworthy foreign aristocrats, visiting baritones, and policemen on the prowl. Because I sometimes "worked" in this congenial atmosphere, it would seem that my private life was inextricably mixed up with my work. But that was true only to the extent that neither then nor at any future time was I ever anxious to get away from my job.

Neither did I get myself emotionally involved with any Femina girl (the ruin of many a man in these days: I once helped Bosel to extricate a relative from the attractive clutches of one of them), but I was on very close terms with a ravishing young dancer who answered to the curious name of Lili Mouton, hailed from Frankfurt, and later became a typical Parisienne. Gjon Mili, that fine Albanian-American photographer, described her as the most attractive fading beauty he had ever met. Although I never shirked battle in Vienna's ferocious war of the sexes—pursuit and conquest, males and females frequently reversing their traditional roles—and boasted of an astonishingly big turnover, in this promiscuous atmosphere my real affections were reserved for a comparatively small number of rather un-Femina girls.

It was a few weeks after my return from London when a dark-haired, modishly flat-chested girl five or six years my senior talked to me in the Café Central, where formal introductions were easily dispensed with. Well dressed, a coffeehouse pallor hidden beneath a layer of cosmetics, languid, heavily mascaraed eyes, cigarette in the corner of her mouth (all of which rather Bohemian manifestations failed to disguise a *petit bourgeois* background), she surprised me by pretending to recognize me as a famous water-polo player, though I was quite sure she had never seen a water-polo match in her life. "Won't you teach us some of the finer points of swimming?" she asked bluntly. "We could go to the Dianabad now. . . ."

The time was 1:15 P.M., but our favorite corner of the old café was so gloomy, one easily forgot that the sun was shining outside and that many Viennese with sufficient time and money were in the habit of enjoying a midday swim in the pleasant big pool in the center of the city. Another girl was standing a few paces away, a striking blonde with an angular face and an acrobat's figure, strong but still feminine. "This is Vera," the dark-haired girl said, "and I am Klara."

We were fooling around in the pool where I had contested many hard fought water-polo matches when Klara turned to Vera: "Didn't I tell you? Never go by a face! Hasn't he a marvelous figure?" I had never thought of my figure in these terms. It was very flattering and, considering my current fifty-inch waistline, constitutes a very happy memory. The two girls had obviously decided to inspect me more closely before proceeding with their rather transparent project. We repaired to Vera's flat where they consummated what they had taken home on approval: me. Vera, the blonde, was much more to my taste, but I eventually fell for dark-haired Klara. She was single and single-minded, while Vera was less determined and married, and I dreaded complications. Within a few weeks I was deeply in love with Klara, a reflection—I am inclined to think now—of her intense love for me. Although we were both promiscuous, our association was happy and lasted for over three years, during

which time we spent many hours gambling in cafés, drinking
(too much) in wine gardens and nightclubs and snatching em-
braces at my home, in her father's flat, after parties when we
often neither knew nor cared where we were. We were a couple
of well-scrubbed, properly dressed, and generally prosperous premature beatniks.

A crisis in our relationship developed when Klara admitted
that she was determined to marry me. I was far too immature for
such a proposition. The very thought of it seemed utterly ridiculous to me. The problem created a tension that settled on us like
a dead weight. On awakening in the morning, instead of anxiously looking forward to meeting her, I began to dread our
tearful and quarrelsome encounters. The crisis lowered resistance
to temptation. I had been meeting pretty girls every day and had
come to know one or two intimately, but the thought of leaving
Klara for another woman had never occurred to me. Now, suddenly, there *was* another woman.

We had first met at one of Klebinder's smaller luncheon
parties at the Eisvogel restaurant—crayfish and Viennese *Backhendl*—where she struck me as far too attractive to be the girl
friend of the decrepit Austro-Czech businessman with whom she
was sitting. He was, I think, the European representative of a
chain of American stores. She was very chic in an English,
tweedy sort of way, and switched her busy conversation easily
from German to English. Her features could have been Viennese
or English. The jawline, from an English women's magazine,
went surprisingly well with her Viennese urchin's upturned nose.
Brown hair, blue eyes—I should have thought her perfect had
she not been less than five foot in height, with tiny feet to match.

Susan turned out to be a big-hearted girl. She owned a fashionable Viennese salon for women's hats, and spent several
months a year touring the United States designing hats for big
stores, cutting and shaping them for selected customers with her
strong, deft fingers in full view of an audience. Like many public
performers, she was basically uneducated but had acquired great
poise and social dexterity. Moreover, my curiosity for all things
English was aroused when I gathered that she had been born in
London of Viennese parents. Sooner than expected, we met for

a second time; Klebinder had promised Susan's aging boy friend to give her shop a little publicity in our paper, and handed me the piddling assignment.

The published interview betrayed such unrestrained enthusiasm for women's hats and their attractive designer that Vienna's ever-alert gossipmongers concluded, long before I was aware of it, that I was in love with Susan, and promptly christened me "Al Chapone." Although, as with most adult writers, there is a Henry Miller in me straining to get out, I am resisting the temptation to describe the shabby little trick by which I turned Susan's charming dinner party in appreciation of my story into a bacchanal that left her (but not me) full of shame and remorse but also (as had been my intention) suddenly aware that a young man could offer her what was beyond her elderly associate's power. What she had not known she had not been conscious of missing. Now she knew. For me—and for her—it was a fortunate coincidence that the old gentleman died a few weeks later. Though she had obviously loved him dearly, no woman ever found consolation so quickly.

We were an incongruous pair. Susan was reticent and—there is no other word—ladylike, punctilious, frugal, much concerned with her reputation, a popular hostess to innumerable visiting American firemen. Somewhat removed from parochial Viennese preoccupations, her interest was directed across the Atlantic or, at least, across the Channel. The temples at which she worshiped were Bullocks Wiltshire, Harrods, and other shrines dedicated to the same deity. I, on the other hand, was a fairly tough, no-nonsense reporter, hard-working, hard-drinking, at home in every low dive and elegant hotel, friend of whores and *Herren* (the Austrian equivalent of gentlemen), restless, ambitious, harassed, and free-spending. Susan would not dream of looking at another man; I would not miss a chance to look at another woman. She was not interested in politics, newspapers or sport; I could not have cared less about women's hats or commercial relations with Britain or the United States, but I did like those ever-grinning, generous, naïve, transatlantic characters who visited Europe in the guise of buyers, and their antiseptically smart, middle-aged, adventure-hungry female colleagues.

The sympathies of Susan's family were with the Nazis, although, incongruously, they seemed most anxious to embrace me as a future member of the family. Through my friends in the political police, I knew that one of her brothers, for whom I had found an undefined, not very arduous but well-paid job on the paper, was not only a member of the illegal Nazi Party but, at the same time, kept the police informed about the Nazis and— about Klebinder. It amused me to have a Nazi on the payroll. Since I had nothing to hide, and did not propose to engage in any criminal activities, rubbing shoulders with a police informer did not disconcert me in the least. Susan was unaware of all this. Had I told her, she would not have believed her little brother capable of such calumny. To prevent him from telling his sister of my escapades I was, however, eventually forced to let him know that I knew. We never discussed the matter, but our highly immoral conspiracy of mutual silence worked perfectly, which was all that mattered to me.

It was important because, not long after Susan and I had, to all outward appearances, become inseparable, I met a pair of dewy eyes, moist half-open lips and a scarf covering some unmistakable scratches on a lily-white neck, belonging to a gorgeous girl with reddish-golden hair who was hardly more than seventeen but radiated the desire and the experience of a woman twice her age. It would have been unthinkable not to reciprocate her interest. Mercifully, the girl dispensed with all preliminaries. We were in separate parties, and nobody introduced us. I just went up to her and asked her to have a drink with me. "Let's go home!" she said, and we walked out as if in a trance, leaving our respective friends to speculate as they would. Before I knew it, I was in bed. Before I had recovered from the ecstasy of it all, she said, as if it were the most natural thing in the world: "You'll have to go now. I'm expecting a visitor!"

That was the pattern of our affair. I could not keep my thoughts, my eyes, my hands off that girl. Susan, as a person, was too precious to abandon; deceiving her, I thought, was the lesser evil. She knew nothing and seemed quite happy. But, frequently, when we had settled down for the night—for by that

time I spent five out of seven nights a week in her apartment—
I could not resist the call, the impervious urge, and jumped into
my clothes and, under the flimsiest pretext, left one bed to race
across Vienna and into another. Two hours later, shocked by the
inevitable, "You'll have to go now. . . ." I was on my weary way
back to Susan. Conscience plagued me when I was with that girl;
jealousy consumed me when I was with Susan. My preoccupation with this involved love life was so great that I neglected my
work. Try as I might, nature forced me to neglect Susan.

Occasionally, rather than meet at her apartment, my illicit,
non-Susan assignation would be at the Eden Bar, a fashionable
nightclub where she would appear wrapped in a nutria coat and—
I knew by the expression on her face—nothing on underneath.
We had a few drinks for kicks (as they say nowadays) and
would then drive home, her home. I pestered her to tell me for
whose sake she was forever turning me out of her bed, but she
answered calmly that she did not ask me to discuss my affair
with Susan, did she? There were scenes, but her merest suggestion that, if I did not like it, we would have to stop seeing
each other crushed me into submission. She was obviously a kept
woman—a kept girl—and it was reasonable to assume that her
benefactor turned up every night to claim his rights. Once or
twice I hung about in the street trying to get a glimpse of him,
feeling miserable, humiliated, desperate—but I never did. The
house—how typical of the girl!—had two entrances, each on a
different street. I did not know about the other until it was too
late.

This had been going on for months when a Hungarian businessman whom I had met on and off in the entertainment belt
asked me to join him for a drink at the back bar of the Femina.
"Will you do me a great favor?" he said. "You are the kind who
will understand." He had great difficulty in getting to the point:
"I had to bring my wife with me on this trip, but I am anxious
to take my girl friend out. I have been thinking. If my girl friend
comes as your partner and if we—that is, my wife and I—should
be in the same place . . . we could meet and join up . . . all
four of us . . . and have a jolly good time!" Though I was not

easily surprised by anything in this line, I must have looked puzzled, for he continued: "Have no fear. My girl friend is very attractive, believe me!"

He scribbled a name and an address on a piece of paper. "To-morrow evening, then. Ten-thirty. I shall never forget what you are doing for me." That was how I discovered who was keeping the girl I was in love with. He introduced her to his wife as my girl friend, which of course she was. We were all deceiving each other. I, for good measure, was deceiving Susan at the same time. Still, it was a most entertaining evening . . . but the webs of intrigue were slowly thickening into a cocoon so tight that it threatened to suffocate me. The four of us went out regularly once a fortnight. Finally the burden of deceit, jealousy, inadequacy, bad conscience, neglect of work, ruptures in human relations all became too much for me. Caught between the two women, I began to seek consolation in the arms of any third party who was able and willing to afford me an hour's carefree respite.

Susan decided that we should get married and settle in the United States. If I gave up this futile preoccupation with newspapers and politics and that sort of thing, she suggested, my Continental charm and personality could help turn me into an admirable salesman. In her mind's eye she saw me crowning America's unsuspecting dollar-strong womanhood with hats, thousands of hats. The cash register in her mind was adding up astronomical profits. We would be rich and, consequently, happy. It was an outrageous suggestion. It would turn me into a tradesman, which was unthinkable; it would have meant virtually living on her money, her work, her prestige—I was too proud for that. It might have been worth considering had she suggested London instead of New York, for it would not have needed much inducement to lure me back to England. In the event, the plan collapsed because deep down I knew—although I did not as yet admit it to myself—that I was no longer in love with Susan.

She gave me three months to think it over while she went on one of her annual trips to the States. I was determined to use these three precious months to organize my escape from an intolerable situation. I was lucky. An attractive young German actress, whose response to my advances flattered my vanity, was going to London, and consulted me about ways and means of breaking into English films. She knew Henry Sherek, she said, and that was as good as a contract. (It was, too.) What she needed was someone who could get her picture into the English papers, a P.R. man—this at a time when the profession was as yet virtually nonexistent. It was not much of a pretext on which to throw away your whole life and start again in a foreign country; it was not exactly an advance for the assistant editor of a leading Vienna newspaper, but I was capable neither of pride nor of prejudice. How the gods came to the rescue by conjuring up an important and dignified London assignment out of the blue is a story to which I shall turn presently. I had three women now but only one for whom I really cared, and with her I spent an enchanting farewell weekend in Budapest after which she wrote me a last letter and sealed it with a kiss. They made good lipstick in those days; it is as fresh today as it was thirty years ago. Before writing this, I looked at the seal for the first time in years. I have never reread the letter.

Shortly after arriving in London, I had a note from Susan telling me that she had become engaged in the United States to the kind of man she had always wanted to spend her life with. Would I forgive her? Would I forgive her! I felt a twinge in my heart, but also a heady sense of almost forgotten freedom. I was happy—but not for long. Coming home one night, not much later, to the room I occupied in a delightful, elderly French lady's house in Park Crescent, I found a message telling me in her strange English that "A lady from America telephoned." I could hardly sleep. It could mean only that Susan had changed her mind and come to London—perhaps was only en route to Vienna. First thing next morning I was downstairs asking Madame to tell me more about that call. It turned out that the lady had telephoned *from* America, which was a very different matter.

Susan needed me! It must have been something very urgent if she suddenly wanted to talk to me after such a definite break. For an hour I battled with the operators on the transatlantic switchboards in London and New York. By midmorning they had established the source of the call, a New York restaurant. There was no reply when I asked to be connected with the place; the restaurant was not due to open until evening. Later in the afternoon I called Vienna. Susan's brother was in tears. In his hand, he stammered, he had a cable saying that Susan had been found in a garage—killed by the fumes from the exhaust of her car.

A hectic private life reflected the explosive political atmosphere. The year was 1932. It was almost impossible to escape the pressures. Austria was a microcosm of the world that was shaping up. Name any problem that has beset a nation in the last thirty years—we had it first. Economic crisis undermining the political structure—that sort of thing had long since become old hat. Politics began to take over people nearly a hundred years after the people first tried to take over politics. Austria was divided into two equal political camps, Right and Left; the division spread until the whole world was so divided. Fascism across the border reached out for influence and conquest: Italian Fascism to the south, rising Naziism to the north. No wonder the germs poisoned our atmosphere.

We had underground Nazis terrorizing government and people with widely scattered bomb outrages a quarter of a century before the *plastiques* began to blast in Paris. A fifth column was operating inside Austria—in the chancellery and in my own office—years before the term acquired its sinister popularity in the Spanish Civil War. Ours was a country, like Britain after 1945, vainly trying to adjust itself to the social changes and shifts in international power, all to the detriment of an order to which we had been conditioned for generations. Everything seemed to pile up and then topple at once. Democracy was unable to cope with the emergency. This was a new kind of war.

From a long government crisis in May, 1932, Engelbert Dollfuss emerged as the new chancellor, a compromise choice that commended itself to his party because the inoffensive little fellow was expected to fill the gap until the struggle between more powerful rivals had been resolved and produced an undisputed leader. Dollfuss moved into the Ballhausplatz with a majority of one. When a vote was called on a critical issue, some members had to be roused from their sickbeds and carried into Parliament on stretchers. Democracy became a farce.

Across the border in Germany, democracy was also on the skids. One administration after the other collapsed, unable to grapple with an increasingly desperate situation. The political intrigues carried within them the seeds of self-destruction and a typical German death wish. It was nine-fifteen one morning when news reached Vienna that Reich President Paul von Hindenburg was about to appoint Adolf Hitler Chancellor of Germany. An hour and a quarter later I was on a plane for Berlin—no bag, no clothes, not even a toothbrush. In Berlin that evening, after I had watched a torchlight procession paying homage to the Führer, and with the ecstatic shouts of his transfixed followers still ringing in my ears, I joined several German journalists in the Café Hessler.

"Clever trick," was the concensus. Clever trick? Whose? Everybody was congratulating the powers-that-be—those cunning, masterful Junkers and officers, Major Oskar von Hindenburg, the President's son, and Herr von Papen, a previous chancellor who had "roped in Hitler," "put him on the spot," "tied him hand and foot," "kept him on a leash"—there was no end to the clichés—to let him "make a fool of himself" and "get rid of him and his vulgar Nazis once for all." Did I believe them? I cannot remember. I had nothing but contempt for the Nazis, whose threat seemed to me purely physical, and that did not frighten me.

Diligently I devoted myself to the mechanics of reporting. Official sources were reticent. It was difficult to get the Socialists to say anything for publication. The Communists were rattled— understandably enough. Through a German friend I obtained a piece of sensational news, but there was no time to check it before my telephone call from Vienna came through. If I was not to miss the edition I had to take the plunge. I dictated: "General Hammerstein-Equord has alerted his division of crack troops and is ready to march on Berlin to chase that political upstart Hitler from the Wilhelmstrasse." It was quite true as far as it went. But it did not go very far. Hammerstein *was* ready to march. Only, he never did. Withal, somehow, the historical significance of the occasion escaped me. Berlin was on edge but offered many diversions. Talk was still good, and never had there been more food for talk, if not thought. A few days later I was glad to get back to Vienna. What really interested us was the German elections, due in a few weeks' time. I would be back when the chips were down.

On Monday, February 28, 1933, I flew once more to Berlin on the first stage of a round trip that was scheduled to take me to Munich and Hamburg and wind up back in Berlin on Sunday, the day of the elections. I booked into the Hessler Hotel and again I was with a number of German writers when we were told that the Reichstag was on fire. We jumped into taxis and rushed there. We arrived just before the police cordon closed around the building. The cupola was aglow, a column of smoke rising to the sky. A minute later a cavalcade of fast cars came to a sudden halt at the side door to which we had made our way. Surrounded by a big entourage, Hermann Goering moved quickly toward the entrance. As he passed I saw that his face was purple-red. He looked as if he were clenching his fists deep down in the big pockets of his coat. An official emerged to meet the minister. The noise of cars and fire engines, of excited shouts and clipped police commands could not drown Goering's voice: "A crime," he thundered, "an unheard-of crime!" The men around him echoed his words. Once more, as he entered the Reichstag, I heard him, every word cutting sharply through the air which was thick with dust and smoke: *"An den Galgen mit ihnen!"* he screamed—To the gallows with them!

Two hours later our messages went to the four corners of the earth. My own report said: "There can be little doubt that the fire which is consuming the Reichstag was raised by hirelings of the Hitler government. It seems that the incendiaries made their way to the Reichstag through an underground passage which connects the building with the Palace of the Reichstag President, Cabinet Minister and Reich Commissioner for the Prussian Police, Captain Hermann Goering. . . ." This theory remained undisputed until 1962, when a German publication cast doubt on Goering's complicity in the crime. The new theory, based on involved circumstantial evidence, was rejected by many authoritative historians. I tend to uphold the view I formed on the spot thirty years ago.

German democracy went up in flames—or what was left of it once Hitler had become chancellor. In a wave of mass arrests, Communists and Socialists were carted off to prison. Police occupied the *Vorwärts* building from which the Social Democratic paper of that name was published. When I went to call on a friend, Foreign Editor Victor Schiff, I was not admitted. (Victor, in fact, after a brief detention was released and went to Paris, where he became correspondent of the London *Daily Herald*. He escaped the Nazis in the nick of time when they occupied Paris in 1940. Reaching London in a British battleship, he was promptly clamped into Pentonville Prison as a suspected fifth columnist. After a five-week ordeal—it was no fun being confined in a locked cell when bombs were dropping all around—he was released, and resumed work for the *Daily Herald*. We remained friends until his death in Rome.)

For the first time I was afraid. Afraid of what, I could not exactly say, and this indefinable fear was a humiliating experience. Few people outside Germany realized as yet that there were good reasons to be afraid. People kept disappearing, leaving the country helter-skelter or being picked up either by the police or by one of the Nazi *Rollkommandos*—uniformed gangsters who worked off private scores and political grudges. We did not know at the time, but so many people were detained that there was not enough room for them, and rough barbed-wire enclosures were rigged up to receive the overflow—and thus were the Nazi concentration camps born.

Looking through a bunch of papers and magazines I had bought at a bookstall, I had come across a curious publication edited by Erik Jan Hanussen, a clairvoyant, part of whose variety act was a spectacular feat which he claimed was based on telepathy. Hanussen, whose real name was Steinschneider, hailed from Vienna, where I had met him during his engagement at the Ronacher Variety Theater. Very impressive his performance had been, too. Somehow I had always thought of Hanussen as a Jew, but I must have been wrong if I could believe my eyes and what I read in his newspaper, the front page of which predicted unparalleled international triumphs for Hitler, Goering, and for Count Wolf von Helldorf, Nazi police president of Berlin. The back pages were filled with small advertisements exclusively devoted to soliciting for undisguised homosexual and related perverse purposes. "Strong man anxious to meet beautiful boy . . ." "How I should love to suffer from the hands of a real man . . ." Hurriedly I made notes of this revealing juxtaposition of Naziism and homosexuality. Come to think of it, it was not astonishing at all. When I had finished dictating a report of the day's news, I put over a story off the cuff about Hanussen's double role as political commentator and Cupid of the Queers.

At noon the following day I was at the Café Hessler, pondering whether to watch developments in Berlin or to go on with the trip as planned, when the hall porter came over from the hotel: "I thought I'd better warn you," he said. It appeared that a *Rollkommando* had called at the hotel to take me into custody. . . . So that was it! That was what I had been afraid of. But how to explain to Vienna—to any outsider? I really did have the wind up now. I asked the hall porter to arrange for my things to be packed and taken to the station, where I would meet the man on the platform from which the Vienna train was due to leave Berlin at 8:00 P.M. I had to go into hiding quickly. It was difficult to guess why I was wanted; there could hardly be a warrant out for my arrest—my reports to Vienna had been unfriendly, but I had not committed any offense against the German laws.

From across the road a huge poster beckoned. The beautiful features of a giant Greta Garbo lured customers to a "continuous performance" of *Menschen im Hotel—Grand Hotel*. In the course of this afternoon, comfortably installed in a box, I watched this film two and three-quarter times. I shall never forget it. It was so enthralling that my mind was riveted on the screen even though some very mixed emotions competed for attention. Was I safe? Had I been wise to tell the hall porter what I proposed to do? But then, would he have warned me in the first instance if he had any intention of betraying me? What of the man who was going to meet me at the station with my luggage? What if he were followed? Garbo was her most gorgeous self. I decided to abandon my suitcase if I noticed anything the least suspicious, and take off without it. What if the German frontier guards had been instructed to detain me and return me to Berlin? Should I confide in the sleeping-car attendant? Could I risk going to the dining car? At long last Garbo managed to reconquer my undivided attention, and I settled down to life in Vicki Baum's Grand Hotel.

By taxi to the station, taking my suitcase from the man who bowed deeply in appreciation of a large tip, into the reserved compartment . . . nowhere was there a hint of danger. The train had hardly moved out of the station when I persuaded myself— quite correctly—that nothing could happen to me in the dining car that did not threaten me in the sleeper. My appetite did not suffer. What I felt was embarrassment at being—well, a fugitive. The trip was uneventful. I slept soundly. Neither passport nor customs officials bothered to wake me. Eleven hours later I arrived in Vienna and woke to the unpleasant realization that I had run away without any real evidence of danger—had abandoned my assignment. It would all be very difficult to explain. It was!

A few months passed before any light was thrown on the incident. By then, German-Jewish refugees were flocking into Vienna in large numbers, among them a little man called Pem (the phonetically linked initials of his full name, Paul Marcus) a popular Berlin theatrical columnist. We quickly became friends. One day at the Café Imperial he was about to introduce me to a fellow refugee. Grinning hugely, he said, "Let me introduce one Frischauer to another!" The man's face suddenly hardened into an angry distortion and his fists came up toward me. Pem and I tried to calm him down and to get to the root of his uncontrollable rage. I had never seen him before. It was some time before he was coherent enough to explain.

In Berlin, on the day of my hurried departure, he had quite by chance gone to the Hessler, where a uniformed Nazi S.A. man had asked his name. Truthfully he had answered "Frischauer." Within seconds he had been dragged away. Blows rained on his head, and he was kicked in the groin all the way to Lichtenfelde army barracks, where he was questioned and tortured for two days. Nothing he said could persuade his jailers that they were tormenting the wrong man, that he was not a newspaper reporter from Vienna and—the interrogator's questions gave him the first hint of the reason for the inexplicable Nazi venom—had never heard of, never read, consequently never reported on, Hanussen's newspaper. It turned out that this particular S.A. squad was under orders from Count Helldorf to avenge the insult and ridicule my article had heaped on his friend Erik Jan Hanussen. I was sorry for this poor man but, of course, glad it had not happened to me. It was not the last time I escaped at another's expense, and the next time it was much more tragic.

A strong political wind was blowing from the direction of Germany. Though it was not clear what the repercussions would be, Hitler's assumption of power was bound to shake us to the core. Austria's cardboard democracy was the first to collapse. True, it was assailed from the inside as well as from the outside, but then extremists on either fringe of the political spectrum are always lying in wait for an opportunity to destroy democracy.

Having so recently seen democratic means employed to undermine German democracy—Hitler, after all, came to power because millions of Germans had voted for him—I arrived at certain conclusions which neither time nor experience have modified. Rather clumsily, I first tried to propound them in 1937, when I anticipated the impending Nazi absorption of Austria in my *Twilight in Vienna*, in which I inveighed against "democracy unlimited." No democracy, I argued, could in the long run survive unless it has the will and the strength to keep the extremists of the Left and the Right under control. To permit public denigration of democracy and unrestrained propaganda by the enemies of democracy is lunacy: I will certainly not die for the right of anybody to say that democracy should perish. Democracy was doomed if it did not provide built-in safeguards against its detractors. Democracy as I knew it was no longer capable of controlling the forces to which it was supposed to give free reign;

again, I felt that the time might come—as surely it has come now—when even the near perfect Westminster model would be in need of reconditioning, though, as I write, the danger which threatens Westminster is boredom and public apathy, rather than violence, engendered by specialization, which is inevitable in our complicated, technical, and fragmented society, and the consequent transfer "upstairs" of many important discussions. The closed doors of a committee room are not exactly conducive to imaginative democracy.

In Vienna events moved swiftly. In the course of a heated debate on the floor of Parliament the president (speaker) vacated his seat. His deputy followed suit. The third speaker also resigned. Parliament had decapitated itself. The debate broke up in confusion, the session was abandoned, the deputies went home. There was no legitimate way to call the next meeting; the rules of procedure did not provide for a freak case like this. With a little goodwill, a means could, of course, have been found to make democracy prevail over a mere technicality. But there was no goodwill for a system which, to all outward appearance, was chaotic and inadequate for the need of the hour. Dollfuss—urged on by Mussolini or the native Fascists or both—frustrated the attempt of the Social Democrats to reconstitute the House, and ordered the police to occupy Parliament and keep the Socialists out. It was all done in a rather leisurely fashion. I slipped into Parliament with the police, where I was held for hours before I could induce them to throw me out.

Dollfuss issued a proclamation and set to work on a new constitution, introducing the corporate state. A Fatherland Front was called into being as a Right-wing political cover organization. The way was open for the Heimwehr to make its weight felt. The Social Democratic Party was doomed. The price Dollfuss had to pay for Mussolini's support involved a war on two fronts —against the Nazis and the Social Democrats. Regarding Hitler as the principal threat, I was quite prepared for this price to be paid. Morally, it was not the right decision, but expediency beckoned with almost irresistible logic. Although I have since learned to distrust political expediency, even in retrospect I cannot help feeling that Dollfuss's decision—and Mussolini's self-interested intervention—saved Austria in July, 1934. The inevitable was postponed for four years—four years of life, freedom, and happiness for many, me and my family among them. The Austrian Socialists claimed that a democratic Austria would have been a firmer bastion against Hitler. I have my doubts. The Czechs, when the time came, did not even fight for their own Sudetenland; the French could not save their "Little Entente."

Few people took the new Austrian constitution seriously; fewer even cared. A small number of vain fools who fancied themselves in the pseudomilitary getup of the Heimwehr crowded around Prince Starhemberg. The rest were paid hirelings. From now on, some of my friends would arrive at the Grand Hotel bar every Sunday morning—marching day in Vienna—looking ridiculously martial in their uniforms. Even "Feichtl," Prince Starhemberg's good-looking, modest, and taciturn brother, was glad when the first two or three drinks drowned political arguments and brought more congenial topics to the fore: which Heurigen to visit that evening, what girls to take along, how to come by sufficient money for the purpose, whose cars to use, and of course, more immediately, lunch. It was a sad comment on a country tottering on the verge of ruin.

Chancellor Dollfuss, although a policeman was now stationed outside his house and a detective guarded the door to his flat upstairs, did not change at all except that, on public occasions, he wore the uniform of his old regiment (he had served as a lieutenant in the First World War); it did not become his tiny stature. Many of the jokes about him date from this period. He was called *Milimetternich*, and it was said that his wife objected to him scratching the parquet floor with his steel helmet when he wore it at home.

When I visited him—and I did so as frequently as before— the chancellor was normally in shirt sleeves and braces and in a hurry to get to the office. To gain more time for our chats, I hit on the idea of introducing him to my barber. In Vienna those who could afford it were shaved at the barber's every morning, but Dollfuss was new to the habit. Two or three mornings a week I collected him at his flat at eight-fifteen and rode with him in his official limousine the few hundred yards to the expensive hairdressing establishment in the Kohlmarkt where our respective barbers were waiting for us side by side. Dollfuss talked in snatches, using a kind of verbal shorthand, unintelligible to all but the initiated—and, I regret to say, sometimes even to me. But by and large he kept me fairly well informed.

It was not long before, inevitably, the news of Dollfuss's regular morning attendance at the barbershop got around. More and more big businessmen, financiers, lobbyists, entrepreneurs with bright ideas, and brazen adventurers were anxious to make appointments with the barber at this early hour. In the end—the establishment not being equipped for such an onslaught—they came without appointment, and the salon looked as if the whole populace had invaded the levee of a king. Dollfuss decided to pay a little extra to have a barber come and shave him at his home. It complicated matters for me but made no real difference.

Klebinder and I were no longer so close as we had once been. My extravagances created constant friction, and his political machinations became less defensible and more mysterious as time went on. Although a profiteer from capitalism, his heart was with the moderate wing of the Social Democrats. Much of the information, I knew perfectly well, which Dollfuss imparted to me and which I passed on to Klebinder went straight to them. I certainly did not mind and, besides, I was convinced Dollfuss knew and did not mind either. Feeding the grapevine with carefully selected and well-aimed news, the wily little man was using me for his own political purposes. Every Sunday I called the chancellor on the telephone, and he told me in his usual mumbo jumbo what he thought it useful to disclose.

"Nothing of importance," he said cryptically one Sunday in October, 1933.

"Ah, *Herr Kanzler*," I pleaded, "it is such a dull day, haven't you got just a little bit of news for me?"

"Well, perhaps . . ." was his casual reply. "You can say that I have accepted the resignation of Dr. Rintelen. Goodbye."

It was a sensational piece of news. Dr. Anton Rintelen, the baldheaded, rotund minister of education with the cunning eyes and cynical smile, was a political power of the first magnitude. As governor of Styria, Rintelen had ruled his province with benevolent autocracy and such disdainful disregard for the central government of Vienna that he became popularly known as "King Anton." His influence on the Christian Socialist Party and in the country was considerable. He also had his fair share of enemies. That this clever and ambitious man should have resigned his high office was a great surprise. If anything, it was evidence of strong tensions inside the Cabinet and could not fail to produce grave political repercussions. Just how grave I was as yet unaware.

Klebinder was out of town and incommunicado, and I was left holding the hot potato. The manner in which Dollfuss had told me the news indicated that it was not yet generally known. Anxiously, I scanned the agency reports; nothing. I did not dare write the story before we reached the printer's. I kept the news even from my colleagues until I wrote the banner headline. In Vienna you never knew. . . .

As usual on press day, I stayed till 2:45 A.M. to see the presses rolling and, with the first couple of copies and a few colleagues, went to the Café Europe, where the executives of our rival paper turned up about the same time with theirs. They were green with envy when they saw our headline. We had another scoop. I was triumphant. An hour later, excited but exhausted, I fell into bed. . . . I heard the telephone ringing in the distance but felt that I had not had my ration of sleep. On Mondays it was an iron rule at home that under no circumstances should I be awakened before 10:00 A.M.

Mother stormed into my bedroom—most unusual. My watch said it was seven-thirty. "Ernst wants to talk to you at once!" she said. She looked worried. I vividly remember telling her to tell Klebinder to go to hell; I had been working for him till the crack of dawn; was I not allowed to have any sleep? But I was awake now, and angry, and might as well tell him personally what I thought of him.

"You have ruined me! You have ruined the paper!" Before I could say a word, his voice, wailing and hissing at the same time, drilled my ear like a siren. What on earth was he talking about? He was in such a state it took some time to make sure what he was saying. What had happened, briefly, was that a few minutes earlier he had received a telephone call from Rintelen, who complained bitterly about "the completely and utterly false news" which adorned the front page of the *Sonn-und-Montags-Zeitung* in the biggest, boldest type available. He had *not* resigned; he had not even *seen* the chancellor for a week, and had no *intention* of resigning. Klebinder screamed at me: "Where did you get this crazy information from? Who has hoaxed you?"

"Dollfuss," I answered, and plonked down the receiver.

My mind was made up. In and out of the bath, into my clothes. In the car I broke several traffic ordinances. I was at the Stallburggasse as the clock struck eight. The chancellor had gone. He was not at the barber's. To the Ballhausplatz at great speed, past the startled detectives and the uniformed guard, up the stairs and into the chancellor's outer office: "I must see the chancellor!" Everybody looked perplexed. They all knew Dollfuss had a weakness for me, but this sort of peremptory impertinence could not be tolerated even from a Cabinet minister. It was outrageous on the part of a reporter. Before they could say anything, however, I repeated: "I must see the chancellor at once!" When I am excited my voice carries; it can be very penetrating. It must have been—or was it a fortunate coincidence?—because the big double doors of the chancellor's office opened and there, his head hardly reaching up to the high door handle, was Dollfuss. "Anything the matter?" he asked, looking at me with a strange expression.

As calmly as possible I told him about Klebinder's call. "Rintelen insists he has not resigned!" I gritted.

"I did not tell you he had resigned," Dollfuss answered. He was smiling indulgently. "What I said was that I have accepted his resignation—and that is true!" With that he was gone.

At 10:00 A.M. the midday paper carried a denial of my story in a prominent position: "Dr. Rintelen has authorized us to say . . ." How newspapers love to deny each other's stories! At the office, which was usually dead on a Monday, half a dozen people were hanging around when I arrived. Klebinder had mobilized as many as he could reach to discuss what could be done to restore the paper's reputation—as if this was the first time that interested parties had denied a newspaper report! His secretary told me that, although in a state of low health and high excitement, Klebinder was at this moment on his way back to Vienna. At lunchtime there was still no sign of him. When I went out an hour later, the next edition of the evening paper contained an official announcement to the effect that Dr. Rintelen had indeed offered his resignation, which the chancellor had accepted with regret. After that, Klebinder and I were hardly on speaking terms.

In the next few weeks Dollfuss maneuvered Rintelen into a position where, reluctant though "King Anton" was to remove himself from the center of power, he could not very well refuse an appointment as Austrian Ambassador to Rome. But we knew that he had vowed to avenge his dismissal. From that moment on he was determined to "get Dollfuss"—*coûte que coûte*. He spent very little time at his post in Rome, frequently stayed for long periods in Vienna and in Graz, his provincial capital. His hatred of Dollfuss inevitably led him into an association with Dollfuss's worst enemies, the Nazis. With their leaders he conspired to bring about a Nazi government in Austria, anything so long as Dollfuss was removed. Besides, the Nazis offered him the post of chancellor. The day the Nazis made their play with the putsch, Rintelen was ready. Dollfuss was murdered. Rintelen had his revenge, but it was to cost him his own life.

Early in February, 1934, I went to Le Havre to meet a party of American friends who were coming to Paris on the first stage of a grand tour of Europe. Our arrangement was to travel on to Vienna together. It was not the ideal season to visit Paris, but we still had a good evening sampling the fruits which are forbidden or unobtainable in most places except Paris. Late breakfast next morning developed, via drinks, into lunch when we noticed the atmosphere imperceptibly tensing. The big doors of the hotel were closed, and the staff rushed around in confusion like a flock of frightened hens. Paris was in the grip of grave riots. I slipped out by a side door into the Champs-Elysées, which was chockablock with people. Moving in from the side streets, platoons of dark-caped police swinging wooden batons and supported by their mounted colleagues tried in vain to break up the massed crowds. I was soon engulfed and, though I had not forgotten the lessons I had learned on my own riotous home ground, once involved, it took a long time before I could extricate myself. Nothing is more disconcerting than to be mixed up in a riot in a foreign country.

That evening Paris was under a strict curfew. The Americans were not allowed to leave the hotel. Few of them had any inclination to brave the hazards of this budding civil war. The cause of the riots was "L'affaire Stavisky," involving corruption in high places, political favoritism, and considerable losses to small investors. After a second day's rioting the curfew was again imposed, and it looked as if Paris might not recover its lighthearted charm for some time. I suggested that Vienna could offer diversions of a kind that visiting Americans would enjoy more than being confined to a Paris hotel lounge. We took the train for Vienna on February 10th, arriving pleasantly exhausted.

The Americans spent most of their first day in Vienna resting up while I attended to the office. Having been away for almost a week, I found Klebinder unusually agitated but not very communicative. Somehow I failed to pick up the trend, and what happened next came as a great surprise to me. By 11:00 A.M. on the following day—February 12th—an ominous silence fell over Vienna. The trams came to a standstill once more. Lights flickered on and off, on and off, on and off—three deliberate cuts in supply which were the signal for a general strike. What developed was the long-threatened confrontation of the Dollfuss regime and the Social Democrats, who had been subject to growing pressure and provocation.

My Americans were advised not to leave their hotel. When I called the office, Klebinder was unobtainable. Fräulein Koban, his secretary, a charming girl of whom I was very fond, refused to tell me where he was: "The telephone is tapped," she said. (I doubt whether it was true.) I called one of his sisters: "Ernst had to go to Pressburg on urgent business," she told me. "I have been trying to contact you for an hour. He wants you to keep a sharp lookout and join him in the evening." Pressburg, or Bratislava, was only a stone's throw from Vienna—but it was in Czechoslovakia.

We did not know it at the time, but we were in the throes of civil war, the well-trained and armed paramilitary formations of the Socialist Schutzbund (about 60,000 men) ranged against the military might of the state (as many men again). For months the Dollfuss-Heimwehr government had tried to undermine the authority of Vienna's Socialist city administration, and now breaking-point had been reached. Hostilities had broken out in Linz when the authorities ordered a search for hidden Socialist arms. In Vienna they reached their crescendo the following day when Dollfuss authorized heavy artillery to bombard some of the famous municipal workers' dwellings. He later said he did it in order to save lives.

Whatever the conclusions to be drawn from this admission, the portentous clash of two radicalized factions left me unmoved and uninvolved. Across the wide gap of time I cannot recall any definable emotion except a curse: "A plague on both their houses!"

The Nazis were the enemy. This internecine warfare threatened to weaken the country beyond recovery. I refused to argue ideology on top of a volcano. It was too late now to allocate the blame. There was nothing I could do, no side to which I was attracted. But while I felt that both sides stank, I hoped that this major clash would at least bring a decision one way or another. What I wanted—what the country needed—was a strong government to protect it from the real danger of Naziism.

Walking through Herrengasse and passing the Ministry of Security, I saw a face I knew: bristling moustache, extended nostrils, flashing eyes like a young English Blimp in a paroxysm of excitement. The man's name was Dr. Altmann—Viktor Altmann if I remember rightly. I had first met him in my cub reporting days when he was a police press officer. As a reward for political services rendered to Major Emil Fey, an up-and-coming Heimwehr leader, Altmann was transferred to the Ministry of Security soon after Major Fey became minister. Altmann was regarded—falsely, I think—as the *éminence grise* behind Fey. To me, as he stood there, inveighing against the Socialists, he seemed everything an official should not be—emotional, partisan, political and, as it turned out, personal: "Tell your friend

Klebinder that his hour has struck!" he barked at me from under his moustache. "We shall know how to deal with him!"

Altmann's fulminations proved to me what I had suspected, that Klebinder's association with the Socialists was closer than he cared to let us know and that he was, after all, not too hasty or cowardly to exchange the explosive political atmosphere of Vienna for the safety of Bratislava. (I met Dr. Altmann again in Berlin after the war, when I understood him to be working for an official British agency.)

That evening I took the train to Bratislava. It was a most uncomfortable journey, most of which was spent crouching on the floor of the compartment while shots were fired at the train from all directions, none, however, coming close enough to cause anxiety. At Bratislava I reported to Klebinder, who had, in the meantime, been joined by several of his sisters. All I could tell him was that all hell was loose in Vienna. I repeated Altmann's threat, which seemed to please him. He, too, felt that it was fortunate he had decided to attend to his business interests in Bratislava at this precise juncture.

Next morning I returned to Vienna by the first train—in the same position I had assumed the previous night; the aim of the snipes had improved. Austrian troops were hunting Social rebels trying to escape across the border into Czechoslovakia.

Klebinder had entrusted me with a mission. He wanted me to persuade Dollfuss to guarantee his safety if he returned to Vienna.

Conditions in Vienna were not conducive to social calls on the chancellor. The shelling of the workers' settlements had aggravated the fury of the Socialists—fury which was all the greater for being impotent. For all practical purposes, the Austrian Social Democratic movement was broken. The failure of the putsch or, if you like, the deliberate crushing of Socialism by the armed force, divided the nation into two parts. "There are those who walk in the light," said Brecht, "and those who walk in the dark. And one sees only those in the light. Those in the dark one does not see." Owing to my association with Dollfuss, I would seem to be walking in the light. But I was not happy. All my instincts were for progress and justice, and while I lived and liked the high life, I had—surprisingly—developed a social conscience, even though so far it was no more than a guilty conscience straining to evolve. Alas, I was a long way from doing anything about it. Come to think of it, I never really did.

My interview with Dollfuss when I managed to see him alone after several futile attempts was short and to the point: "Klebinder sits in Pressburg wetting his pants," I said. "I have heard Altmann threaten him. He is convinced the Heimwehr will arrest him."

Dollfuss laughed heartily. "Yes, I have heard your uncle has gathered a party of Socialist leaders around him. Danneberg, Otto Bauer . . ." Both were on the extreme Left wing of their party.

"Herr Kanzler, you know Bauer can't stand the sight of Klebinder. I was in Pressburg with Klebinder only last night and I did not see anything of Danneberg, either."

"I'll tell Fey not to be stupid," Dollfuss said. "You tell your uncle that nobody is going to eat him."

The government had enforced a particularly insidious censorship of the press, involving restrictions on the size of headlines and obligatory publication of government announcements. It was more than a reporter of my youthful exuberance could bear. I did not see Dollfuss frequently enough to protest effectively. When I had the opportunity of raising the subject, he was in such a state of nervous tension that he could not concentrate on my petition. He gave me the impression that he knew, in his heart of hearts, there could be no happy ending to his situation. It was not press censorship that preoccupied him, but life and death.

The Nazis were gaining in strength. Every day we received threats, and I bought a revolver to protect myself. I was driving along the Mariahilferstrasse when the car was caught up in a Nazi demonstration. Brown shirts, swastika flags, slogan-shouting —the works. Before I knew it—perhaps I had driven a little too close for comfort—the marchers surrounded my car, making ominous noises. Still, it was nothing to be worried about, really, until one of the brownshirts recognized me and called out my name, which was greeted with a storm of booing. (My name had appeared over an angry anti-Nazi story only a day or so earlier.)

The situation became awkward. One of the men hit me on the head. Excitable as I was, I forced myself to keep calm. I reached into my hip pocket, pulled out the revolver, and rested it on my knee. The four Nazis closest to me saw the pistol and backed off instantly. One of them said, "He's got a gun," and the message was passed on down the line. As if by magic, the cluster around my car dissolved. The marchers returned to their ranks. The whole incident had lasted barely a minute. The street was clear, and I quickly passed the sullen, silent column.

The Nazi putsch of July 25th was like a festering sore breaking open. For months the all-pervading underground presence of Nazis in every sphere of public and private life had irritated and inflamed the body politic like alien objects under the skin. The intrigues of the secret Nazi brotherhood demoralized society. Frustrated young Socialists were making common cause with the Nazis. Industrialists were taking out "insurance policies" by supporting the Nazis financially. It was impossible to know whom to trust. Personal relations were poisoned by politics.

Alerted by a message from police headquarters, I raced to the Kärntnerstrasse. Heavy fighting was going on in a side street opposite the Femina where a Nazi commando had occupied the Ravag building, Vienna's Broadcasting House. Heavily armed police were winkling out the dilettante raiders. At first it looked like the kind of isolated outrage to which we had grown accustomed. When I asked a senior police officer what it was all about, he told me that this was not the only trouble spot. Something very sinister was going on at the Ballhausplatz.

Within a few minutes I was outside the chancellery, where I joined a quickly swelling crowd. "They are in there," people were volunteering. "Who are *they?*" I asked. People looked at me as if I had come from the moon. "The Nazis!" they answered with resigned finality.

We were only a few paces from the entrance, which was closed. Police arrived to clear the crowd, but a press pass enabled me to stay in the front row of history and stare at the old building behind whose walls a political tragedy was being played out. It was like sitting in the stalls of a theater where a performance is in progress *behind* the curtain. There was nothing to see, but then nothing I have ever seen has stirred the imagination so powerfully as the thought of those Nazis swarming over the old palace from which Austria's fortunes had been guided for generations.

Troops were moving up now, and heavy guns pointed menacingly at the occupied chancellery. It looked as if the order to fire might be given at any moment. A man appeared on the balcony, another one close behind. The one in front I recognized as Major Fey. Only then did I notice Heimwehr Minister Odo Neustädter-Stürmer, who was standing by my side; he had been sent to negotiate with the rebels. Sent by whom? Commands ran down the street until they reached the Ballhausplatz. Meanwhile those guns were likely to go off. . . . Neustädter-Stürmer was trying to find out what was happening inside. He assured Fey that all over the country the situation was well in hand. Whose side was Fey on—the government's or the rebels'?

It was dusk before I was able to piece together the snatches of information picked up here and there—a word with Neustädter-Stürmer, a question to a police officer, a quick exchange with one of the army officers, consultation with other reporters filtering through the police cordon. By the time I knew the whole truth, it was all over. Today it is one of recent history's best-documented political disasters. The truck-load of illegal Nazis of "S.S.-Standarte 89," dressed in Austrian uniforms, driving into the chancellery past the military guard who were armed with rifles but had never been issued ammunition; their leaders storming upstairs toward the chancellor's office, and one of the rebels, a man called Planetta, shooting Dollfuss and wounding him gravely; Dollfuss imploring the assassins to call a doctor and a priest, and they callously refusing, letting him bleed to death.

The confusion; the warnings about the putsch which had originally been scheduled for the previous day; more warnings, as a result of which the ministers assembled at the War Ministry instead of the Ballhausplatz; the abortive plan to detain Wilhelm Miklas, the President of the Republic, who was on holiday in

the pleasant little Carinthian lakeside resort of Velden; the rebels'
vain hopes that police and army would make common cause with
them; and the putsch collapsing around them like a house of
cards. Having at once divested Dollfuss of his powers and entrusted Dr. Kurt von Schuschnigg, as minister of justice, with
the conduct of affairs, President Miklas had saved the situation.
Dr. Rintelen, on whom the rebels relied to take over as the new
Nazi chancellor of Austria, had been detained at the War Ministry, and shot himself through the chest.

The drama was moving toward its close. Dusk was falling at
the Ballhausplatz. Summoned by the rebels, German Ambassador
Kurt Rieth appeared, by his presence involving the wire-pullers
of the putsch, the Nazi government in Berlin. Here was the real
culprit. I was among the people who surrounded the pale, fum-
bling diplomat. I raised my fist—someone pulled me away or I
would have struck him. Having finally been persuaded that their
attempt to usurp power had failed, the rebels were now prepared
to surrender. They asked that the German ambassador arrange
a safe conduct for them to the German border. It was promised
on the assumption that they had spilled no blood, and was instantly revoked when Dollfuss was found murdered. The police
had a hard time holding us back when the miserable band of
traitors filed through the chancellery door, but we got in a few
kicks and blows before they were loaded onto police wagons.
They were tried; several were hanged and the others were sent
to prison. Four years later the Nazis honored them all as heroes.

By 8:00 P.M. it was all over. It left those who were in the
thick of it mentally exhausted. As I wearily made my way to
the Café Herrenhof to revive myself with a stiff drink, I met
the Vienna correspondent of the United Press, who asked me
whether I could tell him of anyone who had been in the Ballhausplatz throughout the afternoon. "He could earn a few dollars. . . ." I wrote the piece and was paid what seemed a fabulous amount. It was a relief to write the emotion out of my
system.

The personal implications were difficult to grasp. Dollfuss was
gone. . . . He had been a loyal friend to me. He had been a
good man. I had liked him from start to finish. What a rotten

way to die! But then so much was rotten in the state of Austria. (The United Press correspondent, incidentally, married a Viennese, and, infected by the moral decay of the city, refused to leave Vienna when the United States entered the war; he became one of the sorry little band of American traitors supporting the Nazis against his native country.)

All I wanted was to get away. My mind was made up. I had already arranged with Klebinder that I should represent the *Sonn-und-Montags-Zeitung* in London. He was as impatient to get rid of me as I was to bring our association to an end. Other papers, too, were anxious to have me as their correspondent in Britain. My plan was to get my hands on what money Klebinder still owed me to supplement the meager pay I could expect for my contributions. I went to take my leave from Minister Eduard Ludwig, the tall, omniscient chief of the Austrian Federal Press Service, a shrewd politician with a fine grasp of international affairs to match his unparalleled "feel" for the intricacies of Austrian politics. "If you have made up your mind to leave us," he said in the sonorous voice that suited his old-style formality, "we may be able to come to certain mutually beneficient arrangements. . . ."

It was a wonderful proposition. Chancellor Schuschnigg had decided to strengthen the country's diplomatic missions in the world's leading capitals by the unorthodox introduction of a number of down-to-earth men unhampered by the inflexible outlook and social affinities of old-fashioned career diplomats. These special emissaries would work independently of their respective embassies and report to him personally on foreign reactions to Austria's predicament. If these men could also put the Austrian case against Germany and explain the danger facing not only Austria but Europe and the world at large, so much the better; they would be doing a service to humanity. The financial conditions were attractive. "Would you like to go to London to do this kind of job?" Ludwig asked. I was prepared to go to London under any circumstances.

I did not shed a single tear for Vienna—not until March 11, 1938, when the double-crooked cross of the anti-Christ bore down on Austria, and Vienna's baroque beauty and sensitive multinational aestheticism were trampled under the hobnailed jackboot of the barbarians and defiled by the vulgar flags of their upstart movement. The Vienna I turned my back on was my very life—which had been distorted by political pressures, by violence, by the excesses of the night as an escape from an intolerable day. Love, politics, sex, intrigue, money—Vienna's values and my own were in utter disarray.

Nor did I shed a single tear for my family. This was a parting for ever, and the sorrow was too great for tears. Oh, yes, we would meet again here, there, everywhere, but these would be fleeting encounters. This was the end of family life as I had known it. I was moving into another world from which I could see no easy passage back. I was alone.

Mother, nearly sixty-five but still smooth-skinned, her strong hair barely discolored by her years, was zestful, emotional, trying to laugh over her tears. "It's only for a short while," I lied, and added more confidently, "You'll be coming to see me in London soon." Father's health was beginning to deteriorate; his sight and hearing were impaired, his joints racked by gout. His powerful body absorbed a great deal of pain, but his spirit was still fierce, his views were belligerent, his flashes of hilarity astonishing in a man of seventy-two. In chorus we recited our old favorites: the Odyssey in Greek, bits of Latin from Ovid, inevitably Goethe (". . . *Dein wärs, sieh' zu ob Du vielmehr nicht sein*"), bursting atonally into students' songs with "*O, Du alte Burschenherrlichkeit* . . ."—our usual mixed repertoire which, try as we might to appear at ease, sounded monstrously funereal. In the end he was silent and, like me, brimful of dry-eyed affection.

From my brothers I had grown apart—in all friendship. Leo was advising tycoons. Edi's interests were devoted in equal parts to his legal practice and his bridge; a bridge player of the first order, he would soon celebrate his greatest triumph captaining the Austrian team which defeated Ely Culbertson's Americans in the world championship in Budapest. Fritz was a real friend but married to an insufferable woman whose mere existence clouded our relationship. Paul, always an outsider, had moved to London a few months earlier.

6 | *Waiting for War*

The psychological break with Vienna was so complete that it amounted to willful amnesia as far as many areas of the immediate past were concerned. Only advancing years have brought, in company with other twinges, hints of atavism and nostalgic memories—an inexplicable *Heimweh* (a more onomatopoeic word than the clumsy "homesickness").

Returning from the United States in the early 1960's I remembered warmly how New York had taken me to its mammoth granite bosom—a bewildering, crushing, but amiable embrace—as if I belonged to Manhattan. No difficulty there in spelling my name. It sounded so much simpler than Polakovski, Tamburetti, Van Dingen—the names on the licenses of three of my New York taxi drivers. With due humility I felt that my English was better than what passes for our common language among half of New York's population.

In London, on the other hand, anybody with a name and an accent like mine remains a foreigner for ever. To become British by any means other than birth is a feat almost impossible of accomplishment. The British nation is a club that accepts out-of-town members and treats them with scrupulous fairness, though to most of the indigenous a foreigner can never become

146

"one of the team." In the United States every new citizen proudly (if sometimes with the most atrocious accent) declares himself an American. Compare him with the naturalized Briton who, desperately trying to affect the correct accent, whispers defensively ". . . I am British." Whatever the color of his passport, the British reaction to the foreign-born is bound to grate on his ego. Amused curiosity is the best he can expect from the ever-insular Union Jack–waving middle class; demonstrative friendliness or a show of studied unconcern cannot hide the condescension of the intellectual *Herrenvolk*.

Easiest to bear is the uncomprehending suspicion, if not hostility, from the mass of the people whose knowledge of his social ideological and geographical background is often pathetically or comically inadequate. (One of the shattering but by no means isolated post-*Anschluss* gambits: "Austria—that's Germany now, isn't it? And you don't like it! Fancy, turning against your own country!")

What often condemns the stranger out of hand is a too perfect, practically accent-free command of the English language, however laboriously acquired and cultivated over the years (How dare he speak English like a native!") or an Anglicized name. I have carefully avoided making either mistake. The naturalization certificate, however ardently desired, alters nothing except for an occasional pat on the back. It rarely goes much further. In spontaneous discussion the reservation, often amounting to resentment, reveals itself.

Typically, Henry Fairlie, the Right-wing political commentator and a friend, countered one of my arguments with the ultima ratio of the patriotic British-born: "What do you know of England?" To which, at a time when he had never set foot on any other country's soil, I could only reply with Kipling: "And what should they know of England who only England know?" The upper classes, particularly, like their foreigners to be foreign. Once they try to be British, they are beyond the pale.

Yet, while, intellectually, nothing impressed me more than New York's generous "We are all Americans" attitude to the Kowalskis, Figlionis, Cohens, Sandstroms, and Braunschweigers, there is something about Britain's reticence which inspires (in me, anyway) a fierce love and unshakable loyalty—not to say dog-like devotion—such as only a tolerated lover can develop. It is less a love of people and place (though London would be a hard place to leave) than of atmosphere, an ideal which is in the mind and which paradoxically does not become less attractive because it is compounded of visions long since lost.

But however rarely the British live up to their reputation, and however frequently they violate it, the basic principles on which their society is based are good and right. Right, as in few other parts of the world, is still old-fashioned right, and no amount of wrongdoing has changed it.

One of my earliest impressions was of a drunken fight in the Strand, London, one evening soon after I arrived. Two police-men ambled leisurely in the direction of the crowd around the two bodies rolling in the gutter. Perceiving from a discreet dis-tance that neither knives nor broken bottles were being used, they shrugged their shoulders, turned, and walked away. No other police force in the world has produced officers who would miss such a fine opportunity to assert their authority, "restore order," and make an arrest. Within a few minutes the fight re-solved itself, the contestants, tearfully in each other's arms, marched off a little maudlin but none the worse for wear. I have witnessed many similar incidents. *Ubi bene ibi patria*, in my translation, reads: Where the police are good, there is my fatherland.

Still, it was with tremulous anticipation that I landed in Dover in 1935. The immigration officer asked me what I wanted to do in Britain, and I replied, "To become a British subject," which, however flattering to the British, in those days when thousands of German anti-Nazi refugees were seeking sanctuary in the narrow islands, was manifestly not sufficient grounds to admit me. But I was well equipped with money to support myself and testimonials to show that virtually every Vienna editor would regard himself as fortunate if I furnished his newspaper with regular reports from Britain. The formalities were short, and I stepped ashore to the surprising but comforting sound of an immigration officer's charmingly English-accented German words, "*Willkommen* Herr Frischauer." It seemed too good to be true.

A darkly elegant room behind the gorgeous facade of the Regent's Park Nash terraces in a house ran by a puckish little Frenchwoman—I would not have exchanged it for the expansive quarters of our Vienna apartment. Susan's youngest brother attached himself to me as a dog's body (shades of my own early London job, with the roles slightly reversed!).

I acquired two sets of friends which touched on two different facets of my life. One was with the late Dick Plummer, his wife, Beatie, and their circle of friends, who were worldly wise, progressive, passionately interested in Europe, alive to the danger of Hitlerism, contemptuous of the growing spirit of appeasement but withal politically powerless. Assistant general manager of the *Daily Express* when I first met him, Dick became better known as Sir Leslie Plummer, chief of the postwar Labour government's ill-starred African ground-nuts scheme which lost a fortune; so did Dick when he took the job at half the salary Lord Beaverbrook had paid him. Twenty years later, Plummer, who went into politics to become a Labour M.P. and a friend and confidant of Aneurin Bevan and Harold Wilson, reached the threshold of high office in the state which would surely have been his in the event of a Labour victory. In April, 1963, while on a lecture tour to the United States, he died suddenly in New York.

The other people with whom I associated—and never the twain did meet—were like a hangover from the bad old Vienna days, the link being one of my old show-girl friends who turned up in London. She was engaged, or so she said, to a young Spanish grandee, an intense, dark-haired scion of a noble family who was so infatuated with the stately red-golden-haired beauty that he not only allowed her to treat him abominably but spent much more money on her than even he could afford. We became friends, and the three of us went out on the town night after night for weeks on end.

At the "400" Club in Leicester Square, I had an up-to-date glimpse of the English aristocracy in a mild, pleasant, permanent state of inebriation ("I can't understand why you allow this nigger in here" one young baronet rebuked the headwaiter, pointing contemptuously in the direction of the Aga Khan's son and heir, Ali Khan). I was introduced to the intricacies of the Bottle Party; apart from paying the entrance fee, each member had to buy his own bottle of liquor. In the "400" he could at least count on finding his bottle intact on a subsequent visit. In lesser establishments it was a new bottle every time. Frisco, the boisterously amusing Negro entertainer, lorded it over another club which carried his own name, dispensing favors to titled ladies. Crooks and aristocrats, indistinguishable from each other, mingled in another club which was the hunting ground of a uniquely light-fingered expert who specialized in clipping diamonds off brooches and rings of the women with whom he danced.

The champagne flowed, the parties grew wilder. My Spanish friend had long departed when I was still enthralled by the people I had met through him. Little did I know. . . . Weekends I would go to Taplow, a beautiful house with a garden gently sloping down to the bank of the river Thames. The lawn was dotted with gates—yes, gates: Spanish wrought-iron gates, German brass gates, high chiseled Italian doors, gates encased in beautifully designed brick walls. They brought back to mind Grock's famous act when he used to stumble into the ring, groaning under the weight of a garden gate which he put down in the sawdust, unlocked with a big key, stepping through and locking it behind him before picking it up and marching off with it. So many gates at Taplow—all leading nowhere. Our host was a charming, amusing, most generous gentleman who had a predilection for people, as many people as possible, and gates, of which he could not get enough either. I should, of course, have diagnosed this gate-collecting as a manifestation of a subconscious fear of being locked up. A year or so later our host was indicted as a share-pusher, and was sent to prison for seven years.

Among my growing circle of friends was a bunch of gay young men about town, on intimate terms with many of the captains of industry and finance whose names I noticed every day in the society columns of the newspapers. Their accents were as impeccable as their associations. I never stopped to wonder where they found the money to sustain their mode of life. A couple of years later—I had been fortunate to lose them in the meantime—the names of some of my "friends" stared at me from the headlines while they stood in the dock of the Old Bailey, accused of one of London's most spectacular prewar crimes—the so-called Mayfair Robbery. Three of them had lured a well-known jeweler into a room at the Hyde Park Hotel and robbed him of the jewels which, representing themselves as potential buyers, they had asked him to bring to the hotel.

One of my favorite associates was a bright young light, heir to an early nineteenth century marquisate, who boasted that he had recently climbed into the current marquess's palace, cut one of his famous old masters from the frame, and pawned it. I do not think it was true. Barely a decade later the palace, the paintings, the estates, the money, and the title of marquess were all his anyway. From Vienna, to drag me back into the private hell from which I had hoped to escape, came some of my erstwhile playmates with doubtful preoccupations: amateur racing drivers, cardsharpers, and an international pimp who had the use of a Mayfair flat, a Rolls-Royce, and an unlimited expense account for no purpose other than having a choice of available girls whenever his Romanian paymaster visited London.

When I could tear myself away from this riffraff, I spent the nights with my attractive but utterly untalented actress friend who was partly responsible for my translation to London. At long last she obtained a part in a film with Edward G. Robinson. It was the worst he ever made. I spent many of my waking hours persuading art editors to print her picture. That I had come to do a job for Austria, for the Vienna newspapers, for myself, I had almost forgotten.

The day before the outbreak of war—I was then living on the corner of a busy London road facing Regent's Park—I carted a mass of papers from the flat on to the paving stones with which the landlord had covered our front garden. In full view of the passing traffic and people, I set fire to the papers, the smoke rising to the September sky as from the chimney of an embassy or a spy's hideout in the heart of enemy country. The papers I burned in public view included four years' correspondence on heavy, embossed notepaper, and carbons of my own letters.

What worried me about them was that they were in German and entirely political in content—most suspicious, to be sure. In the state of hysteria that grips people and officials (including police) in any country on the eve of war, there would have been no time or inclination to examine these documents and give their owner the benefit of—actually, there was no doubt about them; they were wildly anti-Nazi in character, that being the purpose they served long before the British recognized Hitler's Germany as a deadly enemy.

What a poor diplomat I was! As a spy I would have been completely useless. Assiduously though I devoted myself to my little fire, half as many papers as were burned, their ashes fluttering over Regent's Park, survived in an old box I had overlooked. They have enabled me to salvage a few illustrations of the work I was expected to do in 1935 and—how time flew!— in 1936 and 1937. Much of it was not to my liking; a great deal I never attempted; the bulk I was not in a position to accomplish. When I had sown my wild oats, I settled down to the routine stuff quickly enough.

". . . it is requested that in future you should concentrate on scanning the *Evening Standard*, *Daily Mail*, *Daily Express*, *Daily Herald*, and *News Chronicle*, as also the more important political weeklies for references to Austria. Several copies of the London *Times* are available in this office but in urgent cases it might be advisable to report by telephone as you did in a previous instance. . . ."

Eleven-thirty every night found me dutifully at my post, in Piccadilly Circus outside the Criterion Restaurant, where the early editions of next morning's London dailies were on sale. If a hurried search of the foreign news pages revealed no reference to Austria, the night was still young and mine. If there was a dispatch from Vienna—well, I usually decided that 8:00 A.M. would be early enough for the Federal Press Office to know. Occasionally I retired into the kind of telephone booth from which it was difficult to shut out the noise of a jazzband or the squeals of the dancing girls, and, over the trans-Continental wires, dictated to a sleepily morose Austrian official what the wicked British correspondents in Vienna had dreamed up against us.

The Schuschnigg government's bugbear was the Austrian exile Socialists. Having been forced underground in their own country, they set up headquarters across the border in Brno (Brünn) on Austria's doorstep. From Brno they spun massive political threads to most foreign capitals. As to the resident British correspondents in Vienna, it was much easier for the illegals to prime them with information than for the legitimate government to get its views across. The British press, in particular, will always champion the cause of the underdog. The Brno group published an excellent, miniature clandestine version of their now suppressed Vienna party organ, *Arbeiterzeitung*, which was a real thorn in the side of the government.

"Wien, 7 December, 1935 . . . regarding the Brno *Arbeiterzeitung* I beg to inform you that as a result of the recent polemical paragraphs of the *Manchester Guardian* I had a long conversation with the Vienna correspondent of that paper who told me that these hostile articles are being produced in the editorial offices which obviously maintain certain contacts with the Brno center of Socialist emigrants.

"Regarding the correspondent's own activity—in spite of his Left-Democratic inclination he generally refrains from hostile comments—I have arranged for him to obtain balanced information from the highest quarter.

"But I should be grateful if it were possible for you to find ways and means of explaining the background of the emigrants' policy to the *Manchester Guardian*. A copy of the *Arbeiterzeitung* which I enclose might help. I am referring particularly to its leading article. . . . The notion that the Austrian government could and should be removed in order to facilitate the victory of revolutionary Socialism while the National Socialists will stand by and watch idly is so simple-minded that it's wrong-headedness cannot escape an objective observer. I realize that it may not be easy to influence a paper which is proud of its independence, but experience has taught me that a sober, practical presentation of facts devoid of any apparent propaganda rarely leaves the British unaffected. . . ."

It was not long before the Vienna reports of the *Daily Telegraph* began to worry the Ballhausplatz even more than those of the *Manchester Guardian.* A long document reached me the purpose of which was to draw my attention to an article in the clandestine *Arbeiterzeitung* which described the Conservative government in Britain as an example of brutal class rule whose catastrophic policy was bound to lead to war. . . .

"It is doubtful," I was told from Vienna, "whether such trains of thought would find expression even in the London organ of the British Labour Party. But what are we to make of Mr. G. E. R. Gedye, the Vienna correspondent of the *Daily Telegraph,* a government organ in the narrowest sense, who is known to maintain the closest personal links with these quarters, and sees political developments in Austria solely through the spectacles of the Brno Social Democrats?" (Gedye's brilliant *Fallen Bastions* later became a standard book about central Europe.)

Talk to Victor Gordon-Lennox (diplomatic correspondent of the *Daily Telegraph*); talk to Vernon Bartlett (diplomatic correspondent of the *News Chronicle*); watch the trend of Reuter reports and the Exchange Telegraph Company; keep an eye on anything of a cultural and political character concerning Austria!

With every week it became more difficult. I had an interview with Dai Grenfell, the fiery old Welsh Labour M.P. whom I saw on his return from a trip to Vienna. It was published in a Vienna newspaper. The illegal *Arbeiterzeitung* promptly published another interview with "Comrade Grenfell" in which he denied virtually everything he had told me. According to the *Arbeiterzeitung,* he had been two hundred miles from London when I asked him to talk to me on the telephone. The German version of what he said, he claimed, did not correspond to the statements he made in English. Grenfell denied having told me that he had discussed the political and economic situation with Chancellor Schuschnigg; I still wonder what else they could have been talking about. Neither was he supposed to have said that the Austrian amnesty for imprisoned Socialists had enhanced

the prospects of a reconciliation . . . and so on. *De mortuis,*
etc. . . . The incident taught me never to trust a politician's
denial of what he said to a reporter.

As time went on, instructions from Vienna became less single-
minded. I was unaware (it is the sort of thing they never tell
you) of the grim struggle for power going on in the Austrian
chancellery. The press department was deeply involved. Dr.
Schuschnigg inclined toward a policy if not of appeasement, at
least of avoiding anything that might irritate Hitler. Minister
Ludwig, my chief, was as irreconcilably anti-Nazi as ever. I was
confused. Looking at my instructions, it seemed as if I had been
sent to London to fight the Austrian Socialists rather than the
Nazis. A new document informed me about the impending trial
of sixteen leading Socialists accused of having taken part in an
illegal conference of the "United Socialist Party" in Brno—
among them Bruno Kreisky. Kreisky, who was sentenced to one
year in prison, escaped from Austria before the Nazi invasion,
spent the war years in Sweden, and returned home to become,
first, secretary of state and, later, foreign minister of postwar
Austria.

Frederick Joss, the Vienna-born cartoonist of the London
Star, was in close touch with the Austrian emigrés; he also had
many friends among London newspapermen. Through him I was
able to find out what, in the view of Fleet Street, the Austrian
government could do to mollify the British press. Several suggestions which Joss passed on to me I, in turn, sent on to Vienna.
One of the things that seemed to worry people was the health
of Herr Sailer, political editor of the *Arbeiterzeitung,* who had
been indicted with Kreisky and sent to prison, although he was
a sick man. One suggestion was that Sailer should be examined
by a British medical delegation. "Austrian doctors," I was told
in an emphatic answer to this request, "enjoy a great reputation
the world over and require no outside control. Neither has anybody yet been tortured in Austria in a sadistic manner. Sailer
suffers from a serious eye complaint and is receiving careful
medical treatment." Other points raised included the tapping and
recording of foreign correspondents' telephone conversations:
"Does not exist" was the answer, "but it may happen occasionally

that foreign letters are checked in case they contain illegal propaganda material"; double penalties (administrative and criminal) for political offenses; and the impending elections for the government-sponsored trade unions. I also mentioned a request that the illegal Socialists be permitted to make their unchanging opposition to the *Anschluss* publicly known, only to be reminded (sharply, if pointlessly) that at a time when a Socialist government was in office in Berlin, they had been very much in favor of union with Germany.

"I find the political shopping list which I received through your friendly offices richly arrogant, and an imposition of the kind which only a . . . tribe in central Africa would be prepared to accept!"

A little discouraged, and determined to let Fleet Street find its own bearing in the maze of Austrian politics, I tried my luck in a different direction. From a long list of public personalities who could be expected to support Austria's independence, I interviewed three. One of them was young Duncan Sandys and, when published in Vienna, what he said bucked Austria up no end. Sir Archibald Sinclair, the leader of the Liberal Party, whom I saw at his London office, turned out to be a great Austrophile. I was less happy about George Lansbury, the pacifist and former leader of the Labour Party who believed that he could divert Hitler from his path. Lansbury's travels in pursuit of peace were about to take him to Vienna where he was to meet Dr. Schuschnigg. I asked him to write a message for Austria in his own hand, and he complied, ending with these words: "Every nation wants Peace. Since we shall secure Peace only through Goodwill, and being willing to do to others as we would they should do to us, this is my respectful message to all the world."

"The last words of this message are the same which I used in the memorandum I presented to Adolf Hitler at the start of our recent conversations," Lansbury told me. But he would not tell me anything about his talks with Hitler—"strictly private" he said—"But I can tell you that, of all the great statesmen with whom I talked, Hitler was most emphatic in his assertion that he wanted peace and that Germany would not go to war because of any of the questions concerning German relations with other countries which are currently under discussion."

Rather depressed as a result of my discovery that appeasement was as rampant on the Left as on the Right, I dispatched this political hogwash to Vienna, where it was printed in a prominent position. I could only pray it would not raise false hopes.

Another of my—on this occasion, most enthusiastic—sallies into the undergrowth of Fleet Street resulted from an exposé which the Vienna Federal Press Office sent to me, and which originated from the so-called "Long-Name Association"—"The Association for the Promotion of Mutual Interests of Rhineland and Westphalia"—with headquarters in Düsseldorf. The exposé drawn up by this powerful German industrial pressure group, which enjoyed the active support of all Ruhr industrialists, together with an accompanying map, was first published in 1931 in *Volk und Reich*, a publication under the association's control. The exposé—as illustrated by the map—envisaged a European bloc under German domination incorporating a population of 220 million. *"Germany: bigger than the United States, richer than Great Britain"* said the headline; and, make no mistake, Britain was very rich in those days. Now, it so happened that, late in 1936, Baron Ludwig von Neurath, Hitler's foreign minister, was touring central Europe on a secret mission. Austrian Intelligence discovered that this journey was entirely devoted to a promotion of the Long-Name Association's 1931 aims. The signposts of Hitler's intentions pointed toward Vienna, Prague, and Warsaw—at first. But the ultimate aim was the Europe Hitler held in 1942. Surely that was a matter of immediate concern to Britain and the whole world! I decided to approach the only British newspaper that had consistently shown a full appreciation of the Hitler regime's true character, the *Daily Herald*, and wrote to its distinguished diplomatic correspondent, W. N. Ewer, offering him a précis of the important document. What an international scoop, I thought to myself, I was handing to this man on a platter, and without even asking for payment. Three days later I received his reply:

"DEAR DR. FRISCHAUER,

"I am sorry, but I am afraid I shall not be able to use this material. You see, *Volk und Reich* of 1931 is rather hard to present as news in 1937.

"Yours sincerely,

(*Signed*) "W. N. EWER."

Eighteen months later it was hard catastrophic fact. What Ewer wrote represented the views of the British press as a whole —which is my only reason for quoting it. It is frightening to think how wrong responsible people can be, for the press, in turn, only reflected the views of Whitehall.

It was impossible for me to carry on under these circumstances, and imperative that I should visit Vienna for a frank discussion of my position and the position of the Austrian government. When I asked for permission to interrupt the London service, I received a letter telling me that there was "no objection to your visiting Vienna for a few days, in which case you should inform this office well in advance." But so as not to allow my enthusiasm for the cause to run away with me, the message continued: "It should be added that there can be no question of a refund of your travel expenses."

I was still pondering whether to invest in the airfare in order to save Austria when I received formal news of changes in the Federal Press Office. The redoubtable Minister Ludwig was replaced, and the department with which I was dealing was moved from the Ballhausplatz to lesser premises. But Ludwig wrote to tell me, surprisingly, that he would, after all, continue to deal with my reports, following this up almost immediately with another letter in which he informed me out of the blue that the Federal chancellery would reluctantly have to dispense with my services. I protested vigorously—to tell the truth, rather tearfully—and Ludwig promptly sent me a very kind note saying in effect (what was eminently true of everything concerning Vienna) that "*es wird nicht so heiss gegessen wie gekocht,*" which, briefly, means that nothing is eaten as hot as it is cooked. There would be no immediate change in my position.

Strange things seemed to be cooking in Vienna. Not being

one for blind, unthinking obedience, I became more and more rebellious. Austria and Nazi Germany concluded a cultural agreement (at the time Germany needed a Ministry of Culture about as much as Switzerland needed an Admiralty). There was so much political shilly-shallying it augured evil for Austria's future.

One night in November, 1937, I received a call from the chancellery warning me that strong steps against a subversive Nazi organization would be taken the following morning but, in order to avoid anxiety in Britain, asking me to minimize this incident when it was reported in London. A strange request. What I was expected to do is still not clear to me. But the request was put to me in a tired, resigned voice, and the official at the other end seemed to suggest by implication that it would not be a bad thing if I did the opposite, which is exactly what I decided to do.

At 10:00 A.M. the following morning I was on the telephone to the *Daily Herald*'s foreign editor, asking him to send his Vienna correspondent (whom I knew to be Dr. Friedl Scheu, Socialist son of a famous mother) to the Teinfaltstrasse in central Vienna, where he would find a police raid in progress. If he—the foreign editor—receiving confirmation to this effect, would call me back, I would tell him the full story. Sounding a little bewildered and dubious, the foreign editor nevertheless agreed to do as I asked.

An hour later he was on the phone in a high state of excitement: "Bill Towler speaking," he said. "You know, you were quite right. The Vienna police are certainly going to town on the Teinfaltstrasse. . . . Will you tell me what it's all about?"

Teinfaltstrasse was the headquarters of the Austro-German Cultural Institute which Dr. Schuschnigg had brought into being as a gesture of goodwill to Hitler. True to form, the Austrian Nazis had turned it into a cover for their subversive fifth-column anti-Austrian activities. It was Hitler's Austrian Hell's Kitchen which Herr Schuschnigg, belatedly realizing that the Nazis had betrayed his confidence, had given orders to raid. The *Daily Herald* had a scoop, and Bill Towler sent me a check for £5, the beginning of a long association with the *Daily Herald* and a friendship with Bill Towler that lasted until his death in 1962. It was at the *Daily Herald* that I received a solid grounding in Fleet Street newspaper technique.

The seriousness of the political situation helped to bring me to my senses. The rhythm of my private life slowed considerably. Although I was working harder, I suddenly had time to think—and fall in love. She was a tall, fair-haired artist with permanently paint-stained fingers, French-born, but brought up in a German convent, living in Munich, currently on a brief visit to London from which she never returned home. We were married quietly, moved into a flat on the other side of Regent's Park, and before long were awaiting, happily, if a little nervously, the birth of our baby—a daughter. I was working harder than ever now. With the impending doom of Austria (I never had the faintest hope that the country could be saved) about to sever the last ties with my old life, I reviewed the past, personal and political, and began to write down what I thought—my Vienna testament.

What emerged was not a pretty picture. I seemed to remember very little of the sedately solid atmosphere into which I was born, of Vienna's infectiously gay baroque beauty, of the Opera, the schools that taught me to appreciate the classics, the Habsburg tradition the miniature Republic of Austria had inherited, the cosmopolitan spirit, admittedly oriented to the East rather than to the West. What stuck in my mind, and my gullet, and had to be coughed up, was the chaos and violence of postwar politics, the economic instability that caused rapid deterioration of moral standards, the heartbreaking unemployment . . . the social volcano on top of which I had been dancing the years away. Page after page in long-winded German, abstract ideas and factual examples jostling with each other, I tapped out on the typewriter for long hours every day and night. Sustaining myself with a bottle of port a day, I carried on until it began to add up to a book.

My original title for the book was *Men Without Morals*, and what I wrote was autobiographical in a loose sense. From our amorality and the lowering of standards in our private lives, I moved to parallel symptoms in politics, and what I said about Vienna equally applied to Berlin. Politics without inhibitions, deceit and dishonesty that are the hallmark of fifth columnism— not to speak of the violence—were bound to produce a reaction from the top. Extraordinary measures were needed to deal with extraordinary circumstances. Faced with the implacable hostility from Left and Right, the ones in the middle, the anti-extremists, the moderates, had no choice but to establish a regime strong enough to guarantee survival if they wanted to maintain their position. If it was called a dictatorship, I saw it as a dictatorship of the moderates. True enough, Dollfuss and Schuschnigg suppressed many traditional freedoms and abolished conventional democracy, but theirs was, in essence, a moderate regime if compared with that which Franco was introducing into Spain by means of civil war, or with the genocidal Nazi system that we tried to keep away from our gates.

The news from Vienna was getting worse. Klebinder was mixed up in a nasty affair, involving funds from "Phoenix," Austria's biggest insurance company, which erupted when Dr. Berliner, the eccentric general manager (he owned only one suit, had no home, and was constantly on the move from capital to capital), took his own life. The vast sums Klebinder was said to have received from the company funds were too big even for a Vienna newspaper proprietor's appetite. Only much later it appeared that Klebinder had acted as a man of straw for no less a person than the former Austrian vice-chancellor, Winkler. A onetime chancellor was also thought to have been among the recipients. Although in this instance completely innocent of any malpractice, Klebinder—no hero he—took to his heels again and made off to Yugoslavia. Our relations were strained, and I was already in London when he again appealed to me, as he had done four years earlier, to intercede with the Austrian government on his behalf. He asked me to see Schuschnigg, with whom he had been on very friendly terms, and to obtain an assurance that he would not be prosecuted if he returned to Vienna.

It was not a practicable proposition. My only means of getting Schuschnigg's ear were my London reports; I was not at all certain he would want to receive me on such an errand. I had to tell Klebinder that I could do nothing for him. Mother, who entertained equally misguided notions about my influence on Dr. Schuschnigg, added her own tearful appeal. (I should have explained that Mother came to London for the birth of my daughter, stayed on for several months, but returned to Vienna just as the Nazi storm clouds began to gather over Austria. Later I reproached myself for having allowed her to return to what I should have known to be certain death.)

Klebinder told his sisters that I had been his last hope. The Nazis were at the gates, the *Sonn-und-Montags-Zeitung* was doomed, its owner a man marked out for terrible vengeance. He was a human plant that could flourish in no other soil but Vienna's. His peculiar talents were Viennese. He thought and dreamed Vienna. At last his spirit cracked, and he put an end to a life that had been a true mirror of his times.

As soon as I heard that Schuschnigg was planning to visit Hitler at Berchtesgaden—to become the first of the many European statesmen to be nailed to the cross by the Führer—I arranged to be in Vienna at the time of his return. No longer concerned with my unofficial-official position, I was reverting to type and thinking in terms of journalism. In Vienna a strong political pressure group was urging Schuschnigg to compromise with Hitler. If I gained the impression that these people were liable to succeed, I was determined to resign and speak out. The few Cabinet ministers, diplomats, and civil servants who have done this sort of thing have my greatest admiration. It is easier said (or demanded of others) than done.

Vienna was unreal, uncanny. It was the bad old days all over again, only worse. A nightmare, political and personal. Father greatly aged. Mother resigned, unhappy. Brothers erratic, alternating between extreme gloom and unwarranted optimism. Lily Mouton was there—with the same Spaniard in pursuit.

Schuschnigg had opened the doors of the Cabinet to Hitler's Nazi stooges. One of them was Minister of the Interior Dr. Arthur Seyss-Inquart. "Be careful," I was told at the Ballhausplatz. "If you cross the street against the run of the traffic, you are likely to be arrested; Seyss-Inquart will see to that! We shall not be able to help you. The chancellor wants to avoid all friction with the national element. . . ." This phrase was a euphemism for the Nazis. It sounded like an urgent invitation to go away as quickly as possible. That was what I intended to do.

My interview with Dr. Schuschnigg was brief and singularly unilluminating. About Berchtesgaden he would say no more than the official communiqué had already told the world. The chancellor was visibly on edge, his mind seemingly racing far ahead of the topics we were discussing. I had to tell him truthfully that he could not expect anybody in Britain to lift a finger if Hitler moved against Austria. There would be expressions of sympathy galore, dire warnings by a few farseeing British statesmen such as Winston Churchill, whose unique sense of history would not deceive him so easily as others who were being led up the political garden path. But no action; nothing but a silent gnashing of teeth. A number of prominent people would even be relieved because they were convinced that, once Hitler had his way in Austria, there would be peace on earth forever. I came away from Schuschnigg with the conviction that Austria had only a few more days to live.

At home I tried to persuade Father to go abroad, and implored Mother to come back with me to London. She simply pointed at Father, who did not seem to see, to hear, or to care. Looking out of the window I could, in my mind's eye, already see the familiar Viennese policemen transforming themselves into brownshirted stormtroopers. It was horrible—more than I could bear. I telephoned the airport to inquire about the next plane out of Vienna: "In an hour—to Amsterdam." That was the plane I caught.

Two days later in London, in a friend's flat, I listened on the wireless to Dr. Schuschnigg taking his leave of the people of Austria. The *Wehrmacht* was moving in; the Gestapo was already in Vienna. Hitler—Schuschnigg having roused his ire by asking the Austrian people to decide by plebiscite whether they wanted Austria to remain free and independent—had advanced the date of the invasion, which had long been planned. Goering directed the operation by telephone from Berlin, trying to form an Austro-Nazi government. On his instructions, Seyss-Inquart invited the Wehrmacht to enter Austria. The date was Friday, March 11, 1938. Good God! What was to become of my family? No need to worry about myself. There is no surer guarantee of success for a journalist than to be on intimate terms with disaster.

Two days later, on Sunday afternoon, we returned from my daughter's christening at St. Mary's, Camden Town (we called her Ann after Mother), and prepared to raise our low spirits with a small celebration, when the telephone rang. It was the foreign editor of that fine liberal newspaper the *News Chronicle:* "We've just received exclusive information that Dr. Schuschnigg has escaped to Budapest. You are probably the ideal man to interview him. Will you go?" It was the first I had heard of Dr. Schuschnigg's escape. Though information from Vienna was scarce and unreliable, I understood Schuschnigg to have been taken into custody by the Gestapo, which, anyway, was more in keeping with Nazi practice than to let a man slip through their fingers whom their own propaganda now described as the villain of the Austrian piece. Another difficulty was that I could not very well ask the *Daily Herald*'s permission without giving the *News Chronicle*'s secret away.

The opportunity was too good to miss. Within a couple of hours I received detailed instructions. I was to meet a Mr. Morris of the Cinque Ports Flying Club at the Three Horse Shoes Inn at Laleham near Staines, Middlesex, at 3:00 A.M.; to proceed with him to Lympne Airdrome, whence I was to take off in the general direction of Budapest. Studying the map and considering the most likely type of aircraft to be available, I could see no easy route to take me to Hungary without touching down in Germany or in Austria, either of which was out of the question for a rather well-known Austrian anti-Nazi. The foreign editor promised to advise the Flying Club accordingly.

As a London taxi carried me toward the unusual rendezvous in the dead of night, I could not fail to ponder on the cloak-and-dagger aspects of this assignment. As soon as I had alighted at the agreed spot, the taxi driver decided to return to London, and left me in the middle of nowhere. The world was dark and sinister. I could not see a hand before my eyes. I did not know where to turn. Misery enveloped me. I was a man without a country, without a future. *Quo vadis?* God only knew what had become of Otto and Annerl—as we often called our parents —or of Leo, Edi, and Fritz—Fritz, so helpless compared with the others, so inflexible, so obstinate.

The roar of a sports car's engine grew louder until it came to a halt by my side. "You Mr. Frischauer?" the driver asked, distorting the name. It was Mr. Morris, fresh from a party. We motored on toward the river, transferred to a small boat, and rowed across to the small cabin which Morris shared with a fellow pilot. After a few stiff drinks we motored on to Lympne.

"Everything's ready," said the manager, David Llewellyn, a famous pilot who had made a record flight between London-Johannesburg in 1935. "First stop Paris, next Nuremberg . . ." he showed me the map. "I beg your pardon," I interjected, "but have you not been advised that I am not in a position to set foot on either German or Austrian soil?"

"But that's virtually impossible with the type of aircraft— wait a minute! Let me see. . . . Actually, old man, if we have a good tailwind, we can clear Germany with ten minutes to spare."

"Getting where?"

"To Austria."

It was 9:00 A.M., and the upshot of the argument was that he sent me off to sleep for a couple of hours. By 11:00 A.M. he would have a new route mapped out. I was back at the airport at 11:30, but by that time Mr. Morris was too tired to take off on such a long flight to a part of Europe with which he was not familiar. No other pilot was available. Mr. Llewellyn informed me a little apologetically that there had been a fatal accident involving one of the club's planes the day before and the pilots were a bit shaken up. But he had telephoned Croydon to ask for another chap; they would be flying him in in an hour or so.

We were off in a rickety old box of a plane. The pilot was a chubby, cheerful fellow in a lounge suit with a toothbrush sticking out of his breast pocket. "Supposed to get to Zurich tonight," he said, as soon as the thing was off the ground, "but can't make it—no night-flying equipment!" There was nothing else to do, he added, but to spend the night in Paris. I was in a state of high tension, overtired, despondent about the complications. Paris beckoned like a haven, an escape from the cares of the moment and the future. "Suits me fine," I said.

Leaving the pilot at Le Bourget, I drove to the center of the city. I knew exactly what I wanted. When I woke up next morning, my head was so heavy I could hardly raise myself from the bed without assistance. The evening seemed to have played havoc with my finances as well; I had only just enough money to get me back to Le Bourget. The pilot met me waving a paper: "It's all off," he said. "We are to return to the U.K." The telegram from the *News Chronicle* said that their diplomatic correspondent had established that Schuschnigg was not in Budapest after all, but a prisoner of the Nazis in Vienna. I was disappointed and relieved at the same time.

The return flight was pure Mack Sennett. It was a misty March day, and the pilot had difficulty in making Lympne. "Over there, isn't it?" he kept asking as soon as we had crossed the Channel, diving steeply to get a glimpse of the signs at various railway stations. "No good asking me," was all I could mumble. I was not feeling very well. He gave up in despair and decided to land at the first airstrip that came into view. It belonged to the Kents Flying Club at Canterbury and was not authorized to take foreign flights, but we landed anyway. I took the train from Canterbury and returned home with a moral and physical hangover.

Next day I reported for duty at the *Daily Herald*. The salient facts of my Paris escapade had already reached the office via the Fleet Street grapevine. The editor, Francis Williams (now Lord Francis-Williams), whose comfortable roly-poly appearance disguised an acute brain and a strong personality, offered me a retainer, extra work to be paid separately. I was to cover Austrian and German news and undertake occasional reporting assignments.

My first job was to deal with a brief agency report about a Nazi outrage in the palace of the Cardinal-Archbishop of Vienna. The only way to defeat Nazi press censorship and to obtain reliable information, I decided, was to telephone the archbishop's secretary. In spite of the telltale crackle in the line which indicated that it was being tapped by the Gestapo, the courageous priest told me in great detail about the vulgar Nazi gang who had broken into the palace (although Cardinal Innitzer had, surprisingly, welcomed Hitler to Vienna) and thrown a high church dignitary out of the window and to his death.

A copy of *Der Stürmer*, Julius Streicher's Jew-baiting journal, was on my desk a few days later. Staring at me from the front page was the gaunt, unshaven face of Baron Louis von Rothschild, whom Himmler had personally ordered to be under arrest. Baron Rothschild was held in a room on the fourth floor of the Hotel Metropole, which had been turned into the Vienna headquarters of the Gestapo. (He was eventually bailed out by his English relatives, who paid the Nazis a stiff ransom for his life.) Two doors further along the corridor was the Nazis' other star prisoner, Chancellor Schuschnigg.

Thirteen years later, in the course of inquiries into Himmler's life, I lunched with the former S.S. Upper Group Leader and General Karl Wolf, who had been Himmler's adjutant and confidant for years. In the final stages of the war, Wolf, who was Nazi commander in chief in northern Italy, traveled to Switzerland secretly and against Hitler's orders to meet Mr. Allen Dulles. Acting on behalf of Himmler, who was anxious to curry favor with the victorious Allies and saw himself as a "peacemaker," Wolf agreed to hand over his territory to the American forces without a fight. After the war he was sentenced to six years' detention. After his release he quickly built up a prosperous advertising agency but was arrested for a second time in 1962, when information about some of his undisclosed wartime activities was laid before the German authorities.

But in the Cologne restaurant where we met in 1951, he was at his confident best, a dapper German ex-officer ("To us the S.S. was what the Brigade of Guards is to a young English gentleman") who talked freely about his long association with Himmler and even more eagerly about his brief encounters with Allen Dulles. With Himmler, he said, he visited Schuschnigg and Rothschild in the Hotel Metropole. Himmler was impressed with

Rothschild's bearing and appearance ("the man does not look like a Jew") and promptly responded to Baron Rothschild's only complaint—that the lavatory was filthy dirty—but was disappointed because Schuschnigg refused to make any request at all. The Gestapo leader had been anxious to show himself magnanimous—up to a point. Out of a sense of frustration, Himmler gave instructions for Schuschnigg to be given back his spectacles.

One of the many mysteries arising out of the annexation of Austria was the fate of Frau Alwine Dollfuss, who since the death of the chancellor had been living quietly with her children in Vienna. It was certain that the Vatican had helped the tragic widow to escape from the invading Nazis. She was bound to be safe. But where was she? I was as anxious to know for myself as the editor was for me to find her. No more poignantly effective witness against Hitler could be imagined—and, God knows, strong medicine was needed to rouse the apathetic British to the implications of the rapidly spreading Nazi menace. (French and Americans were not too quick on the uptake either.)

It was July before I discovered that Frau Dollfuss had escaped to Switzerland. I approached the Italian Foreign Office for help. A friend of hers told me of a letter she had received from Mussolini after her husband's murder in which the Duce assured her that he would always be at her service. Now the Fascist Foreign Office wrote bluntly that it could not intervene in any way. Frau Dollfuss wrote a personal note to Mussolini—she intended to come to see him in Rome, she said, in reply to which she received a curt note from his secretary to the effect that she would not be welcome: "The Duce offers you a free passage in an Italian luxury liner if you will consent to leave Europe for ever and settle in South America." The Abysinnian adventure had weakened and isolated Italy to such an extent that Mussolini, Austria's "protector," had not only sold Schuschnigg down the river but was so frightened of Hitler's disfavor that he did not dare to lift a finger for his old friend's widow.

A few weeks later I was advised that Frau Dollfuss had arrived in Britain—in Wales, to be exact. Without losing a minute, I drove up to see her and found her in a friend's house in Llandrindod Wells. It was impossible to hold back a tear as I embraced her silently. Rudi, her little boy, was playing with that happy unawareness of life's harsh reality which is the privilege of children. As always since July 25, 1934, Alwine Dollfuss was dressed completely in black. She was quite content to have found refuge in this quiet Welsh backwater. It was a little too early to talk about the future: "I am absolutely penniless," she confessed with a wry smile, but it was obvious that money was the least of her worries. Rudi was learning English fast, and now Eva, her little daughter, was brought into the room. She was already going to school. Frau Dollfuss told me how she had escaped from Vienna to Bratislava, thence to Switzerland. She refused to say a hard word about Mussolini: "Politics," she said, "politics . . ." and shook her head. We talked a little about her husband. "You know, he wanted nothing for himself," she said, "not wealth, no honors—only the best for our country."

What a poor reporter I was! The occasion was so personal, so deeply touching, I did not find it in my heart to press for statements that would have made good copy. But the interview, when it was published, stirred people deeply. It was reprinted all over the world. I like to think it gained the cause of Austria a few new friends.

Events were moving so fast that, in terms of daily journalism, interest in Austria was soon beginning to fade. We were scanning the horizon for signs of Hitler's next move. We did not have to wait long. The Sudetenland, the German-speaking frontier regions of Czechoslovakia, were already receiving the same political propaganda treatment to which Austria had been subjected a few months earlier. The outline of another of Hitler's "last territorial demands" was taking shape. In London, as far as I could judge, while much had changed, everything was the same as on the eve of Austria's downfall. Appeasement, if anything, had taken even stronger root. The nearer war came, the more determined the inveterate appeasers were to feed the insatiable Hitler with political successes in the idiotic hope that he could be deflected from turning on targets nearer home.

An English mission under Lord Runciman went to Czechoslovakia to study the Sudeten problem and report on Hitler's claim that a suppressed German minority was clamoring to return—as the phrase went—"home to the Reich." One could only expect the worst.

It so happened that King George VI and his queen were about to visit Paris to demonstrate the strength of the Entente Cordiale. By that time I had sources of information which are not normally available to newspapermen. From one of these sources I received a cryptic message suggesting that I go to Croydon Airdrome on a certain date to await the arrival of some very interesting passengers from Berlin. "If you do that," the message said, "you will discover something of great interest to you. . . ."

Dutifully, I went to Croydon and waited—I did not know for whom. One aircraft from Germany arrived . . . and another. . . . Nothing. I had no intention of giving up my vigil, however. The third arrival rewarded my perseverance. I immediately recognized the dumpy but well-dressed, middle-aged little woman who emerged from the aircraft as the so-called Princess Stefanie Hohenlohe, a Hungarian who had married into the German aristocracy and had for years engaged in mysterious political activities. If she was the person whom I had been told to expect, I could foresee great difficulties. How was I to find out what she had in mind? No point asking her; I was the last person in whom she would confide.

There was no time to pursue this line of thought for long. A tall man followed the princess from the aircraft. Looking at him, framed in the door, his face seemed familiar, but his name eluded me. I had seen pictures of him but was sure I had never met him in person. It was—wait a minute! Of course, it was Captain Fritz Wiedemann, Hitler's company commander in the First World War and now his close friend and principal adjutant. Hitler frequently entrusted Wiedemann with highly secret missions. The problem now was to establish the purpose of his visit, and whom he had come to see.

When the couple left Croydon in a big limousine, I followed them in my car. It was not easy to keep up with them, but I knew the princess occupied a house in Brook Street, Mayfair, and that was where I was heading. Although I lost contact several times, we arrived at Brook Street within seconds of each other. As they entered the house, I parked the car outside Claridge's, pushed a pound note into the hand of a disdainfully condescending doorman, and waited. Twenty minutes later Wiedemann emerged alone and hailed a taxi. Off he went, with me in pursuit. At Number Thirteen Eaton Square he got out, paid his fare, and entered quickly through a door which opened before he had even pressed the bell. Three-quarters of an hour later I watched him leave.

It was time for me to return to the office. "Thirteen Eaton Square," "Trilby" Ewer, the diplomatic correspondent, repeated, and thought for a moment: "Halifax," he said cryptically. "Are you sure that's where he went? Can you prove it was Wiedemann?"

To stumble across a scoop was one thing. To get it printed was an entirely different proposition. Lord Halifax was the foreign minister in the appeasing Chamberlain administration. Trilby wanted proof. From a little notebook he produced Lord Halifax's former directory telephone number. "Call up on some pretext," he told me, "and we'll see what they say. . . . With your accent, they're sure to think you're a friend of Wiedemann's."

"I am speaking on behalf of Captain Wiedemann," I said in halting English, summoning up all the gutturals at my disposal. "I am afraid the captain has forgotten his umbrella. . . ."

"Just a minute," the stern voice of a butler replied, and, after an interminable interval, intoned solemnly into my ear: "It is not here. The captain must have left it somewhere else!"

Trilby went to work. The next morning the *Daily Herald* headlines blazed the foreign secretary's guilty secret across the land. These backstage negotiations between the British government and Hitler on the eve of the royal visit to France were likely to undermine French confidence in Britain's Continental policy. The Foreign Office issued a belated, rather weak-kneed communiqué admitting that the conversations had taken place. Wiedemann himself departed—as far as the pursuing reporters were concerned, he disappeared into thin air.

I seemed to be the only one who knew where he was. I followed him to Paris and the Ritz Hotel, where I moved into the room next to his. Wiedemann saw Foreign Minister Bonnet, which I reported dutifully. The Quai d'Orsay denied emphatically that Wiedemann had seen Bonnet or any other member of the French government. The statement said it was not even known whether the captain was in Paris. In the bar of the Ritz, Wiedemann and I—at separate tables—were reading that statement at the same time. I could not help smiling and I thought I saw him smiling too.

Back in London, my world was collapsing around me. Central Europe was doomed. I felt in need of a holiday. Paradox? Callous? Childish escapism? Well, I must have felt that it was a bit of each, for I decided to carry on and, looking at it as a compromise with my conscience, send my wife on holiday instead. Her destination was the early colony of international painters in Saint-Tropez at a time when Sagan and Bardot were babes in arms and the fashionable trend-followers had never heard of the sleepy little port. I felt virtuous because I had sidestepped the problem of enjoying the Riviera sun while the political horizon was dark with war clouds. My good intentions collapsed at 9:00 A.M. on the morning when my wife called a taxi, picked up her bag, and bade me a dreamy farewell.

No man ever dressed more rapidly. Without a bath or a shave I was on my way to the Côte d'Azur. I worked out that my wife's £40, plus the reporter's emergency allowance that I always carried on me for all contingencies, would see us through. My wife did not seem too happy about the arrangement, but I was. After a day crossing of the Channel and an arduous, sleepless night we arrived in Nice but, instead of going on to Saint-Tropez, turned east to Cannes, where I decided to spend a few days. We moved into the Carlton Hotel, where the cash on hand was not likely to last more than a few days. Never mind! It was 3:00 P.M. and very hot when we reached our room. We were weary. I revived myself with a bath and shave, but by the time I emerged refreshed, to give myself over to the pleasures of Cannes, my wife had fallen into a sleep of utter exhaustion.

The £40 in her handbag beckoned. But not for long. Armed with all the money available for this unorthodox holiday, I made straight for the summer casino. Gambling stories bore me, and I shall make this one very short. It reversed the accepted pattern. Having lost all but a few of the £40, I hit a winning streak, first at roulette (number 23—it has cost me a small fortune since), then at *chemin de fer*. When I left the casino after twelve hours' solid gambling and arrived back at the hotel at 4:00 a.m. I found my wife in hysterics. She thought she had lost her husband and, worse, her money. I had great difficulty pacifying her, although I was able to show her my winnings of over £700, a small fortune in those days.

We stayed in Cannes for a luxurious but uneasy holiday. The next three weeks' gambling halved my net profits. I was not really happy. With one eye on the girls who were incongruously dancing the "Lambeth Walk" in bathing suits in Juan les Pins and with the other eye on the newspapers which chronicled the heightening crisis, I lost sight of my wife, who began to go her own way and—in a manner of speaking—never really returned to me.

At Munich, Britain and France agreed to the dismemberment of Czechoslovakia. Hitler's Wehrmacht occupied the Sudetenland as bloodlessly as it had taken Austria six months earlier. In London we shouted ourselves hoarse at protest meetings. It was futile. Czechoslovakia was doomed and so was peace. The further Hitler was allowed to go unchecked, the stronger his challenge to the free world.

My book appeared under the title of *Twilight in Vienna* and was intended as a warning to the West. I thought we were on the brink of war, and said so. Once Austria had been abandoned to Hitler, his appetite was bound to grow. Czechoslovakia and Poland were next on his list. Such unequivocal predictions impressed the reviewers. There were few critical voices. One I remember fastened on a description of Vienna when it was still gay with wine, women, and song: "Now I know," the reviewer wrote, "why the Austrians did not fight the German invaders. For how can you be gay if you are dead?" But you can remain alive and not be very gay either.

Leaving my parents behind, Leo and Edi and their respective families took a train out of Vienna a few hours after the Wehrmacht began to pour into Austria. Of all their belongings they rescued only what they could carry with them in their baggage. At the Austro-Swiss frontier, Nazi irregulars with swastika armlets were in charge of passport and customs control, searching and scrutinizing travelers. Most of the luggage was confiscated, and hundreds of people were turned back and ordered to return to Vienna. My brothers had almost given up hope of getting through when they saw the familiar face of Ferdi, one of the Café Herrenhof waiters, resplendent in a black Nazi uniform and jackboots, lording it over the civilian Nazis. For a split second his eyes met Leo's. Leo had always tipped him lavishly, and Ferdi had shown himself duly and deferentially grateful. There was a glint in his eye; he was the master now. Being a typical Viennese, he decided to show off. Without a second glance at Leo and his frightened party, he issued an authoritative "*Geht in Ordnung!*" —all correct!—and let the whole Frischauer clan pass.

Fritz, as I might have expected, refused to leave Vienna. He was an old officer, he insisted, a highly decorated one who had been fighting by the side of the German Army. They would not dare to touch him. Three days later, his decorations pinned to his chest, he was leaving home when he was stopped by two Gestapo men and was asked if he was Dr. Frischauer.

"Colonel Frischauer," he replied.

"Frischauer?"

He nodded agreement, and they promptly dragged him away. A little farther down the street a Nazi commando was forcing Jews to clean the road and to use their jackets as rags. With kicks and blows Fritz was put to work. In the light of this grim experience, he revised his plans. As soon as arrangements could be completed, he traveled to Vorarlberg, Austria's western province, where a guide was to take him across the mountains into Switzerland. Occasionally, to feed their superior officers' thirst for action, the corrupt Nazi frontier guards, in cooperation with the guides, swooped on selected refugee parties. The captured refugees would be taken back to Austria to face trial and punishment. It would have to be Fritz's party which was caught in this way! Fritz was taken to Feldkirch, given a prison sentence and ordered to be removed to a local concentration camp. A Feldkirch lawyer wrote to me, informing me of his fate. At a price, he hinted, it might be possible to obtain Fritz's release. A distinguished officer, no political background . . . it would not be too expensive, but I would have to produce a permit for him to enter Great Britain.

The amount required was not prohibitive. A British visa was a harder problem. Thousands of Austrians and Germans were clamoring for admission. I appealed to Sir Adrian Bailey, Conservative M.P., and to Sir Archibald Sinclair, the Liberal leader who became Britain's wartime secretary of state for air. In an emergency like this the British (and, incidentally, the Americans) are incomparable. Both Sir Adrian and Sir Archibald interceded with the Home Secretary, who issued a visa without delay. We had a family reunion in Paris, where Leo and Edi had settled in the meantime; but all the brothers, once so proud and self-confident, were clearly suffering from the dreadful corrosion of personality that is so apt to afflict the refugee. At every turn something or other heightened the tragedy that had befallen us and so many of our compatriots.

Being only dimly aware that, soon after I had left Vienna, Fritz and his wife had separated, I did not know that she had escaped to Britain and found employment as a domestic servant. While Fritz and I were lunching in a small restaurant in Paris, a fellow Austrian came up to Fritz, pumped his hand sympathetically, and said in a graveyard voice, "I was so sorry to hear about your wife's death." Fritz went very pale and shook all over. He had no idea that his wife had died. Being unable to reconcile herself to her humble circumstances in a foreign country, she had taken her own life.

Fritz and I traveled to London, leaving Leo and Edi behind.

March, 1939. Hitler summons President Emil Hácha of Czechoslovakia to Berlin; German press and wireless fulminate against the Czech rump state, as the Nazis contemptuously call the country they had dismembered. . . . The next act in the European tragedy was about to unfold. The Wehrmacht was marching in for the kill. The end of Czechoslovakia was at hand. The news editor asked me to go to Croydon, where the British authorities were trying their best to cope with planeloads of panic-stricken refugees arriving from central Europe. There was pandemonium in the big hall. Refugees afraid of being sent back and some of their friends and relatives who had come to meet them were staging a sitdown strike.

In one corner huddled a mysterious group of important looking men—not at all the usual run of refugees—carrying big portfolios, surrounded by a posse of solicitous but watchful policemen. Instinct and curiosity drew me toward them. "What's going on here?" I asked one of the policemen, who seemed completely confused by the babel of foreign voices. I cannot have sounded very English, for he pushed me gently but firmly inside the police cordon, where, willy-nilly, I joined the strange group. I suppose they thought I had come to help them, for they badgered me with questions in Czech. The police assumed I was one of them, and would not let me out. Presently our police escorts moved us toward two big coaches, ordering everybody—including me—to climb aboard.

That was going too far. With one determined effort I broke out of the police ring, but not before I had been able to gather from snatches of conversation that these men were Czech technical and scientific experts from the Skoda Armament Works in Pilsen who, with their most precious secret plans and designs, had been spirited to England in the nick of time. I had stumbled on a very good story.

From the first telephone booth I could find, I called the office and dictated a report, hurriedly marshaling the facts and shaping them into a printable story. Exhausted from the effort, I heaved a sigh of relief before noticing the broken glass at my elbow. I looked straight into another telephone booth and the laughing eyes of a *Daily Express* reporter who had heard every word of my story, which he now proceeded, within my hearing and to my intense mortification, to dictate to his own newspaper with much greater flourish and certainly in better English than I could muster.

7 | *One Man's War*

*L*oneliness. That was what war meant to me when it came. No elation. No depression. Just a feeling of utter loneliness. My wife and child had been evacuated to "somewhere in England." By a cruel coincidence letters went astray, and it was days before I traced them to Cambridge. At the office I felt like a man apart. Now I was not only a foreigner; I was an enemy alien.

It was Sunday, September 3, 1939, and getting on towards 11:00 A.M. when Bill Towler said, "Chamberlain will be speaking presently; it'll be interesting to know what's on the German wireless when he declares war. . . ."

The radio set was in a telephone booth in a recess of the "big room," the main editorial offices. The soundproof door shut out the voices of half a hundred executives, reporters, and secretaries, all chattering with subdued excitement. I put on the earphones and was transported to a different world. A thousand thoughts besieged my consciousness and hammered away at my nervous system. I could not concentrate on the German gutturals that attacked my eardrums like a battering ram.

Impossible to say how long I had been sitting in the airless, stifling booth. When I opened the door, a complete stillness hit me so hard it almost hurt. I jumped up and looked. The vast big room was empty, completely empty. . . .

I hurried past the deserted desks with indecent haste. I ran stumblingly—afraid and embarrassed at the same time. Once outside the swinging double doors I heard voices ebbing away downstairs. Following the direction of the improvised arrow I made toward the shelter. Just before reaching the low cellar level, I caught up with the stragglers.

I had missed the air-raid siren which had sounded while I was in my booth. We stood around in the cellar, stiff English upper lips making stilted conversation. I tried to relieve the tension by saying the first thing that came into my head: "Isn't this the cellar which was hit during the First World War?"

There was a shocked silence. I cursed myself. But it was quite true. A bomb dropped from a German zeppelin had hit the building that used to stand in the place of the big Odhams Press block opposite Covent Garden. A direct hit, it killed ninety people. Now we were in the same rattrap, below ground, waiting. . . .

The all clear sounded sooner than we expected.

Upstairs again, the atmosphere was strained. Each to his own problems. The call-up. The exemption. The job. The family. The house. The mortgage. A forced smile when a glance happened in my direction: "Don't look so worried!" But I was.

Police instructions for aliens had already been announced. There was a wide coastal belt that was out of bounds for us. I was handed a reporter's pass, stamped by some authority and signed by the editor, stating I was an accredited reporter and requesting the police to give me any assistance required. "You can go anywhere with this," I had been told. The executive in charge of foreign and home news broke the ice in which I felt as if I were freezing to death: "Got a quid? I'm in a tearing hurry. . . ." I was a touch—a human touch. How grateful I was that he asked me to lend him a pound. (I never got it back.)

Fritz was at home, uncertain what to do. Both of us had written to the authorities, offering our services in the event of war, in any capacity as long as it helped the war effort. I also wrote letters to the press, saying how anxious we were—Germans and Austrians in England—to do our share. I had a sheaf of official replies: "You have been good enough to express your willingness to offer your services to H.M. Government in wartime. I am now to say that your name and address, together with a record of your qualifications, have been entered in the Central Register. . . ."

Our Irish maid was giving shelter to her sister, and both girls were nervous. So were Fritz and I. We were asleep, nevertheless, that first night of war when the piercing sound of the siren roused us. The two Irish girls, coats over nightdresses, were in a panic. Fritz took command—last war, old experience, keep calm! He put his arm round the younger girl. . . . She might have been better off, I thought, taking her chances with the German bombs.

The owners of the basement apartment were out of town. Fritz decided we should shelter there. With a blow of my fist wrapped in a handkerchief, I broke the window and opened the hatch. The four of us cowered behind the window, looking out into the empty street and the yawning, dark Regent's Park beyond. Nothing disturbed the deadly hush. The girl in my brother's arms giggled. Nerves? I felt like crying. This cowering in the dark was humiliating. Hell, if that was war, it was worse than anything I had imagined. I was not afraid to die, but this . . . was impossible. "I'm going back to bed!" I announced. "You stay here," Fritz said in a muffled voice. The all clear resolved the argument. No German aircraft had come anywhere near Britain; the two air-raid warnings of Sunday, September 3rd, were dress rehearsals for the real thing, which was a long time in coming.

The policeman at the door frowned when he noticed my accent: "You British? No? I'm afraid you'll have to come to the station."

He had come to inquire about the broken window downstairs, and I had told him I was quite prepared to take the blame. But going to the police station was more than I had bargained for. For an "enemy alien" on the second day of war, it could well be a one-way excursion. "Breaking and entering . . ." I knew the police terminology. If they wanted to make something of this it could mean prison, internment. . . .

Nothing of the sort happened. The common sense of the British! The deep-seated fairness! The police sergeant did not exactly wish me luck; he dismissed me with a "get-the-hell-out-of-here" gesture which I shall never forget. The next-door neighbors returned and gave me my wife's letters which had been put into their mailbox by mistake. I brought the family back to London. If it had not been for the blackout, we would not have known there was a war on.

Office life reverted to the old routine, but the midday and evening drinking sessions grew longer. I started a daily column, under the general title of "Inside Germany," compounded of news from the German wireless to which I listened for a few hours every day, and the Nazi newspapers, which reached us with only a little delay via Lisbon and Stockholm. Letting the British reader judge for himself, I quoted news and views from the Goebbels-controlled Nazi press with as little editorial comment as possible. The column was intended to add up to a general picture of Germany at war.

To mention a few items haphazardly: I quoted evidence that indicated that the manpower resources of the Gestapo were inadequate to deal with their task; it looked as if political offenses were on the increase. An order requiring bereaved women to produce proof before being permitted to buy widows' weeds pointed to a severe shortage of material. The obituary columns, by their phraseology, revealed the attitude of many Germans to the war and to Hitler; as time went by, the standard phrase ". . . gave his life for Führer and Fatherland" was omitted from an increasing number of death announcements. Workers being forced to make up time lost during air-raid warnings; the difficulties of Stettin Harbor; mocking references to Austria in the *Völkischer Beobachter;* the anti-British activities of German aristocrats who only a few months earlier had been lionized in the salons and country houses of British society—these were some of the facts of German life that filled my column.

As in intelligence work, I used the mosaic technique to good effect. I made mistakes, naturally. Sometimes I misjudged the news. But it was good to learn after the war how accurately I had, on the whole, reflected the situation. At the time, it impressed Victor Gollancz, who wrote to ask whether I had enough material to expand it into a full-length book. I could have filled a library. Rising at seven every morning, I spent three hours working on the book before going to the office. I called it *The Nazis at War*.

Hannen Swaffer, the aging, eccentric "Pope of Fleet Street," one of the great newspapermen of our time, bestrode the *Herald* office like a veritable collossus, gray hair straggling over ears and forehead, lips stained with nicotine, his lapels covered with ash ("I see you're wearing Players today," an American correspondent once told Swaffer), picking up items from reporters, editors, office boys. Some time earlier Swaffer had already used me as a convenient example to demonstrate the folly of the authorities in classifying people like me as "enemy aliens." Now he offered to write an introduction to my book. "I have for many months," he wrote, "heard Frischauer explain the latest happenings in Germany and interpret them with his intricate knowledge of Hitlerism and its past. . . . I venture to prophesy that his book will be a sensational success!" Good old Swaffer!

The book, which took me only five weeks to write, was published in May, 1940, almost simultaneously with *Failure of a Mission*, a volume in which the British ambassador in Berlin, Sir Nevile Henderson, described his futile and sometimes naïve attempts to persuade Hitler to keep the peace. Reviewing both books, the late A. J. Cummings, one of Fleet Street's most respected political commentators, wrote: "If Henderson had known a tenth part as much of Nazi Germany as Frischauer knows . . . his 'mission' would have been of a very different order." Yet the sources were available to anyone who could read German. The appeasers did not want to know or believe anything that did not fit into their narrow conception of the world situation.

Fritz was sick. He did not like to talk about it, but he had suffered some rough treatment during his brief detention by the Austrian Nazis. Now he developed all sorts of complaints. His eyes gave him trouble, and he had a minor operation. An infection developed in his nose, and another operation was necessary.

He was not a good patient. He seemed to be losing the will to live, and made no effort to recover. Fritz had always been unlucky. Lovable fellow that he was, he was hampered by psychological *gaucherie* and was emotionally accident-prone. Something went wrong during a routine checkup on his nasal cavities, and blood poisoning set in. Within a few days he was dead. There was talk about negligence and "taking the matter further." I loved Fritz more than anyone except my little daughter, but no complaint or investigation could bring him back to life. The war, though still in its phony period, weighed heavily on us all. The slightest mischance grated horribly. We were in a permanent state of exasperation, yet I resisted the futile raking over of a mishap—it could not have been anything else.

One of the few people of the *Sonn-und-Montags-Zeitung* days whose memory I had fondly carried with me to London was Annemarie Selinko, a clever and attractive girl whom I took on as a reporter the day she left high school and who developed into a fine novelist. Caught in Vienna by the war, Annemarie, of Jewish parentage, met a young Danish student who was on a brief visit to Vienna. Providentially, they fell in love just at the right time and married without much ado. Under the protection of her new Danish passport, she was able to leave Vienna. The couple settled in Copenhagen.

Denmark was still neutral, and it was to Annemarie I wrote about Fritz's brief illness and sudden death. A few weeks later I had her reply. In the meantime—as I had fully expected her to do—she had written to my parents, and informed them of the tragedy. They had written back asking for news of me. It was the beginning of a clandestine correspondence with my parents through the good offices of Annemarie which lasted until Denmark, too, was occupied by the Wehrmacht. (Annemarie and her husband escaped to Sweden where they worked tirelessly for the liberation of their country. He is now a high-ranking government official. Later, Annemarie's mammoth novel *Désirée*, which deals with one of the lesser-known episodes in the life of Napoleon, received a good deal of international attention, and Marlon Brando starred in the film Hollywood made of it.)

Having caught the proverbial "last boat out" of France before the outbreak of war, Leo and Edi settled with their families in the United States—Leo in New York, Edi in Hollywood. In due course both became American citizens. We wrote to each other regularly, but it was difficult to build a bridge between isolated England at war and the United States, still safely if nervously at peace. My own letters suffered from conditions which were not conducive to self-analysis and intellectual honesty. Writing letters makes me introspective, but in these days the less I was forced to think, the easier I found life to bear. The strains and stresses of my anomalous position began to tell. Although I felt at one with my surroundings, the "enemy alien" label acted like a constant irritant.

In April, 1940, I drew the attention of the office to certain Nazi activities in Ireland to which I had found indirect references in the Nazi press. The existence of a Nazi fifth column in Eire was much in the public mind. "I'd love to go to Dublin and blow the lid off this Nazi business," I said. The suggestion was taken up. To my surprise, I, the "enemy alien," promptly received an exit and reentry visa. Permission to visit a neutral country was a privilege not accorded many British subjects. "It might be better if there were two of you; we'll send another reporter with you." That I did not like very much. To my suspicious ears "another reporter" sounded like "a British reporter"—a watchdog. In the event, the man chosen was young Ritchie Calder—now Professor Calder—who had already earned literary distinction through having worked with H. G. Wells. For the time being his assignment was cooperation with me.

The crossing of the Irish Channel by night was unremarkable except for dangers that were in the mind rather than tangible. Not surprisingly, in view of the talk about Britain being an island under siege, one was prone to magnify the danger to shipping from German surface raiders and U-boats in the quiet backwaters of the Irish Channel. Yet I could not get the U-boats out of my mind. Lying awake in my bunk, I visualized the highly cinegenic situation of a warning shot being fired across our bow, the hulk of a Nazi submarine looming up in the dark, the young Nazi

seadog with the duelist's scars on his cruel face boarding our
vessel, scanning the passenger list, and hauling me unceremoniously off to Nazi captivity. I did not sleep a wink. Never was I
so relieved as when Dún Laoghaire approached us in the gray
April morning's mist.

A bulky Englishman in the lounge of Dublin's Hibernian
Hotel—gray flannels, sports coat, patriotic red-and-blue veins in
a rugged, round face: "You've just arrived?" His voice rounded
off the impression of a perfect Blimp. His eyes were friendly,
although I noticed in them the typical English condescension to
which I am so susceptible. Talking to strangers—in wartime? I
was forgetting that this was Eire, a neutral country. But then,
what was this gentleman, so evidently out of uniform, doing
here? There could be only one explanation. His barrage of questions bore out my guess. How very alert the British Secret
Service was, spotting a newcomer so quickly! How naïve of him
to ask so many questions! I humored him with a few harmless
answers but still left him guessing—and asking more questions.

"Telephone, sir!" a waiter called out to me.

"What—me?"

"Yes, sir!"

Nobody knew, nobody could possibly know that I was in
Dublin. The mystery was resolved as soon as I reached the telephone booth. Ritchie Calder was waiting for me: "I called you to
warn you to be careful. . . . That man . . . British Secret Service!"

All I could say was that I had nothing to hide from the British
Secret Service. Ritchie continued to fuss over me like an old hen.
He warned me against a chap whom I sought out because of
his notorious connection with the Irish Republican Army and
the Irish Republican Army's well-known contacts with the Nazis.
He warned me again when, at long last, I made contact with a
genuine Nazi. . . . But he was a skilled investigator, in many
respects much more competent than I was. We got on well together.

Robert Smyllie, the famous Anglophile editor of the *Irish
Times*, put me in touch with the former Czech consul in Dublin.
From him we learned about a radio link between the German

Embassy and Berlin. The messages were being monitored by "interested" parties. In a wood not far from Dublin, three hundred German Nazis, all resident in Eire, were meeting every Sunday for military exercises under the command of a typical Wehrmacht sergeant. One official of the Germany Embassy was pointed out to me as the Gestapo representative in Eire. I shared a bottle of champagne with him at the bar of the Gresham Hotel, which got me no further. I wondered whether he knew who I was or suspected the nature of my assignment. Although the Nazi underground organization on Britain's doorstep was small, within a week our notebooks were bulging with information. Elation about the success of our mission tided me over the return voyage, and I gave little thought to the U-boats.

It was "Undress!" at Liverpool when we landed. I was searched most thoroughly. Ritchie was carrying all our notes and, as a British subject, he had an easier passage through customs and immigration. Our report added up to sixteen installments. The *Daily Herald* was preparing to publish the sensational disclosures when Francis Williams, recognizing the implications of the secrets we had unearthed and the value of the information to the country, sent the manuscript to Mr. Attlee, leader of the Labour Party, who—if I am not mistaken—passed it on to "higher authority." In war it is not only important to know the enemy's secrets; it is as important not to let him know that you know. Our revelations about the Nazis in wartime Eire were never published. I am rather proud of that.

However prestigious, this unpublished reportage was my swan song at the *Daily Herald*—for the time being. The phony war was coming to an end and the bridges were drawn up everywhere. (I rented a farmhouse in Hertfordshire to which I moved my wife and child.) At the office, too, the desks were being cleared for action. Destined for high office, Francis Williams handed over the editorship to his deputy, Percy Cudlipp, one of three Welsh brothers who have spread their wings wide over Fleet Street. Emanating from Percy, a cold ridge moved in my direction, percolating to Bill Towler and, however hard he tried to infuse a little warmth into the situation, through Bill to me. The glorious English spring was turning into summer. The hot

European sun was shining on a rapid, frightening advance of the Wehrmacht through the Low Countries and France. I felt ice cold.

"Thank you for your letter of May 29 resigning your position on the staff of the *Daily Herald*. . . . I am sorry circumstances have brought to an end your association with this paper, and I should like to thank you. . . . I wish you luck in anything you may take up in the future. . . . Percy Cudlipp, Editor."

It was the end, as if Percy had signed my death warrant. I felt like death (I could not guess that twenty-odd years later *I* would be writing *his* obituary). Down to our farmhouse at the back of beyond. No money. No prospects. But there was Paul— Paul Frischauer. We had not hit it off very well in England and had seen little of each other. But you can always turn to a brother! We met, and he told me that all Germans and Austrians in Britain were about to be interned. It was only a matter of a few days. He was exempt, of course. Anyway, he was off to Brazil. As soon as he reached South America he would arrange for me to follow him. That was the last I heard of him for twenty years.

I am not the rustic type. I dug the garden listlessly; suffering from lumbago, I made sure that my back was always turned to the sun, and so produced wondrous patterns in the soil. I played with my little daughter, went to the local pub, strained my eyes watching wave after silvery wave of Luftwaffe squadrons making for London. From one high field I could see the explosions racking the capital. I was numb, almost without feeling. Petrified with something worse than fear . . . Hell, who could that be?

The two men who arrived at the door introduced themselves as detectives of the Hertfordshire County Police. "Could we just look around . . . ?"

"Certainly."

Funny—it never occurred to me that this house search concerned me. What they were looking for remained a mystery for years until it suddenly dawned on me that, around that time, police were searching all over Britain for secret wireless transmitters or other means of communication with the enemy. Only a month or so earlier, I had been engaged in unearthing lines of communications between Berlin and the secret Nazis of Dublin. The wheel had certainly turned full circle! The detectives went away apparently satisfied that I was not sending messages to Hitler.

A few days later they were back—or was it two others? I never really noticed their faces. This time they came for me. All I remember is my wife standing in the doorway, my little girl by her side, and me in the back of a police car which sped down the long drive and turned quickly into the road. The babel of my thoughts hummed with a hundred different inflections. What was befalling me was not the common fate of a nation at war whose sons must fight and whose daughters must weep. I was worse than an outsider—the outcast, the enemy.

A thousand questions begged answers, the most important of them—would Hitler invade? I never contemplated the possibility of a successful Nazi invasion. Yet I felt I was facing dangers every bit as grave as those confronting a front-line soldier: the soul-destroying uncertainty, the loss of freedom, interminable imprisonment, the breakup of my family, the impending collision with a new set of people whose outlook and values were not mine. . . . Indeed, my prospective fellow prisoners frightened me more than my British jailers.

There were bound to be a lot of unregenerated Nazis; or I might be joining a multitude of bewildered, terrified, and unassimilated refugees. Both were terrifying possibilities. And questions again: Where were they taking me? Where would I be tomorrow? The day after? Next week? Next month? Next year? It was Kafka-esque.

The small police cell in Hatfield was already occupied by two elderly amiable hobos. There was nothing wrong with them except that they had both been born in Germany and in twenty-odd restless years on the English road had not bothered to change their nationality. The police having overlooked the fact that, being over fifty-five years of age, they were not subject to the general order for the internment of Austrians and Germans, they were released a couple of hours later, presumably to resume their wanderings.

After another two hours I was taken to the local school's

gymnasium, where a few hundred fellow internees were already beginning to bed down with an air of utter resignation. When I collected my thoughts it occurred to me that I had left the farmhouse in the clothes I had been wearing—a pair of threadbare old slacks, a shirt, and a tattered and torn sports jacket. But what really troubled me were the dilapidated suede shoes with big holes in the soles. No soap, no toothbrush—nothing!

A pleasant Viennese boy of seventeen or eighteen attached himself to me and offered me a share of his big soft blanket. He had come prepared. He chatted with such utter unconcern that, much to my surprise, I found his conversation diverting. His mother was worried, he said, that he might not get enough to eat; she had asked him to behave himself, as if he were going on an outing. The tall fair-haired lad looked more like a member of the Hitler Youth than like a young Jew. Indeed, there was no need for me to worry about Nazis here—all these people were refugees from Naziism, mostly Jews, with a sprinkling of Catholics. Their social background ranged from working class to "society" as represented by Baron Leopold Popper-Podharagn, husband of the Vienna Opera's greatest and certainly most flamboyant soprano, Maria Jeritza.

NOTHING is to be written on this side except the date, signature, and address of the sender. Erase words not required. IF ANYTHING ELSE IS ADDED THE POSTCARD WILL BE DESTROYED.
I am (not) well.

I have been admitted into Hospital sick/operation and am going on well.
I am being transferred to another camp.
I have received your card dated

              Signature: Willi Frischauer.
          Camp Address: c/o Chief Censor, Liverpool,
                         Aliens Internment Camp,
Date: 11/7/40   Lingfield Race Course,
                         Surrey.

I struck out everything except "I am well" and sent the regulation card to my home address where it arrived ten days later—

the first sign of life from me since my detention. Although internment was probably the worst ordeal I ever underwent, curiously little resentment against those who ordained it has survived—if it ever existed. Britain was in grave danger, yet the sudden gathering in of German-Austrian anti-Nazi refugees— on the pretext that it was wiser to lock up the lot rather than allow a single spy to remain at large—was evidence of a complete misunderstanding of the character of the war as an ideological contest. It struck me as the automatic reaction of the kind of politician whose prewar flirtation with the Hitler regime had left him nursing a guilt complex that he tried to cure by taking stern measures against people who had always been anti-Nazi—and right.

Lingfield was the first of several race courses that I inhabited as an internee. I did not take well to confinement. Except for the absence of women, an internment camp is a microcosm of the world outside, only worse. Once the shock of detention has worn off, the ruthless grabbers revert to type; the masterful begin to kick others downstairs; the little sneaks try to ingratiate themselves with those in control; the campaigners, the intriguers, the complainers, the greedy, the boastful, the rumor-mongers, the know-it-alls, the pessimists—no observation post provides a closer insight into the darkest corners of human frailty. Each category was represented by several types ranging from timid incompetency to assured expertise.

My own vice was egocentricity. I was chiefly, if not exclusively, preoccupied with myself, even concern for my family turning into self-pity. Looking back on these months, it is apparent that I had a streak of each and all the vices required to make life bearable under such circumstances.

An old *Daily Herald* interoffice memorandum—in itself irrelevant—and a cutting from the *Times Literary Supplement* with a review of *The Nazis at War* which I discovered in my wallet were the weapons for which I reached. Armed with the *Times* clipping, I approached an officer and suggested that it might be useful if I could read some passages from the book to a gathering of internees. Seeing my name in the *Times* so confused the good man that he was almost inclined to believe that the War Office (which was responsible for the internment policy) must have detained the wrong man. Those fools in White-hall! No wonder, I could see him thinking, they never promoted him, an old Territorial, beyond the rank of captain and, instead of letting him gather glory in the field of battle, forced him to deal with a lot of incomprehensible foreigners—albeit some distinguished ones like me.

The *Daily Herald* memorandum I waved in the faces of the gang of silkily smooth German-Jewish clothes-and-suiters who, being first on the spot, had cornered all the desirable jobs allocated to internees: interpreter, liaison, labor control, clerical, and kitchen. Asserting boldly that I was a person of some consequence "on the outside," I suggested that they would be wise to share their privileges with me. Every one of them had a bedroom to himself, while the rank and file bedded down in improvised dormitories fifty or more to a room.

They came quickly to heel. The following day saw me dispensing patronage with the best of them. Having moved into my own bedroom and secured a place at the "staff" dinner table, I installed myself in the "office" where internees assisted the military staff with clerical work. Anticipating Parkinson, I moved another rung up the ladder by acquiring as assistant—the kindly youngster who had comforted me at the gymnasium.

"We have a writer feller here," the officer was saying over my head as he conducted a half-colonel into my presence. "We can put him in charge!"

The colonel agreed. What I was put in charge of was the copying in sextuplicate of a list of the camp inmates: "All names with a cross . . ." I was told. I picked three other men who could type fast; the job had to be completed before next morning and there were over five hundred names. It would have been impossible for a couple of British Army orderlies to copy names like Grezsinsky, Frischauer, Hackenschmidt and the like in the available time. I was going strongly when I discovered a notice attached to the packet of War Office foolscap sheets with which I had been issued: "The following will be assembled at 0700 hours for transport to Liverpool where they will board . . ." or words to that effect. One sentence at the bottom of the notice revealed the destination: Australia.

My finger shook as I ran down the list of names. Only twenty or so were without a cross. Altweg, Berger, Deringer, Dessau, Ewald, Ernst, Frankel, *Frischauer* . . . There it was—and a cross against my name! Me to Australia? Never! It was really quite simple. I simply erased the cross. For a few hours we typed away furiously. By midnight the lists were ready. An officer bringing a whiff of bitter beer to our monastic quarters congratulated me. Next morning at the stroke of 0700 hours, I waved goodbye as all but twenty-two of the camp's complement mounted the heavily guarded army lorries to be taken to Liverpool—and Australia.

Having staved off the threat of deportation, I next began to call for help in all directions. My wife bore the brunt of my hysterical appeals.

July 10th: "My Dear . . . this is slowly getting me down. Please write to me about the people you have approached about my release and their reaction. You must get somebody to help me—Gollancz preferably. Send off an application to Private Secretary, Sir Archibald Sinclair, Air Ministry. . . ."

July 13th: "My Dear . . . Application for my release as a "valuable enemy alien" should be addressed to the War Office."

July 18th: "My Dear . . . still without news. From today's papers I see there is a chance for me to join the forces. Application on my behalf should be phrased so as to make it clear that I prefer service in this country to emigration, but emigration to internment. . . ."

July 20th: "My Dear . . . I need at once two towels, two bedsheets, dressing gown, slippers, pair of shorts, sports shoes, pajamas, saccharin, a cigarette lighter, all in a small suitcase and £5 in cash. . . . There are still £35 on your account; £25 must be reserved for me, please. Further, I must at once be registered with the American Consulate. . . ."

July 23rd: "My Dear . . . Please ask Kenneth to go to 17 Dukes Road, Euston, the Recruiting Center for the Auxiliary Military Pioneer Corps, and enter my name on the list of those who want to join, mentioning that I originally wanted to join the R.A.F. . . ."

July 24th: "My Dear . . . As I expected, the Home Secretary's statement does not indicate any change in the Aliens Policy. I want either to serve in the Pioneer Corps or the R.A.F. or to emigrate—preferably to the U.S.A. or any South American country. . . ."

My appeals were getting more frantic every day. Using every subterfuge I could think of to get hold of the specially treated, invisible-ink-resistant official prisoners' notepaper, I managed to dispatch at least a letter a day, sometimes two. With the connivance of a wonderfully humane and patient intelligence officer, I was soon sending off telegrams in rapid succession. And demanding replies by telegram.

FRISCHAUER INTERNMENT CAMP LINGFIELD RACE COURSE 25 JY DONE EVERYTHING STOP CONTRACTED BARTLETT SINCLAIR GOLLANCZ GRIGG STOP CHEER UP

July 28th: "My Dear . . . am now being transferred to another camp, Kempton Park Race Course, near London. . . ."

FRISCHAUER KEMPTON PARK 31 JY WAR UNDERSECRETARY GRIGGS ASSURANCE WILL DO HIS BEST STOP VISA APPLICATION NO PROGRESS STOP AWAITING ANXIOUSLY GOLLANCZ SUPPORT

FRISCHAUER KEMPTON PARK 2 AU GOLLANCZ MAKING BIG EFFORT

MRS. FRISCHAUER BROCKHOLDS FARMHOUSE 4 AU AM BEING TRANSFERRED TO ANOTHER CAMP STOP SHALL LET YOU KNOW NEW ADDRESS SOON STOP WILLI FRISCHAUER 8195

August 7th: "My Dear . . . I am at the Aliens Internment Camp, Sutton Coldfield, near Birmingham. I cry all night and laugh all day. Everything hopelessly muddled. . . ."

Sutton Coldfield was a disgrace. Rough army tents were pitched on ground covered with brushwood. Every step stirred up a cloud of dust. It might have been all right for prisoners of war, but it was hard on the elderly Jewish refugees who formed the majority of the internees. Spirits dropped; general appearances deteriorated. I was one of the few who bothered to shave and to take a daily shower. The mood was ugly. I led a revolt. At the head of a long column of internees, I marched toward the officers' quarters. The military mind reacted promptly. A platoon of troops, bayonets at the ready, faced the pathetic, disorderly rabble behind me. I did not know whether to laugh or to cry.

An officer appeared and handed me a newspaper—the London *Evening Standard*—pointing to an article by Michael Foot entitled "Why Not Intern De Gaulle?" De Gaulle, head of the Free French exile administration, was the symbol of Europe's *resistance* against the Nazi conqueror. I read out the article aloud. We were so jubilant that our revolt collapsed.

August 11th: "My Dear . . . cannot see the end of all this. There seems to be no chance of joining Pioneers. Therefore I need visa and money to emigrate quickly but not to Shanghai because I do not want the Japanese to extradite me to Germany. South America! . . ."

FRISCHAUER SUTTON COLDFIELD 15 AU HAVE WRITTEN ABOUT YOUR CASE TO BARBARA GOULD LATE CHAIRMAN OF LABOUR PARTY STOP SIR ARCHIBALD SINCLAIR AND SIR EDWARD GRIGGS INTERESTED (*signed*) GOLLANCZ

August 16th: "My Dear . . . it is my conviction that it is better for you and the baby to go to the United States without me. The Pioneer Corps is now acute. Whether it is the best solution I do not know. . . ."

August 19th: "My Dear . . . I'm waiting and waiting for Home Secretary's new statement but do not think anything will alter my decision to join. What do you think?"

An intelligence officer came to the little office in which I was sorting incoming mail. "Frischauer?" He looked grim and sounded angry. "What is the meaning of this?" He handed me a telegram from my wife. It contained only four words: OPPOSED YOU JOINING PIONEERS.

The dutiful intelligence officer's mind took off on a flight of fancy. Opposed to joining the Pioneer Corps? That was clearly anti-British bias! Or, even worse, I might have been a conscientious objector! "Are you a 'conchy'?" he asked.

He listened suspiciously to my protestations of loyalty: "You have censored all my letters," I said. "You must have read a dozen of them in which I offered my services." It took me some time to dispel his doubts.

Backward and forward it went. Letter after letter and telegram after telegram asking for help. Asking as of right. Feeling that every decent Englishman would want to atone by a good deed for his government's folly which imposed such suffering on people like me. Roughly twenty thousand refugees were interned. If I remember rightly, over 60,000 applications from friends pleading for their release reached the authorities. They were snowed under with appeals. Our own shrill impatience defeated our purpose. Even deserving cases could not be dealt with because it was difficult for a wartime staff to dig out the relevant files. But the tide was turning. Some people were already being released, the method of release exposing the hollow pretense that mass internment was necessary on grounds of security. Earliest to be released were enemy aliens with skills that could aid the war effort. Thus a toolmaker, only recently rounded up as a potential fifth columnist, was allowed to take a job in a war factory.

Internees were encouraged to join the one army unit open to every alien—the Pioneers. It made sense. Though not a combat unit, the Pioneer Corps was subject to strict military discipline. It is simpler to supervise a potential enemy inside the army than as a civilian.

Now that I look at them again, my letters, however frantic, betray a complete ignorance and unconcern about the course of the war and the danger the British Isles—and we internees ourselves—were facing. (When France fell, tens of thousands of German-Jewish refugees, similarly interned, fell into the hands of the Nazis and were exterminated.) Visa for the United States . . . Determined to join . . . Request to *Daily Herald* to appoint me correspondent in Mexico or Cuba . . . Applications for release for a different reason every other day . . . And transfer to yet another camp: Race Course, York. Then, at long last, a new Aliens Policy announced by Sir John Anderson, the Home Secretary.

Paragraph 19 of a new set of regulations provided for proved anti-Nazi writers to be released, subject to the verdict of an advisory committee. Instead of pacifying me, this provision made me even more impatient. Why were they not dealing with my case? How long would I have to wait for a committee to confirm the obvious? Only the admirable attitude of the British officers kept a rapidly developing prison psychosis within tolerable bounds. They broke the rules, dispatched letters by ordinary post to avoid the frustrating delays of censorship, facilitated the exchange of telegrams, acted as friends, big brothers, advisers, nursemaids, doctors.

August 27th: "My Dear . . . the more living conditions improve, the worse I feel. Can hardly sleep. . . . I wonder how long procedure under anti-Nazi writers' paragraph will take. . . ."

August 30th: "My Dear . . . either I shall be out in two weeks or in uniform. . . . I might find myself in Africa one morning; you never know. . . ."

MRS. FRISCHAUER BROCKHOLDS FARM 3 SEPT NO NEWS STOP GETTING RESTLESS STOP TELEPHONE ADRIAN BAILEY WHO IS NOW LIAISON OFFICER WITH DE GAULLE

September 3rd: "My Dear . . . sometimes I do not know what I want, but I suppose the Pioneer business will be quicker and I shall probably take this course to look at barbed wire from the outside for a change. . . ."

The Battle of Britain was about to decide the fate of the free world. As far as I was concerned, it never took place.

September 4th: "My Dear . . . it's getting worse. Lots of people are being released and nothing happens in my case. . . . So far the Tribunal has not even been appointed. . . ."

FRISCHAUER YORK 5 SEPT SOME WRITERS UNDER YOUR CATEGORY HAVE BEEN DEALT WITH BY COMMITTEE AND RELEASED STOP WRITING PENCLUB STOP CLOSE TOUCH WITH COMMITTEES STOP LOVE

September 7th: "My Dear . . . now that the Tribunal has been appointed at last, I hope that things will be moving. Kirkpatrick knows me, of course, but I have never heard any of the other names."

Gradually, the nature of the battle that was being fought out in that other world, where people were free to hide in cellars from the Nazi bombs, became clear to me. UNDER NO CIRCUM-STANCES GO TO LONDON, I wired my wife. DONT DO ANYTHING FOR ME IF IT INVOLVES PERSONAL DANGER. . . .

September 10th: "My Dear . . . my nerves are in such a state that I would not make a very good soldier just now. I have not slept properly for almost a week and am as jittery as a jellyfish. Neither can I eat the food any longer, and my cough is a menace not only to me but to the others also. I am waiting to hear how long that Tribunal business is going to take—if I can wait that long. I have to see the doctor, and he will have to decide whether I am fit for continued internment or not. . . ."

All this was not strictly true. The officers were beginning to despair of the slow progress of release under the various categories. They knew that the government's Aliens Policy had been reversed, but the change was slow to make itself felt. Paragraph 19 cases in particular seemed to take an interminable time coming up for review. In war (come to think of it, in peace, too) authorities are, of course, always most suspicious of the bright fellow. Not my officers. They winked, they nodded—I could be quickly released on medical grounds. No wonder my health was rapidly deteriorating!

September 13th: "My Dear . . . the wife of my intelligence officer and her children might suddenly turn up at Brockholds if conditions in their district get much worse. Please put them up and make them as comfortable as circumstances permit. . . ."

MRS. FRISCHAUER BROCKHOLDS 7 OCT RELEASED STOP HOME TONIGHT STOP

The release was on medical grounds. I never felt better in my life. *Eighteen months later* I received a communication from the Home Office, saying that the Aliens' Tribunal's Advisory Committee dealing with applications for release under Category 19 had recognized me as an anti-Nazi writer. . . .

It took less than a week to shake off the superficial effects of three months behind barbed wire. But I was left with a touch of hysterical claustrophobia that has never quite worn off, and a hint of asthma that began to ebb away soon after the end of the war. I was glad to be back with my family, naturally, but reunion with my adopted family, the English people, was even more pleasurable. Only now did I realize how much I had missed them and how burdening had been the lack of communication between me and the majority of the interned Austrians and Germans. It was a case of national schizophrenia. Alas, the reaction of the two national groups to me was exactly the reverse.

Within a week I was back at the *Daily Herald* office in London only to discover that there was no space in the tiny wartime newspaper for contributions like mine. They did want me, however, to listen to German broadcasts as often as possible, and I recall the utter misery of my sessions in that lonely radio booth when, after every Wehrmacht report, Hitler speech, or announcement of some overwhelmingly successful battle (on the ground, in the Ukraine, or in the air—anywhere in Europe), I had to listen to the "Badenweiler March" (Hilter's favorite), the catchy "Horst Wessel" song, anthem to a pimp; and the inevitable jubilant *Luftwaffe* chorus of *"Wir fahren gegen Engelland . . . !"* The thought of it still depresses me, and to this extent—but no further—I was, after all, vulnerable to Dr. Goebbels's propaganda methods.

The *Daily Herald* was but one branch of Odhams Press, the vast, variegated publishing enterprise for whose magazines I had occasionally worked as a free-lance contributor. The one I approached first was *John Bull*, a weekly publication with an intriguing history. It used to be the *Voice of the People*, opening its columns to all manner of complaints. It unearthed scandals by the score. At one time it was controlled by Horatio Bottomley, M.P., a generous big-time crook whose oratory and imagination fired the electorate. Although respectable now under the aegis of Odhams Press (chairman, Lord Southwood), there clung to *John Bull* something of the aura of its adventurous past. What the paper wanted, the editor told me, were articles dealing with serious problems in popular fashion. Did I have any ideas?

Of course I had! The story of my internment to begin with; focus on the Nazi enemy; the story of the suffering of people in occupied countries . . . Ideas flowed in a rich stream. The editor was encouraging. I was *in* again. The stuff I wrote, I am afraid, was not of the highest quality but it helped to keep alive a sense of urgency and a better understanding of the enemy we were fighting. Yet it did not satisfy me. Francis Williams had become an executive at the Ministry of Information, and through him I resumed my quest for some share in the war effort. The result was a commission to write articles for the Ministry that were syndicated throughout the provincial press. Each of the pieces was reproduced at least fifty times.

Neither could I bear to live in the wilds of Hertfordshire, which was like exile from the center of events. Safety from bombs did not compensate me for the remoteness and the boring, wasteful hours of travel. In the months of separation I had grown further away from my wife. She was anxious to emigrate to the United States; I felt at home in England. I took a room in London—symbolically going back to where I started in England, to the Regent's Park house into which I first moved in 1935.

An official who was impressed by my loquacity invited me to go lecturing on behalf of the Ministry. Traveling up and down the country, I gave lectures—sometimes five a day—under the general heading "Know the Enemy"—all about Nazi Germany. One of the first audiences I was asked to address was the Officers' Corps of three large Home Guard units in the industrial Midlands. They were in charge of an important sector of Britain's civil defense against invasion. An excellent opportunity, I thought, of bringing home to these civilian soldiers (mostly World War I officers) the seriousness of the threat, the ruthlessness of the Nazi paratroops, the cruelty of Himmler's S.S. Black Guards, the nature of a war machine geared to terrorizing the civilian population. On the train from London I preselected the grimmest phrases I could possibly employ so as to leave these people in no doubt about the danger that confronted them.

At Wolverhampton I left the train, raring to go into action with the sharpest verbal weapons at my disposal. "Hallo there!" I was greeted by the adjutant of the Home Guard unit, a cheerful but tough young regular officer. "Glad you could make it." He whisked me off in a jeep. "Incidentally," he said, "let me give you a bit of advice, old chap. . . . Start off with a few funny stories and they'll eat out of your hand!"

It was not long before I was an experienced lecturer. Six thousand workers at Manchester's Fairey Aviation Works had the benefit of thirty minutes of my "inside information" about the Nazis. Lord Beaverbrook would have been horrified had he known that the lecture was holding up production of urgently required aircraft!

Soon I got to know the various types of British workmen whose midday break was disturbed by Ministry lectures. Funny interruptions, demonstrative lack of interest, noisy conversations drowning my brave efforts. What disconcerted me most was the frequent phenomenon of a table just below the speaker's platform at which three or more workers were busy playing cards while I was talking—literally—over their heads. Once, as I was holding forth about concentration camps, I caught myself— Chaplinesque situation—getting more and more interested in the hand of one of the player's and, though continuing to babble on automatically, only just restrained myself from pulling him up over a mistake that eventually cost him the game.

Factories in the Midlands, town halls and Rotary clubs in Devonshire, cinemas in Essex, associations along the south coast, Welsh miners in Methodist chapels—like a grim herald of war I flitted from place to place. Posters announced: "Come and Hear Mr. Willi Frischauer in the Canteen"; "Know the Enemy— Walden Cinema, Saffron Walden"; "Mr. Willi Frischauer, Austrian Journalist Will Describe His Experiences of Nazi Germany." The local newspapers carried advertisements announcing the times of my lectures and interviews with "the famous anti-Nazi." The more remote they were from the war, the hungrier people were for information. The enthusiasm of Devonshire compensated me for the apathy of the Midlands, but then the Midlands were doing their share, while Devonshire seemed to have little to contribute.

The difficulty in lecturing, as in writing, was a question of emphasis—how to avoid exaggerating the strength of the Nazis, which could cause despondency, and how, on the other hand, to destroy the Nazi propaganda image of an invincible Wehrmacht which, if accomplished too successfully, was likely to engender complacency. The dilemma has never satisfactorily been solved. The best I could do was to alternate between the two extremes, but I have been accused of falling into both traps—sometimes even when dealing with the same subject.

From lecturing the provinces I was promoted to the London District, where my services as an anti-Nazi drummer were required during the night shifts in suburban war factories. The switch had the advantage of leaving the days free for my journalistic activities (I was contributing to various so-called "Secret Service" columns in Sunday newspapers), but interfered with my private life. No sooner had I arrived home from a drinking session at the end of the day's work when an official motorcar arrived to take me to the arena for tonight's lecture. More often than not the chauffeur (frequently a chauffeurse) had to rouse me from a heavy, not to say drunken, sleep and help me find my bearings.

Occasionally, my incongruous position—the "enemy alien" urging the British to greater war effort against the enemy—produced incidents. The Canadian Army's Education Officer invited me to address a gathering of his officers at their south-coast army camp, but when I applied for a permit to visit the area, which was out of bounds to aliens, the local police turned me down. The Canadian quickly put things right, but then I sulked and refused to go. The bewildered officer complained to the Ministry, and I was sternly rebuked.

By that time I had formed an attachment to an English girl who is now my wife. Because I thought it was a good idea for her to get a glimpse of a British war factory—and me—at work while everybody else was asleep, I took her with me one night to a factory on the Great Western Road, and before mounting the platform to say my piece, installed her in a seat in the audience. Two days later I received a terrible Ministry "rocket." How dare I violate security regulations by taking a stranger into a secret war factory? It seemed ridiculous to let an "enemy alien" into a secret war factory but worry about his English girl friend. Invitations to lecture became less frequent.

Was I a security risk? Now I was worrying. In the end I was convinced that people distrusted me. According to Freud, that would indicate a guilty conscience or a suppressed urge. . . .

But nothing was further from the truth. Never before or after did I feel such a jingoistic devotion to the British cause; never was I more impatient to see Hitler crushed, Britain triumphant, and Europe liberated. Yet whenever the newspapers reported a spy trial, I was apprehensive: another setback for the foreign-born, the enemy aliens who were a part of wartime Britain.

Apart from my office in *John Bull* I also had a desk in the editorial department of *Illustrated,* as the name implies, an illustrated *Life*-like weekly magazine edited by a brilliant picture expert, H. L. Spooner. The wartime staff had shrunk to a handful of people, among them Air Correspondent Carl Olsen, with whom I shared a room. One day I received a telephone call from a stranger who asked whether he could come to see me; he had a letter of introduction from my bank manager. The state of my finances was not such that I could easily refuse the bank manager a favor. "His friends are my friends," I replied grandly. "Come whenever you like!"

He was there within the hour. "I have a book here on which I have been working for some time. You are a writer. . . . Would you mind reading it and giving me your verdict?"

"What is it about?"

"Well, it's about a very delicate subject. About the methods of escape and the escape routes of R.A.F. pilots shot down over Europe."

Achtung, Achtung! I could almost hear myself mutter. I knew there were few more closely guarded secrets than this dangerous business which saved valuable lives and restored highly trained fighting men to their squadrons that could ill afford to lose them. It was something I would not even want to know about. It was, anyway, unthinkable that anyone with real knowledge of the delicate subject would want me to know. I had no doubt that this man was a British secret agent who was testing me—and not going about it too skillfully. Are enemy agents really so stupid as to fall into such simple traps? Being neither an agent nor entirely stupid, I called my colleague over.

"Carl," I said, "this is clearly a matter for you. It's something I know nothing about. I have neither the time nor the inclination to occupy myself with it, but it's right up your street!"

Before I could get much farther, the man was gone. Carl had been "vetted" years earlier.

Professionals were not the only people who seemed to be probing my loyalty. In bars and pubs, inebriated fellow imbibers were inordinately interested in my views, my antecedents, my work—or so it appeared to me. Because somewhere along the road the popular conception of British Secret Service agents always playing the fool or the drunkard must have taken root in my mind, I began to see in every fool or drunk a British Secret Service agent. Never before can an Intelligence Department have boasted a bigger staff than M.I. 5 had in my imagination.

Carl Olsen, incidentally, was himself involved in a curious security leak a few months later when, one afternoon, he returned to the office from the Air Ministry with his papers and instructions giving details of an R.A.F. sweep—over Holland I think it was—in which he was to take part as a war correspondent early next morning. To celebrate the occasion in advance (having already had a few drinks, he kept pointing out that he might not return from the sortie) we went to a little drinking club frequented by two groups of customers who had nothing in common except the geographical location of their places of work: newspapermen employed by Odhams Press and the husky porters of nearby Covent Garden vegetable market.

We were having our fifth or sixth drink when Olsen said, a little too loudly for my liking, "Twelve hours from now I shall be over enemy territory!" He sounded a little drunk—because he was. A minute or so later he said it again. A thick-set, powerful man with a neckerchief and a cap turned round and shouted, "Shut up, you bloody liar!"

"I am not a liar," Olsen replied, full of drunken bonhomie.

"You are too a bloody liar."

It was time I intervened. "Stop insulting my friend," I said. It was not for me to confirm that he was speaking the truth (he should not have said anything at all), so that's all I said.

What happened next is difficult to recall. I think the market porter meant to hit me. I ducked, and he caught Olsen on the chin. Anyway, Carl went down and remained on the floor throughout while I found myself doing battle with half-a-dozen of the bulkiest men I ever say. The unequal fight went on until I managed to maneuver myself toward the door, and escaped. Battered and bruised, my jacket and shirt torn, I rushed back to the office, cleaned up, and returned to the battlefield to see if I could help my friend. I found Olsen drinking in perfect harmony with his—and my—attackers. (That's English, that is!) He had fully recovered. I had a broken blood vessel which made an operation necessary.

Next morning, at dawn, Carl went on his mission with the R.A.F. He returned safely—although a great number of British reporters were killed on similar assignments. Carl died in his bed not many months later.

Feeling as I did that I was still in disgrace with the Ministry of Information, I was surprised to receive a letter from them— a most astonishing letter—asking me if I was prepared to vouch for a gentleman who wanted to become a lecturer and had given my name as a reference. It was none other than my guardian angel in the internment camp. I, the enemy alien, was asked to vouch for a British intelligence officer!

In the eyes of some beholders I did, indeed, seem to occupy a position of some privilege. It was put to embarrassing tests by two close friends, Arthur Steiner, a Viennese who used to work for the *Wiener Sonn-und-Montags-Zeitung* until the *Anschluss* forced him and his wife to emigrate to London; and Pem (Paul Marcus), the ex-Berlin theatrical gossip columnist who first fled from Hitler to Vienna, where we made friends, thence to London, where I helped to smooth his early uncertain steps as a refugee.

Steiner and his wife, interned at the same time as so many of us, were, for some mysterious reason, sent to the internment camp on the Isle of Man, which indicated that they were not likely to be released for a long time. Pem, on the other hand, a wonderful little man but not exactly a martial figure, was one of the first German-Jewish refugees to volunteer for the Pioneer Corps, to be accepted, and, however incongruously, to don a British uniform.

A year or so later, as it happened, both wanted to get out— Steiner, as staunch an anti-Nazi as you could find, from behind the barbed wire of the Isle of Man, and Pem out of the army. Having served in France, Pem had been evacuated with his unit from Dunkirk only to be arrested, along with the whole strange, foreign-looking, German-speaking gang, as soon as they set foot on British soil. They were suspected of being fifth columnists but were soon released when the mistake was discovered. Having soldiered on in Britain—he even became a military policeman—Pem contracted a nervous rash but was reluctant to press for his release from the army. Now both Steiner and Pem had turned to me for advice and help. I quickly convinced the Home Office that Steiner was no security risk. He was set free and went to live in the United States. On behalf of Pem, I enlisted the interest of Ellen Wilkinson, the fiery Labour M.P., who persuaded the War Office that it was quite safe to continue the war without Pem's services. The generous British Army even gave him a small disablement pension.

Since I was doing a good deal of work for many Odhams publications, my name began to count for something. So it was not surprising that—the *John Bull* offices being on the managerial floor—sometimes when I visited the men's room I found myself standing next to the big, handsome gray-haired general manager, John Dunbar. "You know all about Germany," the usually aloof man said to me one morning while we were standing side by side. "Tell me, how long do you think it will be until we beat them?"

The year was 1943. The Nazis had suffered their first major reverses in Africa and at Stalingrad. "They are weakening now, sir," I said and, throwing caution to the wind, continued magisterially, "I should say nine months will see us through." Dunbar was visibly pleased.

We had several more encounters under the same auspices. Seeking confirmation of my view in the light of the changing news, Dunbar invariably returned to the subject: "How much longer . . . ?"

It was a stupid question. It was even more stupid of me to stick to my guns. How was I to know the big boss was going round board meetings, business luncheons, and country clubs telling his friends that his "German expert" had assured him the

Germans would be defeated by the end of 1943? That was exactly what he was doing. Until the end of 1943 my star was rising in Odhams Press. My work appeared here, there, everywhere. The sun of Dunbar's favor illuminated my progress. Came January 1, 1944—but not the end of the war. Suddenly the air grew chill. The wrath of the disappointed Dunbar pursued me for years. I never met him again face to face—not even in the lavatory.

For the purpose of the work I was doing in 1943 and 1944, I completely and utterly insinuated myself into the world of the Nazis, reproducing the mentality, the thoughts, reactions, hopes and fears of Nazi leaders, Wehrmacht generals, ordinary Germans in the street, whether they appeared to be evil and ruthless, clever and cunning, foolhardy and heroic, hungry and long-suffering. Throughout the war I affirmed my belief in the subterranean existence of a good Germany. Preoccupation with things German absorbed my attention to such an extent that many events nearer home made little impact on me. In my mind's eye I saw Hitler involved in a struggle for power with his generals, and wrote about it. (The attempt on Hitler's life a few months later proved me right.) I noticed significant signs of doubt and weakness among Europe's Fascist puppet leaders. Frantic German efforts to strengthen the Reserve Army (I called it the Ersatz Army) indicated heavy losses. Why, Hitler was even calling up children. . . . The last picture showing Hitler alive is of him decorating *Pimpfe*—German boy soldiers.

The crimes—and the punishments! To an increasing extent the question of retribution loomed large and ugly. Publicly, I marked down Ernst Kaltenbrunner, "Killer" Reinhard Heydrich's successor as chief of the Gestapo, for future attention. (Heydrich was killed by two Czech patriots who were trained in London for their dangerous mission.) I recorded the doings of his Austrian compatriot, the revolting Odilo Globocnik, Gauleiter of Lublin, gravedigger-in-chief of murdered Poles and Jews. The expression *Festung Europa*—Fortress Europe—turned up for the first time—proof, if proof were needed, that Nazi military thought was turning to defense. The Nazi press was devoting much space to the *Westwall*, or Atlantic Wall, the defense of Continental

Europe, and to the German generals commanding the troops who guarded it.

The Wehrmacht's senior officer, Field Marshal Gerd von Rundstedt, stole the Nazi show, a proud, upright figure, serene and steely-eyed. Years later I saw the broken old man as a British prisoner of war. I took a side glance at the Yugoslav guerrillas who were divided among themselves, the underground army of Communist Josip Tito (Broz) competing for Allied recognition and aid with Draza Mihajlović's men of rather doubtful political complexion.

In one of his weekly articles in *Das Reich*, Goebbels talked about "Europe at Stake," which, to set the record straight, I countered with a major feature contrasting Hitler's Europe of Quislings and traitors with Britain's Europe whose representatives had formed exile governments in London. Exile armies were growing and fighting side by side with the Allies: a Polish army in Italy, Czech airmen flying wingtip to wingtip with the R.A.F., Norwegians, Belgiums, Dutch and, last but not least, the Free French. The ideological character of the war was becoming more evident as it began to draw to a close. The B.B.C. beamed hope into Europe. At long last I was permitted to describe in detail the call of truth ("Ici Londre" . . . "Parla Londra" . . . "Radio Cranje" . . . "Radio Polski") that began to penetrate the psychological armor of Nazi propaganda.

Confidence was clearly crumbling in the Nazi camp. The last-ditch defenders were brought into play. One I noticed was General Ramcke, a rough Nazified paratrooper who eventually ended up in a French prison, and immediately upon his release after the war returned to Germany and reverted to type. Himmler's *Das Schwarze Korps* exhorting readers to learn the art of street fighting was another sign of the times. They, too, were expecting millions of oppressed people to rise at the first sign of an Allied invasion of Europe. How strong was Europe's underground? In a piece for the *New York Times* I tended to overestimate the strength of our Allies inside Europe. The year 1943 ended on a note of hope. Count Carlo Sforza, the Italian anti-Fascist statesman, passed through London on his way from the United States to Italy—the first of Europe's exiled democrats to return. I had a long talk with him. It was a symbolic occasion. The tide had turned.

Letters from the United States were optimistic: "It won't be long now!" was their general tenor. We were not so sure. The strain was beginning to tell. Many of us were drinking heavier than ever. Never much worried by air raids, some of my colleagues and I used to make our way through the empty streets of London by night—the danger from antiaircraft shells was greater than the threat of a direct hit by a bomb—to drink at a Fleet Street printers' cellar club till dawn, after which six or eight of us would bed down in a small apartment for a couple of hours before returning to the office.

Many evenings were spent in the old Back Bar (which is no more) of the Café Royal, meeting place of publishers, writers, and artists. Critic James Agate, a bottle of champagne at his left, a young disciple at his right, held court and dispensed epigrams, many of which appeared a few days later in his *Daily Express* column. Percy Cudlipp, having okayed his leading article in a public house nearer the office, moved on to better things at the Back Bar. Britain's Hemingway, bearded, formidable Gerald Kersh, complete with bulldog and stout cane, bit through the coins of the realm with his bare teeth and drank innumerable whiskies (sometimes rather nervously watched by his young brother Cyril, a sailor boy in bell bottoms). Actors and actresses, film writers, poets—Dylan Thomas had just graduated to the Back Bar, and at times I feel remorse because my first contact with him was a biff on his nose in response to one of his usual drunken rudenesses. We soon sobered up and became friends.

A story I wrote as 1943 faded away explained why I revised my estimate of the war situation. It was entitled "The Nazis Secret Weapon." Some nasty surprises were in store for us. Still, 1944 came in with talk of the Second Front; the Soviets would not let their Allies forget. To pacify them the Allied top brass attended a big reception at the Soviet Embassy. The leaders of the Allied invasion forces emerged from their secret headquarters "somewhere in England" to demonstrate Anglo-American solidarity with Soviet Russia. My job at this function was not only to describe it but also to divert a rival paper's photographer while my own colleague, James Jarche, doyen of British camera-men, photographed the elusive "Monty" shaking hands with the Soviet ambassador.

Another subject that occupied me intensely was the massive Allied bomber offensives which were softening up the ground for the invasion of Europe. At length I discussed the implica-tion of "Germany without Berlin" when a thousand-bomber raid crippled the Nazi capital and forced the Nazi government to evacuate most of the remaining administrative centers. Germany has been without Berlin ever since. . . .

One German captured my imagination, even as it did that of most British desert rats: General (later Field Marshal) Erwin Rommel, whose legendary fame as commander of the tough but decent Nazi Afrika Korps in the Western Desert was not dimin-ished by his defeat at the hands of Montgomery. Now that Rommel was appointed commander of an army in Europe, I built up—from details gleaned from the Nazi press—the first com-plete word picture of him to be published in the Allied press (*The New York Times*). To stake a claim to this valuable sub-ject, I announced that I was working on a Rommel biography. A brilliant book was indeed written about Rommel—but not by me. Brigadier Desmond Young, who had been Rommel's prisoner, beat me to the draw and gave the popular enemy a fine literary monument (without political warts). Years later, when *Illustrated* acquired Rommel's photograph album for publication, I spent a few days in Herrlingen with Frau Lucie Rommel, the field mar-shal's widow and his son Manfred—nice people.

"Maybe tomorrow will be Hitler's last birthday," I wrote on April 19, 1944, the day before Hitler reached the ripe old age of fifty-five. I was one year too early. But the trend was in the right direction. Goering disappeared from public view; I specu-lated that he was in disgrace. I was right. I noted the silence that descended on Europe's Quislings as the war's most momentous campaign was about to be launched. The atmosphere was heavy with anticipation. Any moment now . . .

For some time past, in the pages of *Illustrated* we had been trying to anticipate the moves in the war by means of large maps setting out the fronts and the areas toward which the rival armies were expected to move. (One of these maps showing industrial and strategic targets in Austria caused me a great deal of trouble after the war.) Now I prepared an "Invasion Map" and briefed the cartographer about the darts which were intended to point in the direction of the impending Allied cross-Channel assault. Dutifully, as with all material dealing with military matters, I sent a copy of the map to the chief censor. Days passed but—most unusual—the map was not returned to us with the customary censor's stamp releasing it for publication. Neither were we told that the censor had decided to forbid its publication. Inquiries proved futile. Reluctantly, the editor decided to drop the map from the current issue.

One morning a few weeks later I found the office in a state of great agitation. Arguing excitedly, the whole staff was pouring over maps. At the crack of dawn the Western Allies had launched their assault against Fortress Europe. The invasion was under way. One look at the strip of French coast to which the editor's finger was pointing—the Cherbourg Peninsula—opened my eyes to the mystery of the missing map. This was exactly the spot at which the arrows had pointed. I had guessed the exact location where the invasion had been launched—and put the censor in a quandary. He could not release the map for publication; neither could he ban it without giving the war's most precious secret away.

We were elated about the progress of the invasion. This surely was the beginning of the end! But Hitler had not shot his bolt yet. He was about to retaliate with the mystery weapon of which he had been boasting for some time. The "buzz bombs" or "doodlebugs" became a serious nuisance. What I found most disconcerting about them was the buzz of the slowly approaching winged bomb and the sudden cutting out of the engine which indicated that it was about to drop close by.

"Was the Buzz Bomb Hitler's Greatest Blunder?" I asked in print, giving voice to the official view that Hitler had gambled recklessly by concentrating on mass production of the new weapon at the expense of conventional bombers and, even more important, fighter aircraft for the defense of Europe. Which did not stop Hitler's "greatest blunder" from harassing us considerably. It was now impossible to get a good night's sleep in London. As my little girl was already with friends in a safe rural district barely thirty miles from the center of the city (my wife had died a few months earlier), I decided for the first time in this war to retreat to the safety of a village in the evening *pour de mieux avancer* the next morning.

We were in the Café Royal drinking our cares away as usual when there was a thud, and a blast shook the building to its foundations. Five minutes later I was in a car on the way to the railway station. Another hour and I was with my daughter in the country. I did not know the bomb had hit Odhams Press and caused considerable damage—German-induced lightning striking for a second time. Next morning we found our desks covered with dust and broken glass. For the next five weeks I commuted every day.

Events began to move more swiftly now. From downstairs (the *Daily Herald*) came the assignment for which I had waited a dozen years. I was asked to prepare the obituaries of all the Nazi leaders I could think of. While busy "burying the Nazis," I also occupied myself with the future of Europe. With Czechoslovakia's exiled Foreign Secretary Jan Masaryk, the quick-thinking, amusing son of his country's founder and first president, Tomáš Garrigue Masaryk, I talked about central and southeastern Europe, the powder keg of the Continent, and he blamed the great powers for having used the little countries as pawns in their contest of power politics. But Jan was confident that the lesson of the war would be learned and that Czechoslovakia—in fact, the whole of central Europe—would become a useful bridge between East and West. "See you in Prague!" were his last words to me. How misplaced his optimism was! After the war Jan Masaryk returned to Prague as foreign minister of a liberated Czechoslovakia. But when the Soviets claimed their sector of the spheres of interest into which the Great Powers divided the world, the Communists took over Masaryk's model democracy. Jan jumped—or was thrown—from a window of his office. I think he would not have found life worth living as an exile for a second time.

Germany was being battered mercilessly while the ring of

Allied armies tightened around her. In several broadcasts I marked the stages of Allied progress and infused a little life into these staid commentaries by almost bursting into song when, for the benefit of a few million B.B.C. listeners, I talked about the history of the Rhine and rendered the "Watch on the Rhine" in my own none too perfect English version: "You hear a call like thunderstorm, From rattling sword and wave-clash born . . ." lyrics now pregnant with new meaning.

By April, 1945, on the eve of victory, the problems confronting the victors made some of us feel very humble. "Victory's Problems Hardly Less Grim than War's" I tried to explain to British readers, few of whom, I know, gave much thought to the miserable human flotsam and jetsam left stranded throughout the Reich by the ravages of war—evacuees without homes or any idea of how to get home, prisoners of war waiting for repatriation, foreign legionnaires and slave workers—altogether more than twenty million derelicts whom victory had dumped into the Allies' lap. No sympathy, I thought, need be wasted on Germans who brought ruin, starvation, and utter wretchedness on their own heads. Yet they would have to be fed, housed, and medically attended if the spread of chaos and disease was to be avoided.

We had been shocked to the core by the discoveries in the concentration camps of Dachau, Belsen, and Auschwitz. With the grave food shortage in Britain in mind, I wrote: "There are people among us who ask whether we should tighten our belts so that the kinsman of the concentration-camp murderers, the people who produced a Himmler, a Goering, a Streicher, shall not starve to death. People . . . do not think of Germany in terms of humanitarian expeditions. But," I concluded, "the British people have a duty to civilization. . . ."

I still thought we were about to discover the good Germans beneath the thick, hard twelve-year-old Nazi hide.

8 | *The Stench of Defeat*

*O*ne week on German soil, and the stench and degradation of defeat choked my nostrils. The struggle for survival had scarred the soul of the persecuted. Relaxing—morals and all—after the strain of battle, the victors were not very pretty to behold, either. All values were gone by the board. Germany was like an isolation ward crowded with sick and infectious people suddenly thrown open to the world.

The journey was slow, exhausting, oppressive. The unaccustomed war correspondent's uniform added to my discomfort. Lugging a heavy bedroll, a canvas bag bulging with unnecessary equipment, a heavy briefcase, and a typewriter from the cross-Channel ferry at Boulogne Harbor to the improvised railway station, I nearly broke down before I got going. Seeing the ugly chaos in a countryside laid waste in the wake of war's steamroller, I felt numb. The stuttering progress of the train, hobbling along a makeshift track—stop-go, stop-stop-stop—rumbling past waiting crowds in stations, halting inexplicably in no-man's-land, grated on my nerves. In darkness we headed toward the Rhine, on which I looked down as we inched our way over the narrow rough army bridge as if floating on air—and about as secure.

Germany: the ragged, stunned people with empty expressions; the starving children foolhardily rushing toward the moving train, arms outstretched and begging for bread (sometimes slipping and screaming as death took its toll of the youngest to bring postwar misery to breaking point); the idling Allied troops who had lost their *raison d'être* . . . On and on toward Oeynhausen-Herford, hub of the British Military Administration. And yet another night, this time past the shadowy figures of Soviet troops in their crumpled pants and wrinkled boots. It seemed as if this journey would never end.

My companion was E. G. Malindine, who, a few weeks earlier, as one of the British Army's official photographers, had recorded the revolting sights of liberated Belsen. Unlike me, this experienced warrior was well versed in the art of making army life tolerable; sandwiches appeared as from a hat, beer flowed at deserted stopovers. Malindine even managed to get reasonable answers to obvious questions (which was by no means easy), could tell an officer from an N.C.O. from a private soldier, which was more than I could in the motley army crowd that camaraderie and informality in action—and Montgomery's example—had tarred with an egalitarian brush (corduroys, colored scarves). Most important, he was word-perfect in the language of war— monosyllabic, foul, but expressive and stimulating.

After a fitful sleep huddled in the corner of a compartment shared with nine others, I woke up feeling rough, sticky, unwashed, unshaven, and unappetizing, hands and face covered with the all-pervading film of dirt and grime, none of which disturbed my companions but made me, the newcomer, the spoiled civilian, feel sick and even more of an outsider than I was already. My British Army officer's uniform emphasized the oddity of my heavily accented and unsoldierly remarks. It was not really done to notice much, to feel, to register surprise, or to comment beyond an occasional "They've had a bashing, all right" or some such euphemistic reaction to the monotonously stomach-sinking view of desolation. At long last the train pulled into the only workable station in the British sector of divided Berlin.

The conducting officer introduced himself: "We have a little

Volkswagen outside. . . ." A German driver, a gaunt, stubble-faced shadow of a man, looking older than his sixty years, was at the wheel, giving off the sour whiff of poverty and hunger.

"How are things?" I asked him—anything to start a conversation and to get a German viewpoint. He was too dull to wonder how I came to speak idiomatic German.

"Must do," he replied. "I thank God that I have work."

He had to look after a sick wife, he added. "She is very bad; very, very ill. . . ."

"What's the matter with her?" I asked casually. Interested in general social conditions rather than in special cases, I was about to abandon this avenue of inquiry as unfruitful.

"Gonorrhea," he said softly. "Infected by the Russians. It's hard on a woman of fifty-five to be raped."

Into the Kurfürstendamm, pride of Berlin's West End, now a narrow path between two rows of ruins from which mountains of rubble spilled into the road. The Hotel am Zoo, Public Relations Mess. On duty at the reception desk was a hall porter who had seen better days. With him was a British Army corporal, the combination highly efficient as an army billeting team: "Room 84, first floor, sir. I'll get an orderly to take your things up." A big, pleasant room.

Off came the uniform, the shirt, the pants, the socks—after forty-eight hours or more. Into the bathroom. Ah, the tap disgorging a gentle flow of hot water which soon added up to a bath, much better than I had been led to expect; and, dead tired, I settled in the tub, and let the water rise around me and went to sleep. God knows how long I had been in there; all at once it was time to get out. A bit of rationed London soap, eau-de-Cologne, my favorite baby powder, and, refreshed, back into the room. Oho . . . !

She must have been very quiet, because I had no idea I had company when I emerged from the bathroom, bare as Adam. She, wearing nothing except a pair of multiladdered, tattered stockings, was walking across the room, a forced smile distorting her coarse but not unattractive face, giving me the benefit of a full view of her very good young body as she moved sideways like a crab. Of course, now I remembered—like a Numbers Girl on the Berlin variety stage who used to parade in front of the curtain carrying a board which almost hid her vital statistics and which showed the number of the next attraction as per program.

Of all the things I expected to encounter in ruined Berlin so shortly after the end of the war—and my imagination had not been idle—this was about the most unlikely. Never before in my life had I been less prepared, never more surprised than when she threw herself at me with the strength of despair. It was almost like rape with the roles reversed. I just managed to escape her clutches, and truly shocked her when, in reply to her plaintive, "*Ich bin ja zufrieden mit ein paar Zigaretten . . .*" I explained in German that this was not the best way to go about getting them from me.

I asked her how she had got in here. She smiled dejectedly, sitting down on the bed just as she was.

"I am the parlormaid," she said, and added quickly, "only temporarily, until things get better. You see, I am an actress, really. My last job was—" I had guessed correctly—"a Numbers Girl."

She had been famous, she said. Her picture had been on many front pages. But what could she now do? Father missing; mother suffering from nerves since the bombing; younger brother hiding at home—he had been lucky to avoid capture by the Russians. Tears were beginning to run down her cheeks; her hands, roughened by hard work, twisted awkwardly. I was so distressed by this confrontation with utter misery that for a few moments I completely forgot that we were both naked.

"Here are some cigarettes. Now get dressed and go."

Money—German money—was valueless. Cigarettes, first to satisfy a craving, later too precious to be smoked, had taken over as currency. Twenty English cigarettes were worth £2 10s. at the current rate of exchange. It was enough in these days to supply a whole German family with the necessities of life, which was more than they could buy anyway. I recalled Vienna's middle-class women deliberately going out to sell themselves on the open market for a few extra luxuries; I had met scores of venal women, but this was the first time I had run across a case of stark hunger compelling a woman to sell her body.

Throughout my stay at the Am Zoo I was never quite safe from her. She was determined to give herself, the only asset she had, in exchange for cigarettes. Never before or after have I paid so much in order *not* to sleep with a woman.

The hotel bar was crowded, buzzing with conversation; the scene was decorated with a few attractive girls from the Women's Services. From the counter an unending supply of champagne cocktails issued forth, the barman rapidly filling row after row of glasses from bottles of French champagne with *Reserviert für die Wehrmacht* labels. I reached for the "Authorization to pay Mr. (Col.) W. Frischauer the sum of . . ." in my wallet. It was addressed to the army paymaster general and—I should have known—cashable only at army pay offices. The conducting officer offered help: "Did you bring plenty of cigarettes?" I was not falling for that. No man could have had a more conclusive lesson about the value of cigarettes. "Or a personal check, perhaps?" That sounded all right. "Yes, I have my checkbook with me."

All I wanted was a few marks. "I can get you 750 for a fiver"—£5. Considering that the official mark rate was 40 to the pound sterling, it was a tempting offer. The transaction was completed. Ten minutes later I was briefed about my privileges as a (civilian) member of the armed forces, one of which was the right to draw £5 in sterling notes from the army paymaster in exchange for 200 marks—the official rate—and to send the money home in a registered envelope. That is what I did next day. Having covered my check, I was left with a net profit of 550 marks (£13 5s. at the official rate). No wonder the British Exchequer lost over £20 million on such transactions within the first year of occupation!

Dark looks from the barman when I offered mark notes as I gave my order, indicating with a sweeping gesture that I wanted everybody to have a drink on me. "That will be twenty-six large champagne cocktails at six marks each," the barman said. Pointing to my marks, he added: "But they're no good to me. Haven't you any cigarettes? Twenty cigarettes for the 26 cocktails, right?" I accepted his proposition. Word got round quickly that I was throwing my cigarettes about in a reckless manner, which was bad for my reputation. It was all right to be called a womanizer or a drunk, but a man who wasted his cigarettes was a fool!

Malindine and I went to work, seeking out the first German democratic leaders to emerge from the political vacuum. One of them was Jacob Kaiser, chairman of the Christian Democrats in the Eastern, Soviet-occupied, Zone of Germany, who eventually became minister for all-German affairs in Dr. Adenauer's Cabinet. We photographed and talked to the "rubble women"—nondescript female figures covered in rags who were digging for dead bodies in the mountains of debris. Our assignment was to convey an impression in words and pictures of the desolation and destruction of bricks and mortar and human beings. Within two or three days we had some very dramatic shots in the can. My notebook was filled.

Slowly I acclimatized myself to the strange military/social setup which revolved around the bar of the Hotel am Zoo. But unlike most of my English colleagues who treated the defeated "Jerries" with the contempt implied in the "nonfraternization" order, I (whose most cherished animosities have often wilted by personal contact with the foe) made friends with some of the hotel employees, among them an East African boy whose Berlin accent, in strange contrast with his dark skin and wiry hair, sounded a reminder of Germany's colonial past. Incredible that this young African should have survived extermination by the Nazis, who rated Negroes as subhuman as Jews and gypsies! Showing his big white teeth in a broad smile, his eyes flashing, this lively youngster was doing odd jobs around the hotel, picking up a cigarette here, a cigarette there and, I suppose, making a living.

Early on the sixth day of our Berlin operation I was waiting for Malindine to venture out once more into the wilderness of Berlin. I waited and waited. He was late, very late. At long last he arrived swearing like the good trooper he was, trailing a gang of excited hotel staff behind him. A big case containing all his cameras had disappeared from his room. He had last seen them the previous afternoon. Only a member of the staff could have taken them; that a fellow newspaperman or an officer might be guilty was inconceivable. The value of the cameras in the Berlin black market was inestimable—enough to buy a villa or an old master or any number of luxuries which hungry Germans were offering for sale. The cameras were never seen again. Neither was my young Negro friend. Whether there was a connection between the two disappearances, who can say? Without cameras our mission had to be abandoned.

A few weeks later I was back in Berlin. "They have caught the woman who betrayed Goerdeler," I was told. None of the correspondents seemed to care. Dr. Carl Goerdeler, former mayor of Leipzig, was the civilian head of the anti-Hitler conspiracy of July 20, 1944. While many of the implicated generals were arrested at the Bendlerstrasse War Office, Goerdeler had disappeared completely. The Nazi authorities offered a reward of 100,000 marks for his capture, and Frau Helene Schwärzel, a pathetic middle-aged rural postmistress, recognized the dignified, tall ex-mayor in her village, and told the police. It was not a question of pro-Nazi sentiments—poor little woman!—she did what she thought right, and knew no better.

Now she had been caught and put behind bars. Thousands of Nazis, Gestapo officials, S.S. generals, exterminators, and Gauleiters were in hiding or had escaped across the border, yet how proud the Allies were of this fine catch! Frau Schwärzel had never touched a pfennig of the 100,000 marks which were recovered intact from her account. Although to her Goerdeler was a traitor, she had been shocked when she read that the man she had betrayed had been executed. We drove to North Berlin Police Headquarters in the Alexanderplatz and saw her in her cell, tearful, bewildered, blinking at the flashbulbs of the photographers, a human casualty buffeted in the bedlam of war.

Otto Grotewohl, pre-Hitler Social Democratic Reichstag deputy, one of the few to survive the war inside Germany, was a man of the future: no record of collaboration with the Nazis, a small party organization already in being . . . I was anxious to meet him. Waiting to be admitted to his office, I talked to his young secretary, as usual asking questions about things German, looking for the "human angle" to illustrate the renaissance of

German party politics and to help break down the barrier of incomprehension between Germans and The Rest.

Our conversation was just beginning to come alive when the telephone rang and she told me that her chief would see me now. He was a tall, stooping, earnest man who talked sense—not so sickeningly submissive as most Germans in those days; not protesting his anti-Nazi past, as all the best Nazis did; critical of certain Allied attitudes but neither carping nor arrogant. I liked him. I hoped to see him again, and said so: "Come to my house one evening. Come on Monday. I shall be there at 7:30 P.M.," he responded. He seemed to be as eager for contact with the outside world as I was to get a glimpse of a 1945 German at home.

But first I wanted to meet his secretary again. She agreed to come to the Café Wien, next door to the Hotel am Zoo, which was out of bounds for "Allied personnel." As I had no coffee coupons, I paid with cigarettes. She would not accept any, which was most extraordinary for a *Fraulein*. She was also very reticent about Grotewohl. When I told her that I intended to go to his flat the following evening, a curious steely glint came into her eyes—but she said nothing.

She was with Grotewohl's wife when I called the following evening, nearly an hour late. The two women seemed glad to have a visitor. They were in a frightful state. Tears gathered in Frau Grotewohl's eyes, and the secretary looked petrified with fear. Was there anything I could do, I asked. Where was Herr Grotewohl?

They exchanged a quick glance, and I thought I saw the secretary nod. I knew they were consulting whether to let me in on their secret. "*Mein mann . . .*" Frau Grotewohl began slowly. He was not here, she said. That much I had already noticed. But soon emotion burst the gates of reticence, and her story erupted like the sea breaking over a dam: "He is in Karlshorst. . . ."

It was not easy to find my bearings across the rapids which, sometimes tearfully, sometimes defiantly, sometimes uncertainly, cascaded from her lips. This evening, for the fifth time, a car from Soviet Headquarters in Karlshorst had called for her husband at seven-thirty, had taken him away and—after tormenting hours of waiting—brought him back at the crack of dawn, a

nervous wreck, bathed in perspiration, shaking all over, and refusing to say anything except: "Zhukov wanted to talk to
me. . . ." Zhukov was the supreme Soviet commander in Germany.

A few months later I knew what Zhukov and Grotewohl had
talked about, although I visualized the conversations as being
rather one-sided. It also occurred to me that Grotewohl had
probably asked me to call on him at this particular hour in order
to have a British-uniformed witness of his departure for Karlshorst, a place from which no German could be sure to return
alive. In Grotewohl's case, as I found out later, the choice was
between the two roads out of Karlshorst—one leading into the
political camp of the Communists, the other to a slave-labor camp
in Siberia.

Grotewohl chose the Communist camp, and took his Social
Democrats into alliance with the Communists in a newly formed
Socialist Unity Party. When the Soviets set up the Communist
German People's Republic in East Germany, Grotewohl became
the first prime minister. He also divorced his wife and married
his secretary. By a curious twist of fate, his new secretary did
not stay at her post very long either. She was unmasked as an
agent of a West German espionage organization, tried in secret,
and executed.

I saw Grotewohl again on two or three occasions before the
Iron Curtain came down. But when, some years later, I braved
the hazards of an unauthorized crossing into Communist East
Berlin, and asked an official of the East German Press Office to
take me to Grotewohl, I met the maddening, uncomprehending
—intentionally uncomprehending—stone-walled, arrogantly-cau-
tious expression which is my personal "image" of Communist
officials at work. I hate it.

It was just as hateful in 1960 when I went to Berlin to advise
a team of television operators on a fifty-minute program about
The Divided City—as everybody called it. The coverage of West
Berlin was a foregone conclusion: the new buildings, the hustle
and bustle of the Kurfürstendamm cafés, the small Jewish community that survives in Berlin, Mayor Willy Brandt, a repre-

sentative of an agency which collects information from East Berlin whom the East Germans would call a spy. . . . But there was the problem of projecting East Berlin. Three times I conducted my television friends through the Brandenburg Gate; three times we returned with vague promises and no results. We had to give up. I have no quarrel with the East Berliners, but I am emotionally incapable of dealing with Communist officials. I never wanted to go back there again.

Yet I did. And under the most curious circumstances. Instead of a holiday in Venice I decided to take my wife to Berlin in August, 1961. We landed smack in the middle of the biggest East-West crisis in Europe since the Berlin blockade. The night before we arrived at Tempelhof Airport, the East Germans had started to put up the now infamous Berlin Wall. For hours we stood and watched, flabbergasted as bedraggled, sweaty East German troops, guarded by machine-gun-toting N.C.O.'s, set block upon block of concrete and strung mile after mile of barbed-wire fencing along the boundary of the Soviet sector. Two days later we knew that the Soviets intended Berlin to be permanently bisected. We were in the Café Kempinski in the Kurfürstendamm when the crowds gathered and a column of 1,500 newly arrived American battle troops paraded demonstratively down the tree-lined avenue; "The *Amis*," a couple of middle-aged German women exclaimed in chorus behind us. "About time, too!"

Frankly, I never believed that the Soviets would encourage the East Germans to go further and occupy West Berlin, or that they intended to occupy it themselves. Every child knew the Western Allies could not let them get away with that. The nervous anticipation of the Berliners did not communicate itself to me, and I did not share the excitement of the many foreign correspondents who had come to report the beginnings of World War III. As thousands of East Germans (over ten million in ten years) crossed to freedom and, more important, prosperity in West Germany, it became clear—at least to me—that the Communist regime would have to stop this ruinous drain of manpower sooner or later. Neither could the Soviets afford the western flank of their empire to be economically emaciated to the point of collapse. However hateful, the Wall was an ingenious device to stop the rot without having to go to war. Dr. Adenauer was apparently of a different opinion. He thought the balloon had gone up and did not even bother to visit Berlin. It was the beginning of his end.

Would my wife, then, never see East Berlin? She did, sooner than I had thought possible under the circumstances. For, making innocent inquiries about ways and means to penetrate the recently reinforced Iron Curtain, I received a laconic reply: "Excursion tours into East Berlin daily at 2:30 P.M. from the Kurfürstendamm." This is how, while the world waited with bated breath for the war to start somewhere along the boundary between East and West Berlin, my wife and I crossed the line in a big lumbering coach crowded with Belgian, Dutch, French, Austrian, and other assorted sightseers. What was remarkable was not what we saw in East Berlin's drab and shabby streets from whose ruins the trees grew green and high, and the flags and banners with Socialist exhortations, but that, in this week of climactic tension, we were able to enter East Berlin at all.

News Chronicle, Wednesday, May 2, 1945:

HITLER DEAD
Doenitz, New Führer, Says: We Fight On
More Big News Today, Declares Nazi Radio

"Hitler is dead. His death was announced last night by Hamburg Radio in a proclamation. Admiral Doenitz becomes the new Führer.

"It is reported from the Führer's headquarters that our Führer, Adolf Hitler, died a soldier's death this afternoon at his command post in the Reich Chancellery, fighting to the last breath against Bolshevism and for Germany. On April 30 the Führer appointed Grand Admiral Doenitz as his successor. . . ."

Admiral Doenitz went to the microphone: ". . . In deepest sorrow and reverence the German people bow. . . . The end of the Führer's struggles and of his unswerving straight path of life is marked by his heroic death in the Capital of the Reich.

My first task is to save the German people from annihilation by the advancing Bolshevist enemy. The military struggle continues only with this aim. Inasmuch and as long as the attainment of this aim is being hindered by the British and the Americans, we shall have to continue to defend ourselves against them as well and shall have to continue to fight. . . ."

The end of the war, victory in Europe, VE-Day, is swamped in my memory by the impressions of my first postwar trips to Germany. That day we left the office after a day's hard work and, passing one of the many public houses where people were celebrating, we ran into a fight. The sound of one man's skull hitting the pavement is still with me almost twenty years later. He died there and then. God knows who he was. I think of him as one of the last victims of the war.

I went to see Mr. Ivone Kirkpatrick, prewar counselor at the appeasing British Embassy in Berlin but, in political acumen, head and shoulders above the hapless British Ambassador Sir Nevile Henderson. Not very tactfully, I described Kirkpatrick to the readers as "Hitler's British Successor" (he had been appointed British representative on the Allied Control Commission for Germany).

TOWLER DAILY HERALD 2140 COLLECT VIENNA JULY 6 HAVE NOW SEEN PEOPLE WHO SAY FRISCHAUERS PARENTS LIVED HERE UNTIL MIDDLE 1942 WHEN TAKEN TO THERESIENSTADT WHERE BELIEVED DIED AT END 1943 STOP BEEN SUPPORTED WITH PACKETS AND MONEY WHILE HERE AND IN THERESIENSTADT BUT AFTER 1943 PACKETS UNACKNOWLEDGED STOP SOME RETURNED STOP AS THEY WERE AT THERESIENSTADT TRANSIT CAMP EIGHTEEN MONTHS UNBELIEVE THEY WOULD BE DEPORTED FOR EXECUTION AFTER SO LONG STOP PROBABLY DIED NATURAL DEATH

Both at the same time? In Vienna several months later I was offered information about the identity of the Gestapo men responsible for rounding up Mother and taking Father, too, when he refused to be parted from his wife after fifty years of marriage. This was no case for personal vengeance.

DUNHURST
BEDALES SCHOOL
PETERSFIELD

DEAR DADDY,

I have made up a poem here it is.

Spring

The flowers are out
The birds are singing
Robbins to their nests are bringing
Little twigs of happiness.

Children are happy
Dogs are snappy
They are barking away
Full of play.

After lessons every day
Children all go out and play
Full of happiness and joy
Springs the best of seasons.

I will try to make up another poem for you one day. I hope you like that one.

Love,
(*signed*) ANN

MISS ANN FRISCHAUER   COMMISSIONER GENERAL
Bedales School   FOR THE U.K. IN SOUTH-EAST ASIA
Petersfield,   Singapore, 25 August.
Hampshire,
Gt. Britain.

DEAR ANN,

I was delighted to hear that you have won the Junior Essay Prize, and I have sent you a cheque for Webster's Biographical Dictionary. I read your essay in the Bedales Chronicle which has just reached me here on the other side of the world. I greatly enjoyed your account . . . a remarkable piece of writing for one in the lowest form of the school, and I congratulate you on it.

I hope you are enjoying life at Bedales as much as I did. I cannot wish you anything better than that.

The best of luck to you always.

(*signed*) MALCOLM MACDONALD

CERTIFIED COPY OF AN ENTRY OF MARRIAGE

Marriage Solemnized at the Registry Office, District of Hampstead in the Metropolitan Borough of Hampstead . . .

Wilhelm Frischauer, widower, Journalist, 43 Eton Place, London N.W. 3.

Ethel Mary Knock, Private Secretary, Rose Cottage, Gubblecote, Near Tring.

By Licence before me:

(*Signed*) PADDY H. READY,
Registrar.

Daily Mail, Friday, September 14, 1945:

HIMMLER'S PLAN IF GERMANS HAD INVADED IN 1940

BRITAIN HAD 2,300 MARKED MEN
CHURCHILL AND ATLEE AND THE V-CABINET

"Berlin: Himmler's plan for 'liquidating' leaders in every field of British activity—a plan that was to have come into operation if the German invasion in 1940 had succeeded—is contained in Gestapo dossiers disclosed here today.

"The list includes the names of the present Prime Minister, Mr. Attlee, Mr. Churchill, the Victory Cabinet, and detailed all those whose arrest was to be 'automatic' after the Wehrmacht's victory."

Among the 2,300 listed by Himmler were: J. J. Astor, Norman Angell, Lord Beaverbrook, Dr. Edouard Beneš, Robert Boothby, Ernest Bevin, Lord Camrose, R. H. S. Crossman, Winston Churchill, Hugh Dalton, Alfred Duff Cooper, Sir John Ellerman, Dingle Foot, Sigmund Freud, Willi Frischauer . . .

Only because I rarely stayed in Germany for more than a fortnight at a time, returning to Britain whenever I could, did I escape the corrosion of sentiments and standards that afflicted many resident representatives of the West: soldiers, administrators, medical personnel, security staff, journalists. In the British Press Club, as in most officers' messes, colonialism ran riot, and I, new to the experience and enjoying it immensely, ran riot as fast as anybody else. The drink was cheap to the point of being free; the food—considering the starvation all around us—fabulous. Traditional British breakfast bacon was served as lunch fare in two-inch-high ham steaks. German cooks transformed army rations into delicious meals. The wine from the cellars of the Wehrmacht, and the whiskey, though rationed, were ample to get a man (and his girl friend) drunk every night. The temptation for "fiddling," army-style, was irresistible. Of course I was not immune. But I was an infant compared with the old hands at the game.

Buying a camera from a German in the street for thirty cigarettes made me feel really wicked. Conscience plagued me, and I was relieved when, only a few weeks later in London, my apartment was burgled and the camera was among other possessions taken. Yet there were British and American officers who ran a highly organized smuggling racket between Berlin and Belgium, taking old masters, silverware, and jewelry to Brussels and returning with butter, shoes, clothes, and other necessities of life that were unobtainable in Germany. Although the army authorities tried to look the other way and let these delinquent officers —many of them fine fighting men—have their last fling, here and there investigations were instituted. A major implored me to help him repatriate a certain Italian barman to his native village in the Apennines. If this man were arrested as a black marketeer, as he might well be, a dozen officers who had earned distinction in the tank battles of Africa and Normandy would be involved and disgraced. At the time it was virtually impossible for a foreign civilian to leave Germany without taking his place in a queue behind a hundred thousand or more, but friends at UNRRA responded to my appeal. The man was back in Italy within three days.

The girls of Berlin, I kept telling my colleagues, used to be the most gorgeous creatures in the world. A Berlin society photographer who had survived the war and the collapse (society photographers have a way of landing on their feet) promised to arrange a beauty parade. Having watched the big-booted, ungainly females hurrying along the streets, their heads covered with thick scarves, I had not spotted a single pretty girl since my arrival, and I was a little skeptical. We met at his studio, and soon they arrived, two, three, four apparitions looking exactly as I expected. My disappointment must have been apparent, for the photographer smiled and asked me to be patient. His Beggar's Opera quartet disappeared into another room.

A few minutes later the four girls returned. Instead of rags they wore bright, flimsy things. It was difficult to believe there had not been a clever substitution. The girls, seventeen or eighteen years old, were ravishing beauties, slim-limbed yet full-figured, with attractive features—all women, yet somehow childlike, except for the knowing look in their dark-shadowed blue eyes. They explained that it was not advisable for German girls to parade their attractions in a city which was the playground for the frustrated soldiers of four armies. Yes, they had some good clothes they had salvaged from the bombing, but they were saving them for better times.

All four girls were separated from their families, temporarily, they hoped. Now that they had survived the war, their hopes flowered once more. Their attitude spelled confidence born of an innate resilience, a typical Berlin quality often misunderstood as cockiness or cheek. In the long years of ordeal that followed, it has served Berliners well.

A few Allied photographers intent on shooting a different kind of game enlisted my help as an interpreter when they decided to approach a number of the much older, less attractive girls who were hanging around streetcorners in the vicinity of the Kurfürstendamm. Armed with a few bottles of German gin (requisitioned), they rounded up three girls, and disappeared. Three hours later they returned looking unhappy and shamefaced. Intending to give them a good time, the men had lavished their gin on the girls but, not having had a proper meal in days, the ladies couldn't carry their liquor. One after another passed out; a doctor had to be called, and an ugly situation was only just avoided. Nonfraternization was still the order of the day. The *Fraulein*—any German girl friend—had not yet matured into a politico-social phenomenon.

The ice was beginning to break, but the misery was unrelieved. From a visit to the Ruhr we brought back pictures of the cavedwellers in Germany's ruined powerhouse. "No Food, No Coal" was a heading in which I summed up the life of a Ruhr miner. German crews under British supervision were lackadaisically implementing the Allied dismantling policy, breaking up machines that had escaped the blanket bombing of the Ruhr. In the skeleton of what was once the biggest shed of Krupp's giant industrial empire, workers were taking the world's biggest steel press to bits; it was due to be shipped to Yugoslavia for reparations. (Before this press, only a year or so earlier, Hitler had stood in silence, giving public thanks for Krupp's capacity to forge his weapons of war.)

Ninety-two percent of Essen was totally destroyed but a few hundred yards down the road fourteen- and fifteen-year-old boys, sons of Ruhr steelworkers, attended technical classes in the midst of ruins—their own type of investment in the future, in which, incredibly, they had not lost confidence. "It will take fifty years to rebuild this city," I heard an Allied officer say— with a degree of satisfaction. No, friend, if these boys have their way, it will be less than five, I thought.

Villa Hügel, the great manor of the Krupp family, was the seat of the British North German Coal Control. In a damask-tapestried room a British officer's desk was situated below a fine portrait of Gustav Krupp von Bohlen und Halbach. (When Herr Bohlen und Halbach, a diplomat, married Frau Bertha, the Krupp heiress and godmother of the 1914–1918 war gigantic German gun, he added her surname to his.) The portrait, like much else in the magnificent castle, was awry under the occupation regime. But over the immaculate huge dining room where we took lunch at a table seating three hundred hovered the spirit of generations of Krupps and their erstwhile political associates. Where I was sitting **Gustav Krupp** had entertained **Kaiser Wil-**

helm II. Hitler had been guest of honor at this table not so long ago. The lawn at the back of the Villa was beautifully manicured, like that of an English country house, its rich green in striking contrast to the gray-on-gray of cloud and dust that hung over the city that had been Essen.

To provide food even at the starvation level of 1,500 calories per person per day was more than the Western Allies' exhausted economies could manage. Food, housing, transport, work, health —and morale! How to set Germany's gutted, creaking, rusty, greaseless machinery in motion again, and to coax a semblance of civilized existence from the chaos of collapse? Contemplating it, the mind did not dwell on retribution. The fate that had over-taken the German people could rouse only one emotion: compas-sion. Their humility was contemptible but understandable. My immediate reaction was to forget the crimes that had been com-mitted, and start afresh.

The major war criminals were being dealt with at Nurem-berg. Not one who likes to gloat, I allocated only a day to the trial, but the glimpse of the War Crimes Tribunal in session, with the rows of deflated Nazi leaders in the dock, has remained firmly fixed in my memory. It was easy to remove men, but well-nigh impossible to bury the past. When I returned to London I found a telegram from Nuremberg waiting for me: "American Chief Prosecutor asks can Willi Frischauer let him know name of Jewish ex-Richthofen Squadron pilot whom Goering personally stripped of decorations, and any details where he was shot, im-prisoned, etc." The query referred to one of my prewar stories. The source had been Conrad Heiden, the first Hitler biographer, and I wired the information accordingly.

Nonfraternization having succumbed to the demands of hu-man nature, the physical and the moral health of the occupation troops became a major preoccupation. For two nights I accom-panied the military police on raids of Bielefeld's entertainment district, and what I saw was so vulgar and verminous, so dis-gusting and depraved that it defied description. A dozen girls whom we rounded up and took to hospital for a medical checkup were not allowed to return home. The hunt for the young soldiers whom they had infected was a frustrating business. Germany was sick, and was contaminating the victorious Western Allies.

The contours of the Cold War were already drawn on military maps. At the demarcation line between the British and Soviet zones in Schleswig-Holstein, troops were watching each other suspiciously across a stretch of no-man's-land, playing a cruel game with German refugees as the pawns, sending clusters of miserable humanity backward and forward as if it were all a huge joke. A constant stream of ragged men, women, and children was clamoring for admission to the West, mostly Germans expelled from Poland and Czechoslovakia, where the Nazi authorities had settled them on lush farms and installed them in rich firms. Tank patrols of the splendid 10th Hussars were on the move night and day catching up and controlling these "line-crossers" who were richly sprinkled with Nazis and criminals (often one and the same) and, I suppose, with the early Soviet spies seeking a foothold in the West. In Bavaria I saw the Americans harassed by similar problems.

The division of Germany was hardening into a political fact. It first struck me in the Berlin City Bank's mammoth safe, which held 1,800 million marks in notes—rows and rows, stacks and stacks of currency. The value of paper money had hardly appreciated during the first few years of peace. If the economy of Germany was ever to be revived, the most pressing need was a currency reform. Prices were still being quoted in cigarettes: coffee was 80 cigarettes a pound, bread 16 a loaf, a good meal two packs. One United States Army sergeant bought a house in the fashionable Berlin district of Grünewald for a hundred cartons of cigarettes. But the British and Americans who were anxious to restore sanity to this crazy situation were blocked by the Soviets, who were just entering the *Nyet* phase of diplomacy. It was impossible for East and West to agree on a single issue regarding Germany and Berlin. . . .

That is not strictly true. Having applied for permission to produce a photo-reportage of the Allied Kommandatura of Berlin, the city's inter-Allied governing authority, I attended a meeting of this august body. The gloom was relieved only by Miss Elizabeth Wyndham (as she then was) who held the rank of an assistant chief of staff in the "British Element" and must surely be the most beautiful woman ever to hold an official position. One item after another was crossed off the agenda as the four Allied commanders, flanked by their staff, sadly shook their heads to signify disagreement. A new water installation to be built? *"Nyet,"* said the Russian. Permission for a publication? *"Non,"* replied the French general in retaliation. "No, no, no!" echoed the British and the Americans in loyal chorus. "Mr. Frischauer, of London, requests permission for photographs to be taken by Mr. Reuben Saidman, both gentlemen accredited to the British Element. . . . It is proposed to take photographs of this meeting and the Kommandatura's other activities in this building."

Everybody looked toward Major-General Kotikov, a bulky man with a shock of white hair, expecting the familiar *Nyet.* Major-General E. O. Herbert, the British commandant, glanced briefly in my direction, shrugging his shoulders in anticipation to indicate his resignation. The American, Colonel Howley, and his French colleague, General Ganeval, were half-rising from their seats to bring the frustrating morning's business to an end. But Kotikov looked up, nodded his head. I thought he said "O.K." General Herbert relaxed. "That's the first thing on which we have agreed for a long time. . . ."

There were not many others. This first and only photo-reportage had hardly appeared in print when the thin veneer of Allied cooperation cracked and the East-West quarrel erupted in full force. In Frankfort, under American auspices, Professor Dr. Ludwig Erhard, an obscure Bavarian economist, was hatching plans for a currency reform which, while it was the only means of putting Germany on her feet, was bound to force the hand of the Soviets, who would either have to follow suit in their zone of occupation or cut the East Germans off from their Western compatriots. Berlin was clearly indispensable to both contestants not only as an economic and strategic asset but even more so for political and psychological reasons.

In the brief postwar honeymoon between the Soviets and the

Western Allies, agreements on access to Berlin were so loosely drawn up that the city was bound to become the focal point of the East-West quarrel for the soul of Germany. If the West proposed to buy Germany with economic reform and (Marshall) aid, the East was determined to recoup its prestige by grabbing Berlin as a political prize. Soviet troops stopped traffic on the narrow supply road between West Germany and Berlin. Interference developed into a tight blockade. But if agreements about access by land were imperfect, there was no doubt about the air corridor through which the Western Allies were by treaty entitled to fly to Berlin. An Anglo-American airlift was mounted and soon assumed the strength and solidity of an air bridge, which was what the Germans called it, one aircraft landing in Berlin every minute of the day and night. It seemed only yesterday that the Western Allies did not know where to find supplies to keep Germany going. Now they flew into Berlin with capacity loads of flour, sugar, semifinished products for Berlin factories, even coal.

The first postwar elections in Germany—the first free and unrigged German elections since November, 1932—were imminent. The campaign was moving toward a final frenzy. But the political meeting of the Christian Democratic Union, West Germany's strongest party, which I attended at Essen, was comparatively sedate, although the Ruhr was one of the country's problem territories. The speaker was one Dr. Konrad Adenauer, the party's elderly leader who would be West Germany's first postwar chancellor within a matter of weeks. Listening to his speech I did not trust my ears. What was he for? He did not say. What was he against? Britain! Britain was unquestionably the principal target of his attacks. The dismantling of Ruhr factories was still an issue, although it had been slowed down to purely symbolic proportions, and for every old factory the British broke up the Americans were helping to build a new one and equipping it with modern machinery. The British this . . . the British that! To the thunderous applause of a thousand good *Spiesbürger* who listened to him, Dr. Adenauer worked himself up into a fine old anti-British frenzy.

At the house of Dr. Toussaint, the local Christian Democratic leader, I came face to face with Dr. Adenauer. "Did you really mean what you said?" I asked him point blank and, so as to avoid misinterpreting a politician who had spoken in the heat of a difficult election campaign, explained how we magazine writers worked: "May I say, *Doktor* Adenauer," I emphasized, "that whatever you tell me now cannot appear in print for another two weeks, by which time the election will have been decided. . . . It takes that long to produce our magazine. I would not want to give the British readers a false impression of your views."

Dr. Adenauer thought for a brief moment: "What I said on the platform was my honest view. I will stand by it at all times. That is how I feel—always will." The way he said it, I had little doubt he meant it.

"Tell me something about yourself," I asked the old gentleman two days later, and added—an old reporter's trick to disguise my ignorance—"I'd rather hear it from the horse's mouth!"

"*Ach ja*" he said slowly, "there is not very much to tell. . . ."

A few minutes earlier, Dr. Konrad Adenauer had admitted me to his villa perched high on the steep bank of the Rhine overlooking the village of Rhöndorf. I knew next to nothing about the new man who was emerging as the leader of the West Germans.

Dr. Adenauer was visibly making an effort to be pleasant to a team—I was accompanied by David Seymour, the splendid American photographer who perished a few years later in the Israeli-Egyptian cross fire of the brief Suez campaign—which could make his face and his views known with one stroke in the United States, Britain, and France. He pointed to the *Drachenfels*, the big rock facing the villa from which a dragon was said to have menaced the fair Rhinemaidens, and discoursed on other local legends. But he was not a man one could take to easily. His Rhenish sense of humor did not harmonize with my own Viennese brand, which had long since acquired an English gloss. Pointing toward the Rhine, as we stood side by side on his balcony, Dr. Adenauer said this was the direction in which he used to look in the final stages of the war when the Americans fired across the river at Remagen: "Shells were coming this way," he said, "but not too close," he added laughingly. (Dr. Adenauer's publicists later placed those American shells closer and closer to him all the time: ". . . He was fortunate to escape unhurt," was the latest version.)

And what had he been doing during the war? Living in quiet retirement, the old gentleman explained. What else was there to do? "The Nazis left you in peace?" More or less, he replied, except after the July 20th putsch when they arrested everybody: "They questioned me but let me go when I proved that I had nothing to do with the affair. You know, I was never a friend of Hitler's," Adenauer said quietly. Since he told me about his brush with the Gestapo, the incident has been magnified out of recognition. He was arrested—not once but twice; he was held in a Gestapo prison. Why, he must have come to believe in his own publicity because he repeated it all in a television interview for American listeners in the spring of 1963.

Dr. Adenauer had never been very popular in Germany. He was suspected of separatist inclinations after the First World War when the Rhineland was as sensitive a German area in the West as Silesia was in the East; he was distrusted as a Francophile while nationalist Germans honored the memory of a man called Leo Schlageter, who was executed by the French, and Herr Krupp preferred to go to prison rather than to collaborate with the French.

But he had been a courageous mayor of Cologne even under Hitler. As the representative of this ancient Catholic city, he had refused to put out the swastika flags to greet the Führer. That, however, was long before Naziism revealed its true character. At that time few Right-wing, non-Jewish politicians, however anti-Hitler, were in personal danger. Dr. Adenauer was gently removed from office. Yet his anger was not so much directed against the Nazis who had removed him in the early thirties as against the British local area commander, Brigadier John A. Barraclough, who—Dr. Adenauer having reinstated himself as mayor of Cologne as soon as the British troops drove the Nazis out—dismissed him without much ado because the old boy was disposed to disregard British military government and run the old Cathedral city once more as his private domain.

"You know," he said to me, lingering on the occasion with loving hate, "this English soldier dismisses me. . . . Just like that." Dr. Adenauer professed to have forgotten the offender's name. But he made it quite obvious that he would never forget the day. "Many years ago," he mused, "when I was mayor of Cologne, I was given a silk Union Jack which I treasured. I hid it when the Gestapo came to question me. I did not part with it, although it was a dangerous thing to have about the house during the war. But when this thing happened to me, when this Englishman behaved as he did, I put that Union Jack away, I don't know where. I have not seen it since. . . ."

The eyes narrowed as Adenauer rested his chin on his chest; it was an attitude of petrified anger. This man is a born hater, I said to myself; an irreconcilable man, one who will never forgive. It touched a chord because I recognized it as an unattractive trait of which I have tried to purge myself in vain. I had always regarded this stubborn eye-for-an-eye unforgiveness as part of my Jewish heritage. Here was a Teutonic version of the ugly characteristic. The political conclusions which I drew from this perception helped me to interpret many of Dr. Adenauer's political intentions correctly. "Look for the anti-British bias" was the rule I applied in assessing each of his international moves, very much as Alexandre Dumas suggested, "*Cherchez la femme*," to find the root of all evil. I have been assailed, ridiculed, dismissed as one whose judgment was warped by incorrigible hatred of the Germans until, twelve years later, the penny dropped and Dr. Adenauer's anti-British bias was accepted as one of the factors to be reckoned with in the political life of Europe. If somewhat belated, it was a most gratifying vindication of my views. The German newspapers castigated Dr. Adenauer's politics and political gaucheries in the last months of his "reign" in almost exactly the same terms that I had been using for years.

In our early conversations I told him that I was shocked to hear him talk about Britain as he did. He replied with undisguised surprise and with the kind of logic that is typical of the man: "But you are not English, are you? From your accent I should say you were born in Vienna."

Because it was an important part of my assignment to help

David Seymour obtain his photographs, I did not pursue the subject lest our tempers take over and bring the interview to a premature and unpleasant end. But I could not leave it at that. I was planning to get my revenge. In the steep garden with the rosebushes which he was so fond of tending, I spied a sheep; it bleated noisily as we approached.

"Dr. Adenauer," I said, "you know how fond the British are of animals. Would you mind being photographed with the sheep?" I was thinking of the new leader taking charge of his German sheep, leading them God knows where. The picture might well become symbolic at some future date. I did not expect Adenauer to agree.

"Certainly," he replied. "I'd love to be photographed with *Nelke*."

"Nelke?"—*Nelke* is the German word for carnation.

"That's the name I have given it because of its sweet smell." He held his nose. "But it is a very individualistic sheep," he added as if he guessed my thoughts.

Dr. Adenauer wrote to me twice in his own handwriting to ask whether I could let him have some of the photographs, and thanked me kindly when I sent them to him. But I came away from this interview with a very nasty taste. What baffled me about him was a kind of political insensitivity; the hard, egomaniacal core of the man would surely render him completely impervious to outside influence in the pursuit of his personal ambitions. No trace here of the traditional British pose of personal disinterestedness—even if it is often only a pose.

From the first Dr. Adenauer assumed a stubborn *l'état c'est moi* position, and the German people, as usual, followed their leader—until things began to go wrong. Nor—again until the very end—would they or their newspapers (with the honorable exception of *Der Spiegel* and *Die Zeit*, two publications which could restore one's confidence in the "good" German) find any fault with him at all. With obstinate disregard of world opinion, he clung to Dr. Hans Globke as his first secretary of state and closest personal adviser, although millions of people on both sides of the Iron Curtain regarded Globke's commentary of the brutal anti-Jewish Nazi Nuremberg Laws as the Bible of practical political anti-Semitism that was bound to lead to disastrous consequences.

To put the reins of power into the hands of such a man, to invest him with authority for important appointments in the civil service, the control of undersecretaries in all ministries, the supervision of intelligence, espionage, and counterespionage, was an affront to a world that had bled itself white in the war against Naziism and everything it stood for. A leading West German diplomat once asked me how the image of his country could be improved. "Get rid of Globke to begin with," was my reply, which echoed influential British, American, and French views. It may take some time, but historians will find plenty of material to assess how much damage West Germany's international prestige suffered by the retention of this man in a key post of Dr. Adenauer's administration. I, for one, came to see Adenauer as the dummy on the knee of the man whom millions of Jews will curse to their dying day.

It was like being in at the birth of a new Germany. I took the baby's pulse and examined the infant thoroughly. Considering its parentage, I was not too hopeful of its chances, but it certainly deserved a chance. I searched for hereditary traits, watched the Allied midwives and the German doctors ponder the unassimilated past and the worrisome problems of the future.

At Travemünde, a once-fashionable seaside resort, people were paying to peer through telescopes into the Soviet Zone, just as fifteen years later Germans would peer over the Berlin Wall into the Communist half of the city. Munich's beer gardens were crowded, and the clatter of heavy steins mingled with the raucous voices of Bavarians arguing in typical *Biertisch* manner. Their talk had paved the way for Hitler. In 1963 the voice of Bavarian politics had hardly improved.

On Lüneburg Heath, barely three hundred yards from the Soviet Zone, occupying a flat in the house of his publisher (the same firm that first published *Das Kapital*), Dr. Hjalmar Schacht, the financial genius without whose clever manipulation the German economy could not have supported Hitler's war machine, received me with his postwar stock question: "Have you any cigars? Impossible to get any here. . . ." Cigars were Schacht's first thought after his acquittal at Nuremberg, when he asked reporters who pressed him for interviews to pay him in cigars. Then as now, his perky, uninhibited personality asserted itself. He was dressed incongruously in khaki shorts, ankle socks, shirt and tie, the gawky head, like an ostrich's, wagging on top of a too long neck. His book, *Settling Accounts with Hitler*, had just been published. It was doing very well, he said, and had enabled him to furnish his flat.

Like so many encounters with canny political practitioners of his kind, this interview did not yield anything very remarkable. He was not ready to tell the whole truth—not to me, anyway—and his calculated views on current affairs did not impress me. A few years later he was once more riding high as financial adviser and banker. Like most intelligent Germans at one time or another, Schacht had eventually fallen out with Hitler—or vice versa—and this is what saved him. I take no charitable view of his past. At a time when the Nazis had everything except talent, Schacht supplied the missing ingredient in the economic sphere. Though not guilty by the arbitrary standards of the War Crimes Tribunal, he was an early ally of the Nazis. That he could re-emerge to wealth and esteem was an illuminating commentary on Dr. Adenauer's Germany.

If the Schacht-built Germany economy was the base on which Hitler built his war machine, the hands to which he entrusted the machine belonged to the German generals. The man I saw sitting in the dock in Hamburg was a general's general, the idol of every aspiring German colonel, the real brains behind the Wehrmacht—if it is appropriate to credit with brains generals who lose every war they start, and shift the blame on any old scapegoat that comes to mind. He was Friedrich Erich Levinski, better known as von Manstein, one of Hitler's top field marshals. Accused of complicity in the mass murders of civilians on the Eastern front, Manstein's guilt was easily established. It did not take his judges—fellow members, so to speak, of the international trade union of generals—very long to hand down their sentence: eighteen years' imprisonment.

What really mattered was the sequel. Manstein's sentence was cut, cut, cut again. The convicted war criminal, having suffered only a fraction of his just punishment, was quickly released. So far not so good; but no worse than expected. But damned if the man was not soon received with honors by Chancellor Adenauer, who thanked him for his support and advice in building up the new democratic West German *Bundeswehr*, whose leaders are *then* surprised if people regard an alliance with these Manstein-inspired soldiers with a certain amount of trepidation. If the Bundeswehr is perturbed about the reserve with which West Germany's allies—the people, not the governments—treat German uniforms, they ought to address themselves to Dr. Adenauer and those German officers who exhort their recruits to model themselves on convicted Nazi war criminals!

In the small North German town of Varel I sought out former Wehrmacht Major Otto Ernst Remer, another monument of the Nazi past. He was busily organizing the neo-Nazi Socialist Reich Party, which gained temporary successes in local elections but was eventually banned. Remer was a relic of the 1944 anti-Hitler conspiracy. More than any other man he had contributed to its failure.

The putsch need not have collapsed when it failed in its major objective of killing Hitler. (A massive table leg took the full blast from the bomb which one of the conspirators had placed in the conference room of the Führer's headquarters in Rastenburg, East Prussia.) The anti-Hitler generals who were assembled in the Berlin Bendlerstrasse War Office waiting to take control might still have succeeded had it not been for Major Remer, who commanded the Berlin Guards Regiment on that critical day. When "suspicious goings-on in the Bendlerstrasse" were brought to his notice, Remer contacted Goebbels. On Goebbels's instructions, Remer's men cordoned off the area. Well in advance of the Gestapo, Remer himself, revolver at the ready, entered the War Office to investigate, and it was through him that Hitler's authority reasserted itself. The officers whom he arrested were tried, tortured, and executed—hung from butcher's hooks. Promoted by special Führer order, Remer became one of Nazi Germany's most celebrated officers.

Now, five years later, his ego still fed on the memory of his one day of glory. He was proud, he told me, to have done his duty to the Führer. The tall, good-looking but gaunt ex-soldier with the high cheekbones of an East Prussian was cast in the same mold—and clothed in the same shabby civilian clothes—as the demobilized German officers of the First World War who incited each other's minds with tales of past glory, their fantasies of "what might have been" turning quickly to "what could be" if only they had their way, and "what had to be done" to get their way. Insensitive to arguments, a prisoner of his own narrow outlook, Remer mouthed political catchwords with automatic monotony. It was inevitable that his short-lived headlong flight to a freak success should end with a crash.

Was there nothing at all in the "new" Germany worthy of praise? What I missed most in my German peregrinations was dignity—a spark of human dignity. Unexpectedly, I found it in the eyes of a balding little man who was working for £2 a week as a storekeeper in the British Army Medical Depot at Rahlstedt. His only complaint was that the pay was low. But the job was all right. The future? At seventy-one a man had no right to expect much of the future. The retired old gentleman doing an honest if humble job of work as conscientiously as he could, neither groveling nor grumbling, his dignity unimpaired by whatever might befall him on the descent from his once high office to his now lowly station was Konrad Eduard Albert, until recently general-admiral and second-in-command of the Nazi navy, known as the finest naval-explosives expert in Germany.

Then there was that fine scholar, author, editor, and educator, Professor Theodor Heuss. He was awaiting a summons to the office of president of the Federal Republic when I called on him. No German has spoken out more magnificently against Nazi atrocities, against the sins of discrimination, anti-Semitism, and violence than this great old humanist. What a pity he should have been the target of anti-German discourtesies, if not demonstrations, when he visited Britain while in office. No man deserved less to suffer for the aberrations of the Adenauer regime.

9 | *The Germans and I*

*W*hen the public house opposite our London office closed at 3:00 P.M., we went to Soho, where members can get served in drinking clubs throughout the afternoon. Around 5:00 P.M. it was time to return to the office, pick up our coats and hats and briefcases to get back to the bar of our local by opening time, half an hour later. In the interval, we were in a happy frame of mind, laughing, singing, fooling around in our three-desk cubicle which was enclosed by frosted-glass partitions. We were a little unsteady on our legs, impetuous, unpredictable, perhaps riotous. Crash!

There was angry muttering in the next cubicle as a paper-weight or a stapler or an ashtray—I really do not know which—went sailing through the glass: "Hey! What the hell . . . !"

Workingmen have a dignity of which their union is the repository, and a union official has access to the boss, and what kind of trade unionist would he be if he missed a chance to lodge a complaint at the highest quarter, particularly—I refer to our membership in the National Union of Journalists—if he could get at members of another union? A workingman had been wounded below the ear! Blood was flowing from a small scratch!

Though my song was loud and clear, I am not the type to

throw things about, so I did not feel guilty. But here was the situation: One of my friends had disappeared—but he was certainly innocent. The other, Charles Hamblett, happened to be married to John Dunbar's daughter, so it could not possibly have been *he*. That left me. Now, my position, as we know, had not been very secure ever since the war had failed to stop at the designated time, but Len Spooner, a fine and loyal editor, disregarding Dunbar's innuendos and generally trying to resist the creeping transfer of Fleet Street power from the editorial to the managerial offices, had kept me in business. Since I repaid him by doing good work, however precarious my hold on the job, I was riding high as an editorial operator.

The undermanager was firm: "We are prepared to give you two weeks' pay. We hate to do this, but when it has all blown over you can resume work as if nothing had happened." He did not continue but I could read his thoughts: Now, be a good boy and go quietly. Make no fuss J.D. (house style for John Dunbar) cannot very well sack his own—

Of course not, I tacitly replied, or he would have to pay Charlie's salary out of his own pocket. . . . It's quite clear I'll have to go. But quietly? No, sir!

How could I go quietly—and where? The day the weekly paycheck failed to reach the bank I was in dire trouble. I had been in that kind of trouble before, of course. Come to think of it, I had been in that kind of trouble for years. Having to see the bank manager; explaining why the account was overdrawn; promising to put my house in order without delay; it was the last time; if he would only help out now . . . I shuddered whenever I saw the expression on his face, the look of stern duty battling with the glint of smug satisfaction as he preened himself because he had me in his power—the roof over my head, the next meal, the school fees, not to speak of my wife's summer coat. To face him again in this hopeless situation required an extra effort. I girded myself. If I could not prevail over a mere banker, what price my future as a reporter?

I was very determined. Must have an overdraft; brilliant prospects in the near future . . . What prospects? . . . Secret for the moment; fierce competition in the writing world; you know

—sort of scoop coming my way; publishers bidding; newspapers all over the world clamoring for rights . . . I could see the man did not believe a word I said—and he was right. But a germ of doubt crept into his adamant refusal and I quickly got my foot in the door: "So you would let me down just as I am on the threshold of success?" I badgered the poor fellow, threw everything at him I had: in-swingers, bouncers, googlies, and Chinamen (consult a cricket dictionary).

The unimaginative mind of the bookkeeper began to reel from my unremitting verbal assault; the cold heart was beginning to feel the strain from the pull on its strings as I juggled images of literary triumph and financial disaster. With a gasp he fainted and slumped over his desk. His assistant rushed into the office, correctly assessed the situation, scribbled his initials on my check which was the obvious cause of all the trouble, hustled me to the counter and extracted the cash from the cashier with extraordinary speed. I was out in the street with a fistful of notes before I knew what had happened. The bank manager, I am glad to say, recovered. But soon after the incident he retired. I never saw him again.

Another Canossa was awaiting my arrival. It was in an English seaside resort to which the head office of the Inland Revenue had been evacuated during the war, and from which it would not return because of the postwar housing shortage in the capital city. Only the most laggard taxpayers are summoned to the presence of one of the hardhearted officials of the evacuated tax collector's office. Visions of the Gestapo accompanied me on the train journey to the coast which is normally made to the accompaniment of children's delightedly expectant shrieks and the grown-ups' inconsequential but happy chatter. The sum I owed was not astronomical, but for all the money I had, it might as well have been.

"Your regular income?" I had to confess that as of now it was nil. But I had had a handsome retainer for a long time, hadn't I? And I could not very well be owing money to the Inland Revenue if I had not earned all these large amounts in the past, could I? So I must have spent it on something else—money which actually did not belong to me but to the state? I should have put that money away, put it to one side. Did I not have any outside income? From abroad, perhaps, since I traveled a great deal? And my house must be worth something? No house? A flat, then—the furniture for instance—that could raise a tidy sum if it was put up for auction, could it not? What? A furnished flat?

"You know how it is these days with flats, don't you?" It was the first complete sentence I could get in edgeways, but it stemmed the wearisome flow of questions, recriminations, threats. A flash of understanding raced across his blankly stony countenance. He was a young man, not unhandsome. I thought the stern demeanor did not become him. Did a worried mortal lurk behind the barricade of grim official demeanor?

"Of course. We civil servants have our troubles, too, you know." He sounded almost human.

"Housing trouble?" Intuitively I knew the gods were still with me. I had hit on his Achilles' heel.

"It's wicked," he said abruptly. "They stick us down here and never concern themselves for a moment whether we ever see our families. . . . If I could get a flat in London I'd quit the service tomorrow."

"Maybe I can help," I suggested with great modesty. "My landlord is a big builder. There are always flats going. . . ." The only recent occasion on which I had seen my landlord was to explain that there had been a bit of trouble in the office, that I was changing my job, and would he mind being patient about the three months' rent due? Until things had sorted themselves out? He had looked glum but agreed to wait a week or so. "Do you want me to contact him for you?" I asked the income-tax inspector.

"Would you do that?" The atmosphere was transformed. Fidgety hands were playing with my file. The sheet with scribbled figures and the sum total denoting the amount of my indebtedness disappeared as he closed the folder and—we kept talking animatedly all the while—put it casually into a drawer. "Here's the address of my digs," he said. "If you would write to me when you have seen the landlord . . . it's a question of my marriage . . . I doubt whether the wife can take it much longer."

"If I catch the 3:20 from Worthing Station, I could be back in town in time to see him this afternoon. . . ."

I was out of his office in two minutes. The landlord came to the telephone. "Things are looking up," I told him. "I have just made a wonderful arrangement with the Inland Revenue which puts me in a much stronger position. Only, I promised to recommend this fellow to you. A very nice chap. Most deserving. I told him what a wonderful landlord you are. May I tell him to come and see you?"

He muttered something to the effect that he did not want many more tenants like me . . . but an Inland Revenue official as a client did appeal to him. I arranged a meeting. My own relations with the landlord remained precarious for a long time to come, and I did not feel inclined to ask him whether he had come to terms with my friend from the Inland Revenue. It was over eighteen months before my tax file came to the surface again. By that time I was able to offer a reasonable settlement.

But for the time being I had to make a living. I was penniless. Spooner's genius for compromise came to the rescue. He felt badly about the whole thing, and secured a moderately adequate payoff for me. So I did go—quietly. Quietly, but determined to get my own back. I wanted not a destructive revenge but a constructive idea to help me rebuild a shattered career. I needed help, of course, needed it badly. Where could I turn? I decided to make the enemy pay. To move right into the camp of the man who had ruined me. Not to ask for mercy, certainly not! But to exploit his bad conscience, to confront him with a dilemma between professional duty and private prejudice.

The moment I asked myself the question, "What next?" the answer came to me and the decision was made. No more offices and bosses, friendly or otherwise. If not a little dignity, at least some elbowroom in the rat race! What better than to set myself up as a free lance? Surveying the rich and as yet largely unexploited field of Nazi history, I picked its most picturesque figure—Hermann Goering. I had seen the man twice: on the night of the Reichstag fire in Berlin and, more recently, in the dock at Nuremberg. Although the defects of his character were glaring and he had done some shocking things, I had never been able to summon up as much hatred for him as for the atrocious Hitler and the unspeakable Himmler. (I had a sneaking respect for Goebbels whose principal weapons, albeit in a wicked cause, were his quick mind and his clever pen.)

Boldly, I sent Dunbar a brief outline of a Goering biography I proposed to write. Turn it down if you dare! You know damn well that I shall go to a rival publisher and, when the book is a brilliant success, will make you look as foolish as the Berlin experts who turned down Remarque's *All Quiet on the Western Front*. Not that I expected to emulate Remarque's success, but it was a nice thought to plant in the mind of this man. It did not occur to me that he had probably never read *All Quiet* if indeed he had even heard of it.

Whenever I am in a difficult situation, clichés crowd in on my vacant mind. As I waited for a decision I kept saying to myself, "As one door closes, another opens. . . ." It stimulated a little hope and confidence in the cunning of my scheme. I did not have to wait long. Trying to avoid an invidious decision, Dunbar sent my suggestion "upstairs" to the chairman—most unusual, but then word about my sacking and hints about sacrifice on the altar of nepotism were circulating throughout the firm. And lo and behold! the chairman had apparently been thinking for some time that a Goering biography might be a good idea. He passed my note to the head of the Book Department with a recommendation to proceed with the project. The result was a good contract, a handsome advance, a firm belief in poetic justice and British fairness. *Faut de mieux*, I was a working writer again.

Munich was full of surprises. In the lounge of the Park Hotel I saw a face I knew, a man I had not seen since Vienna, 1934, when he had scrounged a few schillings off me. I wondered what he had done during the war. He was a most un-Nazi-like figure of a man, a would-be theatrical impresario, a professional *Adabei*, as we Viennese call one who attaches himself to every party or occasion as the wind blows.

"How are you? How have you been? So nice to see you!"

"I say, Frischauer, can you lend me ten marks? I'll let you have it back in a couple of days. You will? Thank you! Be seeing you."

In the bar of the Vier Jahreszeiten Hotel, once the Mecca of good food in Germany and still an excellent hotel:

"Willi Frischauer!"

That man! Now, let me think. . . . Of course! The eve of my departure from Vienna in 1934 . . . drinks at the Grand Hotel, a quick look-in at a *chemin de fer* game . . . a last fling before the responsible years in London. A couple of good hands and then, inevitably, the decline to an empty wallet, I.O.U.'s, arguments with the management: "The limit, *mein Herr* . . . yes, even for you . . . no exceptions!" And then a friendly voice: "If I can help you?"

"I need a thousand schillings."

"Certainly, if I can have your watch as security." Which posed a problem. An unusual watch, a gift from Susan, how would I ever retrieve it? I was due to leave next morning at the crack of dawn. But I handed the watch over, forgot all about it in the excitement of the move to London, wrote to Vienna months later, had no reply, forgot all about it again. Here now, the war and postwar years intervening, was that man again:

"How about my watch? May I redeem it?"

"You may not, certainly not. Do you know what that watch means to me?" For seven years, he said, he had been in Nazi prisons and concentration camps, being shifted from one to another but always, always he had managed to hang onto the watch. While he still had it he felt safe, he said. He had remained safe. Here he was, hail and hearty, fabulously rich, incredibly successful. Banker, financier of the scandal-infested German gambling casinos. A typical central-European prewar weed flowering in postwar Bavaria, Europe's most fertile ground for every kind of political crook and financial trickster.

Stories about this man abounded in Munich. After his release from Dachau, his idiomatic American caught the ear of a United States colonel who appointed him mayor of a town under his command and overwhelmed him with privileges—concessions for this, permits for that. In occupied Germany the smile of an Allied officer was a passport to wealth. No wonder my friend was reputed to be the richest man in Bavaria. It was all perfectly true, he admitted. And my watch had been his talisman. Yes, he was very comfortably off, but his heart was tiring; he was getting old.

Soon I heard another version of this man's rise to eminence. A man of the world and a fine linguist, he was discovered in a concentration camp when the great S.S. scheme (Operation Behrens, after the S.S. officer who organized the project) for flooding the world with forged sterling and debasing the British currency was being put into operation. Experts on fine paper, caligraphers, engravers working in great secrecy in the seclusion of concentration camps, had produced millions of forged high-denomination sterling notes. To circulate them, Behrens had selected a number of plausible men whom he sent abroad—mainly to Switzerland and to the Argentine—to exchange the forgeries for genuine foreign currency.

The scheme almost achieved its purpose. Britain was forced to take all sterling notes of £10 or more out of circulation. But there were two flaws: the idea matured too late in the war, and some of the "circulators" selected by Behrens did not play the game. They did get rid of the forgeries as arranged, but unsportingly kept the proceeds of the transaction to themselves. Many a German-owned hacienda in the Argentine was acquired with this kind of money.

The man who had been minding my watch for so many years was one of those selected for such an assignment. It took him to Switzerland, where he unloaded a small fortune of phony pound notes on unsuspecting bankers and dealers in exchange for solid Swiss currency. Then he settled down comfortably to await the end of the war, after which he returned to Germany. Some of Germany's finest horses were racing under his colors; I attended parties in his house jammed with the dignitaries of the new German democracy. I saw him liberally distributing loans and gifts with the dexterity of a prewar Viennese. He helped and advised people generously and made fortunes for many. But he never gave me back my watch. It kept bringing him luck in everything. But it could not cure the disease of his heart. He died. One day I shall write his full story, and he will make a fortune for me, too.

I first picked up Frau Emmy Goering's trail in Düsseldorf, although Gustav Grundgens, that fine old actor, would not admit to having helped the Nazi lady in distress—as rumor had it. A hint sent me to a tiny hamlet, not far from Nuremberg, and to a wooden hut which shook every time a train passed close behind it. That was where Frau Goering lived, the local innkeeper told me, and Edda, Goering's pretty little girl, whose godmother was Edda Mussolini-Ciano. No, they were not here now; gone to the North Sea island of Sylt—where the Reich marshal (as they still called Goering) once had a house.

It was not difficult to trace the stately fair-haired Emmy Goering on the small island. For a week or so we talked about her late husband. What an attractive person she is! Having failed to discover a single self-confessed Nazi in five years of postwar peregrinations through Germany, here, at long last, I found an honest woman. Of course, she said, she had shared her husband's political creed—could any woman who loved her man do otherwise? In these days it needed courage for the widow of a Nazi leader to speak the truth.

She remained loyal to her husband beyond his death. Much of what she told me about him and their life together was colored by her loyalty, though it was a matter of interpretation, never a question of truth or falsehood. I came to like her very much, though not so much as an irresponsible Walter Winchell paragraph suggested. The lady had already attained a ripe old age when I first met her. The day before I left I sent her a large bunch of roses, and when I went to take my leave the roses were in a vase behind a huge photograph showing Hermann Goering in one of his splendid chamois-leather uniforms. "If my husband knew that your flowers are adorning his picture, he would turn in his grave," she said, laughing—but with tears in her eyes. She cries easily when talking of him. Greatly helped by introductions she gave me, I penetrated the strange world of the surviving Nazis, piecing together from their tales the fragments of Goering's life, working hard to fit the contradictory information into the general picture that emerged from documents in Allied hands, evidence of the Nuremberg Trials, and records in many libraries.

Goering's personal photographer had already published a rather malicious worm's-eye view of his master that contained nothing of historical value. But what many of Goering's erstwhile associates said shed light on important aspects of his career as a Nazi leader. My research completed, it took me seven weeks to write the book, and Odhams, London (as also several Continental publications), acquired the serialization rights on condition that I return to Germany with a staff photographer to obtain pictures of the principal surviving characters in the book.

Thus, with publication of the book scheduled for March, 1951, I visited Frau Goering again in November of 1950. "Have a look at this letter," was one of the first things she said, handing me a note she had received from London. It was written in moderate German, and was an appeal from an English writer, Ewan Butler, for information about her husband; he was just completing a Goering biography, and only waiting to take account of what she might wish to say. This book would be a fairer portrait, he promised, than any produced by a Nazi (Goering's photographer) or a Jewish refugee (presumably me!). "I shall tell him at once that I will not cooperate with him," Emmy Goering stated flatly.

It was still four months before my book was due to be published. What if this other Goering biographer pipped me at the post? "You will do nothing of the sort, my dear lady," I told Frau Goering. "Please write and say that you will be happy to cooperate but that you are not feeling well at the moment, and will be taking a rest cure, but that you will see him, say . . . early February." I sent Odhams a telegram warning them of the threatening competition and suggesting they advance the publication date: "We'll make it early February," they wired back. Early February at El Vino's, Fleet Street's own inn presided over by the incomparable Frank Bower, I met Ewan Butler, who congratulated me warmly on the success of my *Goering*.

For another month or so I toured Germany in search of Nazi contacts. By the time *Goering* was published I was deeply involved in research for a book about Himmler, my next project. Himmler's brother, a pathetic figure, a pauper in the colony of snooty and wealthy ex-Nazis who were by now safely and comfortably installed in the most attractive villas of Wiessenee, the beautiful Bavarian lakeside resort, told me: "I have very good qualifications. . . . I was in charge of all educational activities in the S.S.!" Utterly unconscious of the irony, he asked me to give him a letter of recommendation to the new German authorities, or perhaps the Allies, in exchange for information about his late brother, with a few family pictures thrown into the bargain. I gave him fifty marks. No recommendation.

The old Nazis shook off shame and guilt as snakes shed their skin. They no longer wore the swastika but once more they carried their ugly hearts on their sleeves. Some were still—or again—in uniform. At Lüneburg I stumbled upon a meeting of the reconstituted *Stahlhelm* (steel helmet) the prewar ex-servicemen's organization which the Nazis recognized as their spiritual cousins and smoothly absorbed into the party soon after Hitler came to power. Once again: the same old routine, the same old jargon, the same old blood-and-thunder tirades, the same old sinister physiognomy of the German at his worst. A social gathering—a National-Social gathering—eating pea soup, German Army style, with bits of ham floating in it, exchanging memories about the good old days of the war.

There was worse to come. One of the few occasions when I did not dare to say what I thought was when I came face to face with former S.S. General Herbert Otto Gille, under whose direction the million-odd surviving S.S. men had formed an organization allegedly devoted to the search for missing comrades but more concerned with "fighting for the restoration of the honour of the S.S." (From the Nuremberg War Crimes verdict: "The S.S. . . . embarked on a series of experiments on human beings, which included freezing to death, killing by poison bul-

lets. . . . It engaged in the massacres of the Jews . . .") At Gif-
horn, presenting himself for election as a member of the town
council, Wilhelm Schepmann, the former leader of the S.A.
storm troops, told me: "I am a democrat now." (War Crimes
verdict: "The S.A. . . . acted as the strong arm of the Nazi
Party. It took part in beerhall feuds and was used for street
fighting in battles against political opponents. . . .")

A dealer in Hanover was doing a brisk business in Nazi war
decorations, insignia, jackboots. Eagerly he laid out some of his
treasures for my inspection. The front page of the *Frontsoldat*,
the professional soldier's trade paper, carried a picture of Field
Marshall Manstein with the Knights Cross of the Iron Cross
dangling from his neck. . . . Paratroop General Kurt Student,
who led the 1940 attack on Holland and commanded the first
conquest of an island from the air (Crete), smoked a big cigar
in his pleasant home near Hamburg as he talked about the next
war. . . . I returned to London dismayed, and wrote a piece
under the title "Return of the Nazis." Its publication coincided
with the arrest by British authorities of a group of ex-Nazis, including one of Dr. Goebbels's principal aides, who were accused
of plotting a neo-Nazi coup. The authorities failed to prove their
charges, however, and the men were released.

Concurrently with the return of the Nazis, the German Army
reappeared in the wings, preparing—in suitable camouflage—to
take the stage again. Rumors about secret rearming and the re-
birth of German militarism were ripe when I arrived in Bonn
to take a closer look. Having summoned up all my energy and
determination to storm the sinister fortress and become the first
foreign reporter to penetrate the renascent German Army's sanctum, I felt like a man ramming his shoulder against an open door
when permission for me to inspect the Ermekeil Kaserne, headquarters of the new army, was granted almost as a matter of
course. This being late in 1953, it was equally disconcerting for
a scoop-hungry reporter to be told at once that this organization had been in existence since November, 1950, when Count
Schwerin, a former panzer general, created the nucleus of the
German postwar army.

The new army's political direction was in the hands of Herr

Theodor Blank, a former miner and trade-union leader whose official title was "The Representative of the Federal Chancellor for Questions Associated with the Increase of the Allied Forces" —the operative word being "Allied." This German contingent was intended to become part of a European Defense Community —evidence, it was contended, of the German resolve not to create another independent German Wehrmacht as an instrument of national policy. The hope was that Germany would find a place in an integrated Europe, and her army a place in an integrated European Defense Community.

Suspicious minds like mine, however, interpreted this policy as a clever stratagem to overcome objections to German rearmament and a first step toward a European land force in which, inevitably, the German contingent would be the strongest, investing West Germany with the authority and influence that is the natural concomitant of military strength. Since many of the leaders of this new army were the same men who had served Hitler, this was an ominous prospect. I could foresee the day ten years hence when the American NATO chief's deputy commander of European land forces would be a German, and the man who stood by Hitler's side when the bomb of July 20, 1944, exploded—and standing next to me on this occasion—would be representing the new Bundeswehr on the Allied Staff Committee in Washington.

"Heusinger," the slim, modest little man introduced himself as we shook hands. (How insignificant the dreaded German generals look out of uniform, and how splendid British generals look in civilian clothes!) Heusinger's suit was crumpled. "Tell me, Herr Heusinger," Herr Blank said—it was all very civilian and informal. The man was, of course, General Adolf Heusinger, Hitler's chief of operations and closest military adviser, who, however, like most German generals, became highly critical of Hitler once the Führer led the Wehrmacht to defeat.

But the headquarters of the *Amt Blank,* as the embryonic West German War Office was known, housed a few officers of excellent anti-Nazi antecedents with whom I was happy to shake hands: the heroic Axel von dem Bussche, who had been prepared to blow himself up if he could only succeed in taking the

Führer with him; Colonel Count Bogeslav von Bonin, who refused to carry out Hitler's infamous order to destroy Warsaw and was sent to a concentration camp; Colonel Count Johannes Adolf von Kielmansegg, a nephew of General Werner von Fritsch, commander in chief of the German Army, whom Hitler and Goering framed in 1938 to break the spirit of the army, and eventually drove to his death. (Significantly, neither Bonin nor Kielmansegg had a smooth passage in the new Bundeswehr.)

Kielmansegg, Bonin, and General Gerhard Matzky, commander of the German frontier police (army units camouflaged as police), all received invitations to attend British army maneuvers on the plains of Westphalia. I was heading there too. Two days after my visit to Bonn I was just passing the General Officers' Mess in the British maneuver area when I noticed Bonin and Kielmansegg, soldiers in mufti (wearing trench coats) wandering forlornly through the camp, obviously lost and certainly unrecognized. Their British hosts would, in any case, practice a studied aloofness toward their erstwhile enemies, but it was just an unfortunate inadvertency that nobody at all was there to greet them or show them around.

"This way, gentlemen," I said in German, and led them toward the Mess. "Just wait a second while I alert the British Army. . . ."

When I put my head through the door I was dazzled by more gold braid than I had seen for some time. "Gentlemen, your guests have arrived," I said. Startled by my German accent, two colonels jumped up and came toward me with their hands outstretched in greeting. "No, not me . . . out there!"

Outside, I made the introductions: "Colonels Bonin and Kielmansegg"—but I did not then know the name of the British officer. (It was, in fact, Brigadier R. F. K. Belchem.)

A year later I pursued my studies of the German Army—in Paris. Nobody seemed to have noticed how naturally the Bundeswehr was carving out a place for itself in the Western Alliance. Under General Hans Speidel, a group of German officers was organizing European Army integration in the French capital. They were the first German Army men to walk the pavements of Paris since S.S. General Karl Oberg, chief of the

German Gestapo in France, was driven from his office in the Avenue Foch. The Germans in Paris were rather more coy than their comrades in Bonn. It took a good deal of persuasion and several references back to Bonn before the political head of the German mission, Baron Hasso von Etzdorf, was prepared to co-operate with me. Once the permission was granted, the baron, a professional diplomat whose most prized possession is a silver cigarette case given to him by the Emperor of Japan, was bon-homie personified, most helpful and frank about his mission.

He must have been surprised when I reported our talks fairly and factually, because he and his aides acknowledged my work with fulsome letters of praise. "I hope to see you soon in Brus-sels," Baron Etzdorf wrote. I never made the trip. Later he came to London as German ambassador, but we did not meet again.

In Bonn, a leading politician asked me what I thought of General Speidel, bespectacled scientist-soldier, university lec-turer, diplomat, a Teutonic but on the whole honorable man, al-though his role as a military attaché in prewar Paris has been criticized. Well, what was I to think of a man whose brother, also a high-ranking German officer, said on his release from an Allied War Crimes prison: "My brother Hans has visited me frequently in prison and discussed the problems of the new Ger-man Army with me." War criminal into ally! Perhaps General Hans Speidel was not his brother's keeper.

The campaign for the 1955 Saar referendum was in its final stage when I arrived in Saarbrücken. Although the return of the Saar into the Reich was a foregone conclusion, it was not a stimulating experience. On the Tuesday before the Sunday poll-ing, I received a call from London advising me that Dr. Otto John had returned to the West. Now, that *was* a story! A year or so earlier, on July 20, 1954—the tenth anniversary of the anti-Hitler putsch—Dr. Otto John, a participant in the putsch, had attended a Berlin ceremony in commemoration of the conspira-tors—and had then disappeared.

Otto John! In 1944, one of the few conspirators to escape the noose of Hitler's hangman, he was brought (via Madrid) to Britain where he joined the weirdly effective British "Black

Propaganda" team under former *Daily Express* reporter Sefton Delmer. He returned to Germany after the war and was the only one of six candidates to be approved by the Allies when West Germany, still subject to the Occupation Statute, chose a chief for the Office for the Protection of the Constitution, an internal counterintelligence agency, mainly directed against the Communists.

Suspecting him as a "British stooge"—than which nothing could be worse—Dr. Adenauer and his clique pointedly ostracized Otto John. When, furthermore, the chief of the Office for the Protection of the Constitution turned his attention to the scandal of the surviving, conspiring, and ever more influential old Nazis, whom he regarded as a graver danger than the Communists, he fell fully into disgrace. John was a heavy drinker—not surprising under the circumstances—and an impetuous, highly emotional character, none of which was designed to enhance his popularity in Bonn. When he, a key figure in the country's security service, disappeared from West Berlin on the emotion-laden day of the anniversary (he had been observed with tears in his eyes during the memorial service), the Bonn government was thrown into complete disarray. Minister of the Interior Dr. Gerhard Shroeder, a clever, ambitious man whose record is marred by his candidature for the Nazi S.A. in the early days of Hitler, made an official announcement to the effect that Otto John had been kidnapped by the Communists and was being held in East Berlin.

That is indeed where John turned up, apparently at liberty, and where (later) Delmer, his former London chief, and other British journalists talked to him. Soon Bonn changed its tune. John, according to the new version, had not been kidnapped; he was a renegade who had gone over to the Communists; he had always been a Communist. . . . Otto John's defection—if it was defection—had come at an opportune moment for Dr. Adenauer, who had in any case decided to put his friend, ex-Nazi General Reinhard Gehlen, in charge of West German Security. Otto John? Good riddance! What a slap in the face, too, for Britain, whose tool "traitor John" had been during the war. Time and again Germans told me they regarded John's anti-Nazi work as treason of the worst kind: while they were fighting for their lives John had been "assisting the enemy." Anti-Nazis of German extraction are still regarded as traitors if they fought side by side with Hitler's enemies during the war. (And that, roughly, is the attitude some Austrians and, inexplicably, many Germans adopt toward me, too.)

Suddenly, as mysteriously as he had disappeared, Otto John returned to the West. With the help of a Danish journalist, Henrik Bonde-Henriksen, a friend of Louis Ferdinand of Hohenzollern, John crossed into West Berlin and was promptly arrested. By the time I arrived in Bonn he was being interrogated by the *Sicherheitsgruppe* (Security Group), an indeterminate police branch which operates with Gestapo-like stealth and among whose personnel were a number of former S.S. officers with a criminal Nazi past. ("Every policeman worth his salt was in the Gestapo and the S.S.," West Germans explain disingenuously. "Would you prefer us to have no police rather than a police force including S.S. men?" To which my answer, of course, is "Yes.")

Mine was an undistinguished reportage because I could not compete with British correspondents who had been John's colleagues in the Delmer outfit. But the John case (after a most unsatisfactory trial he was eventually sent to prison for "treasonable associations") moved me deeply. I saw in it a symptom of the East-West tug-of-war for the German soul, an example of German schizophrenia, and a natural phenomenon in a country physically and ideologically divided into two halves. It was a situation custom-made for Cold War espionage, German agents slipping as easily from East to West, and vice versa, as a Londoner crosses from Kensington into Chelsea or a New Yorker from Manhattan to the Bronx. I never believed Otto John guilty in the terms of the verdict, and began to study his case. Having obtained the transcript of a memorandum in which he told his own story, I talked to many people who know him intimately and thought well of him. The result was a book, under the title *The Man Who Came Back*, which, while it unfortunately damaged the market for his own memoirs, was a poor effort on my part. If it sold well it was chiefly because people mistook it for an excellent novel under the same title by another author which was published in the same week.

From the Otto John mystery to the Reinhard Gehlen enigma was but a brief step. No sooner had I made known my intention to investigate "The Man Without a Face"—former General Gehlen, Hitler's expert for "Foreign Armies, East" on the Wehrmacht's wartime General Staff—than I found myself caught in the clammy web of the German political underground. An excellent report on Gehlen had already been published by *Der Spiegel*, the courageous Hamburg magazine, giving chapter and verse of the modern techniques and paraphernalia of espionage and treason: secret cells in offices camouflaged as commercial firms, couriers using dead-letter boxes to hide messages, the art of insinuating agents into the opponents' espionage network—in short, every kind of deception, dishonesty, and chicanery a clever criminal mind could devise in the interest of national security.

Naturally, I was anxious to take it from there—get more material about the man I knew to have been captured by the Americans after the war and to have bought his freedom in exchange for his bulging files of material about Russia which he had rescued from the collapse of Nazi Germany; and who was promptly engaged by Mr. Allen Dulles's Central Intelligence Agency to reconstitute an anti-Soviet espionage network. The result was the "O.G.", or Organization Gehlen, which the good general staffed with many of his surviving collaborators—Wehrmacht staff officers and S.S. men. In the course of my inquiries I made several approaches to official circles which brought no response. Though perhaps they did in a way, for out of the blue some unwholesome types began to turn up at my hotel, offering me material about espionage activities but never mentioning the name of Gehlen. I got a booklet here, a transcript there, a "secret" document from the East, a confidential memorandum from the West. In little bars all over Berlin and Hamburg shady characters sidled up to me offering me "information" for a hundred marks a time. Girls whom I approached with entirely different intentions did not wait for my proposition but, instead, suggested that they had a friend who had a friend who knew some inside stories. . . .

They all, naturally, wanted money, although I had no doubt that several of my would-be informants had instructions from the "O.G." to contact me and lead me up the garden path. Fair enough. But it seemed that only third-hand and fourth-rate practitioners of the German East-West espionage charade had been assigned to me. Every time I went back to my hotel I had to take a bath and clean my teeth to get rid of the bad taste, yet I continued to feel dirty throughout my "investigation." When a more respectable type approached me and suggested that a successful exposé of the Gehlen organization could do nothing but damage the Western cause, and I recognized him as a legitimate American intelligence agent, I snatched at the excuse and washed my hands of the whole sordid business. The decision did not exactly represent a journalistic or literary triumph, but what a relief!

After the spies and peddlers of secrets to the worst type of Nazi war criminal, my new quarry represented a change of pace. He was one of the German academics who had lent his mind to the unspeakable cruelties the Nazi philosophy encouraged. On an assignment from the *Woman's Sunday Mirror*, which managed to infuse a good deal of social significance into its popular human-interest approach, I traveled once more to Germany, this time to meet a certain Professor Carl Clauberg, who had just returned from captivity in Soviet Russia. If he was the kind of German for whose return the Adenauer government had been clamoring for years, he could not expect much sympathy in the Western world. Indeed, when my report about Clauberg was published, it was headed "The Most Horrible Man in the World." He was certainly the most horrible man I ever met, anyway.

When I visited him in Kiel, Carl Clauberg was in bed recovering from the hardships he had suffered in a Soviet prison camp. A bespectacled, bald little man with a Hitler moustache and darting eyes, he wagged a finger at me as he talked about himself with great relish. He was only eight years old, he said, when he decided to become a doctor. Four years later he knew exactly what kind of doctor he would be: "I will be a woman's doctor," he quoted himself as saying at the age of twelve. "Research into the human egg fascinates me." He studied assiduously and carried on extensive animal research. His great opportunity arrived when Hitler came to power and sterilization became the medical catchword of a Nazi Party, committed as it was to the "purification" of the German race and the weeding out of all "inferior" human strains. According to Clauberg, he secured an interview with Himmler, to whom he explained the method he had developed to make barren at least one thousand women a day—Jewish women, gypsy women, imbecilic women, "racially inadequate" women—whatever that may mean—any women the authorities might wish to turn over to him for treatment. Clauberg was a man after Himmler's own heart. He was posted to the Auschwitz concentration camp where a whole block, Block 10, was put at his disposal as a "Medical Experimental Center."

In Düsseldorf I met one of Professor Clauberg's patients from Auschwitz, Frau Augusta Nathan, one of the very few to survive his "treatment." With a trembling hand she showed me the official document certifying that "during your detention in Auschwitz concentration camp you were abused in an unpermissible manner as a medical experimental person for the purpose of sterilization." Her hair had been shaved off, a prison number had been tattooed on her arm, and she had been made to stand naked in line while Clauberg chose the healthiest specimens to be transferred to Block 10. Without benefit of anesthetic, she suffered the agony of internal examination before Clauberg appeared to test a new drug on her.

"Give me half an hour to explain myself to the medical experts of the world, and they will hail me as a great scientist," Clauberg rasped at me from his sickbed. "All I asked for was fifty mentally defective women for experiments. Himmler told me I could have as many as I wanted. . . ."

The public prosecutor in Kiel, stirred up by the publication of my report, ordered Clauberg to be arrested and indicted. The prosecution was collating information to establish how many women had died at Clauberg's hands and how many had survived as physical and psychological wrecks. Before he could be tried, the miserable life of the most horrible man in the world expired.

After this experience I was in no hurry to return to the political mud bath of Germany. When I did go back after a considerable time, I found myself in Munich in the company of a lively, attractive woman who had for years held a place in my imagination as one of Hitler's early girl friends. I was interested in the sexual background of this man, knew all about his strange early affair with his Austrian niece (whom he drove to suicide), and had gathered a fair amount of secondhand information about his association with Eva Braun. But here, facing me in a comfortable Munich drawing room, lively as a cricket, was Henrietta, daughter of Hitler's friend and photographer Heinrich Hoffmann, and wife—as I thought—of Baldur von Schirach, the Nazi Youth Leader and Gauleiter of Vienna, whose order to make Vienna *judenrein* led to the deportation and death of my parents in 1942.

Being opposed to the principle of *Sippenverantwortung* (responsibility of relatives) for the deeds of political or other criminals, I looked upon Frau von Schirach as a fascinating exhibit of the Nazi period, like Emmy Goering a member of the Hitler hierarchy. Was she ever his girl friend? There was no better way of finding out than to ask her.

"Good God, no!" was her spontaneous reply. "I'll tell you what happened. . . ." And she told me the story of how Hitler, after an evening at her father's home, had gone off and returned because he had forgotten his crop; how, dressed only in her nightgown, she had opened the door and how he, wiping his moustache with a grandiose gesture, informed her solemnly that he wanted to kiss her. She was so surprised, Henriette explained, that she blurted out: "Kiss me, Herr Hitler? No, that is not possible!" whereupon he turned on his heel, and left. Henriette Hoffmann, as she then was, was only in her early teens. Hitler was best man at her wedding, and she often visited him and Eva Braun at Obersalzberg or Berlin, but he never made another pass at her.

The conversation inevitably turned on Baldur von Schirach. Henriette had not seen him for some time, but one of the children had visited their father a few weeks earlier. What Frau Schirach told me of the boy's account of the visit worried me. It seemed that while the whole of West German society was permeated with ex-Nazis endowed with wealth and state pensions, the Western Allies and the Germans alike pacified their guilty consciences about this state of affairs by the simple method of keeping Baldur von Schirach (twenty years) and his two companions, Albert Speer (twenty years) and Rudolf Hess (life), incarcerated in Berlin's Spandau Prison. The conditions under which these men were held (since improved) seemed to me shameful, and reminiscent of Gestapo torture.

Not wishing to make journalistic capital out of this conversation, I decided to write a reader's letter to the *Manchester Guardian* which I handed to Gerard Fay, its perceptive London editor, who recognized the importance of the subject. A few days later the *Guardian* published the letter. It explained that "on a recent visit to Germany I was given a first-hand account of the three prisoners of Spandau." For over twelve years, I thundered, these men had been kept in virtual solitary confinement with only a few books and an occasional severely censored newspaper. The rule of silence in the prison had only recently been slightly relaxed, but their guards still did not speak to them. . . . The minds of Speer and Schirach were almost completely blank; they were beyond caring or wanting and hoping for release. They had even lost the will to die.

When his son visited Schirach, I went on, and told him that he had gone completely gray at fifty-one years of age, he was surprised. Though a barbar shaved the prisoners, they had not been allowed to look into a mirror for years. Schirach's greatest wish, expressed after much thought, was to see a dog again—or anything alive. Conversely, Speer had recently made an application that he be allowed to take his meals alone. Though there was no quarrel between them, he could no longer face Schirach across a table twice a day—Schirach and no one else. They had nothing to say to each other, and the silence grated on their nerves. Hess's mental condition had deteriorated so much that a detailed description of his habits would invite the charge of sensationalism.

"Even though," I continued, "these men may indirectly be responsible for the sufferings and the death of others (having lost my parents as a result of a decree signed by Schirach I have a stake in the matter), I still cannot believe there are many people in this country who approve of this form of punishment. Revenge has no place in civilized justice. Neither should psychological torture be applied as punishment for physical violence.

"It is also doubtful whether the detention of these forgotten men serves any political purpose. They are civilians, yet in West Germany recently a military man of high rank who was convicted as a war criminal and eventually reprieved was decorated for helping to reconstitute the German Army.

"I realize that I am pleading an unpopular cause. Yet this at least I have learnt in this country—that in politics it is more blessed to defend one's enemies than one's friends. And I know that Britain's reputation abroad rests largely on her moral courage to uphold the spirit rather than the letter of the law. I believe that if the British authorities were to raise the question of the Spandau prisoners now, they would find the Americans sympathetic, the French indifferent but not antagonistic and the Russians perhaps willing to show that they no longer believe in prisons as a means of breaking the human spirit."

What I wrote then I still firmly believe. The response to the publication of this letter was greater than I expected. It became the subject of leading articles. I received hundreds of communications, only a small minority disagreeing with my view. A man whose brother lost his life in Dachau concentration camp offered his support. On television Malcolm Muggeridge, referring to the letter, remarked that "among all the fantasy and triviality and special pleading with which the newspapers are necessarily crammed, every now and again one comes upon something which authentically expounds the human tragedy. . . ."

Encouraged by the public reaction, Frau von Schirach came to London to hand the Foreign Office a petition for the release of her husband. She was very kindly received. But nothing happened. The editor of the *Daily Mail* contemplated publishing her story but changed his mind at the last moment. The trouble was that she had been secretly divorced from her imprisoned husband and had reverted to her maiden name. For some reason I have never been able to fathom *The Times,* reporting her visit to London and the Foreign Office, kept referring to her as Frau Henriette Jacob. Henriette Hoffmann-Schirach did not protest. Some time later I adapted and translated her reminiscences, which were published in London under the title *The Price of Glory.* The book affords a unique insight into the world of a top Nazi woman.

However trite the observation, there is no denying the impact of first impressions. I was captivated by Berthold Beitz the moment I set eyes on him, and what I have since learned about him justifies my judgment. Beitz is Krupp's *Generalbevollmächtigter* (chief executive) and virtual boss of the reconstituted Krupp empire.

A brief explanation of my attitude toward Germany and the Germans would not come amiss at this stage. It is not, as has so often been falsely asserted, that I cannot forget Germany's Nazi past (a failing which, according to the pollsters, I would be sharing with a majority of the British people). On the contrary, no one is more anxious to forget it. My resentment is directed against those Germans who will not allow me to forget it— against the surviving or revived Nazi attitude, not necessarily in the Hitler mold but similar in mentality, spirit, and sentiment. What I object to is not the survival of old Nazis but their shameless and unrepentant return to public positions with the connivance and support of so-called German democrats. In too many places, when you scratch below the surface, you find a powerful Nazi vested interest.

Irrespective of his guilt or innocence, the presence of Dr. Globke at Adenauer's elbow was bound to encourage Nazi elements in the West German Civil Service, judiciary, police, and intelligence services. It was Adenauer's couldn't-care-less attitude (to put it mildly) that was responsible for the delay of fifteen years or more in bringing to justice thousands of Nazi war criminals with the lives of hundreds of thousands of Jews, Poles, and

Russians on their consciences, until Karl Adolf Eichmann's revelations and Israeli threats of exposure forced his hand. It is today's Germany with which I and many others are concerned,
not Hitler's. I am prepared to see Hess, Speer, and Schirach go
free (even at the price of an occasional excess, such as Doenitz's
brazen lecture to a few schoolboys) if the civil service, the police, the judiciary, the security, and intelligence services and the
political parties—in short, public life—is purged of S.S. men and
ex-Nazi functionaries. The military with doubtful war records
and proximity to the extermination squads, as well as the guilty
generals who are receiving big pensions, are the obstacles on
West Germany's road to full and equal partnership with the
West.

I have the greatest respect for the West German press which
has frankly and fairly recorded the never-ending series of trials
of war criminals, and has openly aired other deficiencies in the
young democratic system, but I have only pity for the pathetic
scribblers in the Allied camp who jumped to the defense of
Adenauer's Germany at the exact moment when the German
press trumped the worst I could say about the old man.

It was in this spirit that I revisited Essen, with no more il-
lusions about the history of the firm of Friedrich Krupp than
I have about the dark chapters in the British or American (or,
for that matter, Austrian) past. What exercised my mind was
whether my built-in political radar system would register a dark
spot on the sensitive membrane of a lifelong experience of Nazi
sounds and sentiments when this eminent industrial Ruhr leader
came into view, heir of the Ruhr captains who carried Hitler to
power on their massive shoulders.

The conditions Berthold Beitz created for our meeting were,
admittedly, not conducive to the reception of unpleasant signals.
We met for lunch at the Essener Hof, a hotel of international
standards that used to be Krupp's guest house. Old-fashioned
elegance competed with modern facilities to mollify the most
fastidious visitor. Beitz's personal history was impressive. The
youthfully slim, elegant industrialist had worked for the wartime Nazi administration in Poland but—unique achievement—
was highly respected by the postwar Polish government because

he had helped to save many thousands of Polish lives. He was employed by an insurance firm in Hamburg when a chance meeting with Alfried von Krupp, the head of the firm, who had spent six years in the Allied War Crimes prison of Landsberg, resulted in their association. These two were very different kinds of men: the staid, ponderous, reticent Prince of the Ruhr, and the slick, fast-thinking, aggressive young man whose philosophy was completely in tune with his times.

Once Beitz was installed in Essen and invested with supreme authority, he rode roughshod over traditions as only a *Ruhrfremder*—a stranger to the Ruhr—could do. He reconstructed and modernized the administrative structure of Friedrich Krupp as thoroughly as the bricks and mortar and machinery of the firm's war-gutted factories. Dead wood was ruthlessly cast out, and a new spirit came in in the wake of the tempest. He weathered the inevitable crises and succeeded in reshaping the old familiar and unpopular Krupp image with his deft handling of the industrial scalpel until it became, if not attractive, at least acceptable. The firm which had devoted 25 percent of its capacity to arms production under Hitler now turned its back on the deadly trade.

Talking quickly and amusingly, Beitz drew a fascinating word picture of Krupp's new destiny, his own, and the work which took him to the four corners of the earth. Although his conversation was studded with references to kings and queens, shahs, imams, rajahs, this minister and that president (on either side of the Iron Curtain) as naturally as others talk about their next-door neighbors, Beitz himself emerged as the new type of cosmopolitan supermanager who seemed to owe much of his professional outlook to his American counterpart, while his personal approach and style was reminiscent of the British aristocracy. A musiclover, a passionate and excellent shot (he was a sergeant in the war but he had never fired a shot in anger), father of three young daughters, Beitz has drive without push, energy with grace, and a sharp tongue with a humorous tip.

He talked of Krupp's $1,000 million annual turnover (a fifth of it in export trade); of the factories he had built and was going to build in India, Soviet Russia, Brazil; of his interest in Australia, the Middle East, the whole world—anything to provide work for his 110,000 workers, 30,000 of whom are based in Essen alone. The Ruhr is Essen, they say in Germany, and Essen is Krupp. It was not surprising that Beitz took the initiative in breaching the political Iron Curtain. He was the ideal person to talk business with the Poles, whom Adenauer hated. He boldly traveled to Soviet Russia to inspect Krupp-built factories and—more important—to talk to Khrushchev. In our world where the flag tends to follow trade, it is men like Beitz whom Germany and the world need.

Erhard likes Beitz—it is one of the many advantages Professor Dr. Ludwig Erhard has over Dr. Adenaur, who looked askance at the politico-economic excursions of Krupp's chief executive. The last time I saw Professor Erhard, at his Ministry of Economics in Bonn, he was relaxed as usual, yet firm and definite in what he said, quite different from the soft, shilly-shallying, undecided cunctator the Adenauer clique tried to picture him as. Suspicious of the political dangers inherent in an autarkic European Common Market, firmly wedded to Britain and the United States in his economic conceptions, suspicious of his compatriot, Adenauer-protégé Professor Walter Hallstein, head of the powerful European Common Market Commission, Professor Erhard stuck by his liberal guns though all around him one country after another was moving swiftly toward state planning.

Professor Erhard is one of those rare politicians who manage to talk to interviewers in the same easy manner that they would use in a private conversation. He conveys the impression that he says what he thinks. Perhaps that is why Dr. Adenauer regarded him as a political lightweight. He may yet confound his critics. Highly intelligent, Erhard is flexible, adaptable, and above all, humane. I believe he will play a most successful Truman to Dr. Adenauer's Roosevelt—if I may be forgiven this imperfect political metaphor.

It was obvious that Erhard had no intention of rushing in to transform Adenauer's Germany in a day. A change of atmosphere was what was required—and no better man to bring it about than the architect of the West German economic miracle. But there was another man who, quite apart from his political affiliations, could convince me that a new spirit prevailed in West

Germany: Willy Brandt, the gallant mayor of West Berlin, a fine, genuine democrat whose ardent patriotism, hardened in the heat of the Battle of Berlin, does not grate because it does not conjure up unpleasant associations. Willy Brandt had to leave Germany soon after Hitler came to power (he adopted his current name in the anti-Nazi underground), and spent the war years in Norway. In the course of the last West German election campaign, he was violently attacked because he had changed his name (shades of Schicklgruber), because he spent the war years in exile, and because he donned a Norwegian uniform to escape from the Gestapo. But he has a kind of integrity and a pure spirit that rise above such calumnies and communicate themselves to whomever he talks to. It was a great boon to meet him, as I did on several occasions, and to listen to a German politician who can call a spade a spade and himself a democrat, but has no need to protest too much.

10 | *In the Picture*

Deutschland über Alles? To hell with Germany! Thinking of Germany robbed Heinrich Heine of his sleep. I seem to have been thinking of Germany night and day, and many impressions I value survive only as loose fragments in an over-crowded memory.

"As the bombs exploded and the rifles cracked," a headline-conscious subeditor blurbed, "Willi Frischauer . . . arrived in Palestine to report on conditions. . . ." It was November, 1945, and I was anxious to embrace my Jewish cousins who had survived another mortal enemy.

A cold wave of hate almost threw me back into the sea. I came eager to tell these people about the Nazis whose faces I had so recently seen ground into the dust, but they treated me, a Jewish mother's son whose life had been one long anti-Hitler crusade, as an enemy. Why? For God's sake, why? The answer did not occur to me at once, for the British uniform which, as a correspondent accredited to the British Army, I wore as a matter of course did not at first seem to me in any way significant. But the Jews of Palestine were not concerned with the Nazis. They were fighting an enemy nearer home—the British.

It was understandable but it hurt. The British, administering

269

the Mandate, were accused of keeping would-be Jewish immi-
grants out so as not to arouse Arab resentment. But my loyalties
were with the British, and my hatred was reserved for the Nazis.
Within days of my arrival I found myself reporting on the
Jewish bomb outrages that were painfully reminiscent of the
Nazi terror in Austria ten years earlier. I was terribly ill at ease.
A Palestine-born young Jewish girl, the niece of a London friend,
spoke in the jargon of the Hitler youth, merely substituting
"British" for "Jew" as the target of her contemptuous vitupera-
tion. "Everybody looks over his shoulder to see when the next
shot will be fired, the next bomb explode," I wrote. The leaders
of the Jewish Agency gave me a balanced account of the situation, but the interview I remember best was with a fair-haired
young man from Vienna, Teddy Kollek, who was vaguely described as being connected with the Jewish Agency—with the
Hagganah might have been closer to the truth—and who spoke
for all young Jews.

Kollek, however, managed to make some sense of the paradoxical link between the stinking, murderous charnelhouses in
which the Nazis had exterminated six million Jews, and the
British, who had staked their very existence on defeating the
scourge of the Jews. "We Jews are on the spot," said Kollek.
"We want a Jewish state. We want a national home. That would
end the cause of all the Jewish trouble—being always in the
minority. We want to bring help to friends and relatives, the
few surviving European Jews. We want a Jewish majority. We
do not trust Arab assurances of a fair deal. . . . We are like a
starving man clamoring for a piece of bread. . . . We shall fight
for our rights and go down fighting rather than refuse to help
our brethren. . . ." There was a breath of heroic despair in his
words but also the authentic ring of confidence in ultimate victory.

Fifteen years later I met Teddy Kollek again. The Jewish
State, born in despair, terror, and bloodshed, was now a reality
—and beautiful to behold. Glamorous villas in the attractive style
of the sixties, their gay colors radiant in the sun, overlooked the
port of Haifa, which was a shambles when I saw it in 1945. The
whole country seemed to defy the proverbial Mediterranean

lethargy. The air was invigorating and so were the people. The swamps had been reclaimed and been made to bloom. The economic miracle of Palestine's transformation into Israel was triumphantly apparent even at a first glance. The infinite variety of the people, among whom tall and blond and, I swear, blue-eyed youngsters belied the notorious popular image of the Jew and made nonsense of Hitler's race theories that find a subconscious echo in so many gentile minds. They had come from all corners of the globe to be in a minority no more.

We were in Haifa to watch Otto Preminger's film *Exodus* being produced on the location of the early struggles I had witnessed. Teddy Kollek, an elder statesman by now, a close friend and adviser of Premier Ben Gurion, was there, and at a dinner at the Hotel Zion we talked of the years during which people from sixty, seventy, or more countries had been transformed into a single nation. "Hebrew," he said. "Hebrew is the explanation. Only by enforcing the use of a common language could we achieve this integration."

I wanted to contribute to the goodwill of the occasion by showing off with the first line of a Jewish prayer, the only Hebrew I knew. Anxious to make my meaning understood in English, I called one of the waiters. "Do you speak English?" I asked.

"Speak English? I speak six languages."

"Well, then translate the following from the Hebrew . . ."

"I'm sorry. Hebrew I don't speak so good."

Teddy Kollek's mood was somber. He looked at me quizzically, his thoughts seemingly far away. But they were not, as I was to learn. Barely twenty-four hours before our conversation took place, Adolf Eichmann had been brought back to Israel and confined in a Haifa detention center less than half a mile from where we talked.

The British uniform I wore so proudly was no more popular in Cairo than in Jerusalem. At the Egyptian Foreign Office I was kept waiting in a long narrow room crowded with people manipulating tiny cups of black coffee in their gesticulating hands with perplexing dexterity. Whenever I opened my mouth to explain my mission to the man at a desk at the far end of the corridor, someone handed me another cup of black coffee. It was only when I managed to get two consecutive sentences out that the high-powered receptionist took notice:

"You are not English," he stated, looking me up and down. "Where do you come from?"

"Vienna."

His face lit up. "*Aus Wien!*" he exclaimed in German with a Viennese inflection: "Very glad to meet you!" He told me he had studied in Vienna—as had so many of his Foreign Office colleagues. It appeared that the conduct of Egyptian foreign affairs was in the hands of a Vienna-educated clique, much as the British Foreign Office used to be dominated by Catholics. To a Vienna-born reporter, in spite of his British uniform, all Egyptian doors were open. Seat of honor at the state opening of Parliament, an invitation to the official banquet of the Arab League, and an interview with the Premier (Nokrashi Pasha)—anything.

For me the climax was a lunch at the palatial home of a well-known senator and chief of several famous Arab tribes. We feasted on slices of delicious roast lamb stacked high on enormous silver trays. Encouraged by my genial host to eat more than was good for me, there was no room left for the beautifully scented digestive tea that followed the meal. I had the place of honor between the graying, balding senator, who did not speak a word of English, and his handsome dark-haired son, who had enjoyed—and he *meant* enjoyed—an English university education.

Presently the old man nudged me and suggested with an inviting gesture of his head that I follow him. Through many wonderfully furnished rooms, he led me to his private sanctum and to a mahogany cupboard on the wall. Opening it with a little silver key he took a bottle of Scotch from it, filled a tall tumbler to the brim, and handed it to me. "Cheers," he said, and smiled. He watched me closely as I put the tumbler to my lips, and frowned with deep disappointment whenever I paused for a second to catch my breath. He was not content until I had downed the lot—more than a third of a bottle. I needed the support of his arm as he steered me back to the dining room. He looked very pleased with himself. The room and the company danced gaily but confusedly before my eyes. I had to hold on to my chair. . . .

As from a great distance I heard the voice of my host's son: "Follow me. . . ." Taking me by the arm he walked me—oh, no!—yes!—in the same direction, through the same rooms, to the same destination. Out came the bottle and the tumbler—and a wide smile on his face. . . .

It was past breakfast time when I woke up in my hotel next morning, but the bevy of tarbooshed servants, in their white burnooses conjured up a dozen small Egyptian eggs that I devoured with gusto. They produced giant prawns, Viennese rolls, and French croissants to go with the coffee. Bless them! After years of food rationing in Britain they tempted my palate with an international cuisine of a quality I had almost forgotten existed. They laid the foundation of a physical expansion that was to change a thirty-inch waistline to a fifty-two-inch girth, now my trade-mark. In a world that expiates its sins by the self-inflicted torture of dieting and slimming, I have, ever since these days of the Egyptian fleshpots, nurtured my corporation with loving care.

The four foreign ministers were meeting at Lancaster House in London (December, 1947), and I went along to describe the scene and render what assistance I could to two colleagues from the photographic department. My broad shoulders cleared a passage for one of them, Eric Auerbach, who was more at home in the sedate atmosphere of a concert hall than in the turbulent arena of a political photo-call.

Endeavoring to convey to Moscow's emissary, Foreign Minister Vyacheslav Molotov, that a brief smile into Auerbach's camera would make a nice change from his monotonous facial equivalent of *Nyet*, I gesticulated so violently in front of his face that next day's newsreel pictures of the occasion, and a series of stills taken by James Jarche, my other photographer friend, showed rather more of me than of Mr. Molotov. These pictures were published in many parts of the world, and I have been asked a hundred times what on earth I was saying to Molotov and, incidentally, when did I learn to speak Russian?

When I began to work with press photographers, most of them were ex-office boys who had graduated to the profession via the dark room. Few British magazine photographers, though excellent at their job, boasted a very high intellectual level, which was a pity because we were entering upon a phase of journalistic mass communication which was unthinkable without pictures. From my early experience of picture journalism I had retained a conception of the ideal photographer as personified by Dr. Erich Salomon of the *Berliner Illustrierte*, which was the world's premier picture magazine until *Life* took its place. With a camera dangling from his neck as if it were the Order of the Golden Fleece, Salomon mingled with the leading statesmen of his generation, discussing world affairs at their own level while casually and unobtrusively working his shutter. He was the first grand master of the candid camera, and while many highly skilled photographers followed his example and even improved on his techniques, it was a long time before another could equal his knowledge and social standing.

In contrast, I was condemned to work with photographers who never really understood the subject with which they were dealing, even though they often produced good coverage. Some of them were extremely prejudiced, idiosyncratic, ill-mannered, respecters neither of persons nor occasions—not blasé but simply impervious to external impressions. One, photographing the deathly sick, one-armed, one-legged, nervously trembling German Socialist leader Kurt Schumacher, the only truly great German to emerge from the 1933–1945 paralysis of the German intellect (and a Nazi concentration camp), barked at him with the authentic "good German, dead German" ring: "Keep still, or we'll never get the bloody picture!" If ever there was a time when I had to lower my eyes in shame in front of a German, this was it.

Later I worked with some of the finest people in the profession, such as Robert Capa, the intrepid, impetuous, Hungarian-born genius who was the greatest war photographer of the last war. I remember Capa when he was sacked from an American magazine, stranded in wartime Britain without valid passport or accreditation, cadging a lift from a United States paratroop unit en route to North Africa and ending up by jumping with them in the American invasion of Sicily—taking pictures all the while; or standing waist-deep in the sea, coolly photographing the first Allied troops to set foot in Europe on D-Day. Bob Capa sought out danger and was doomed to die in battle; it happened in Indochina. Some of my most delightful working weeks were spent with Capa's friend, the mild-mannered, sensitive David Seymour, who knew every back street in Rome and every grape that grew in the Rhineland, his special area of investigation when he had worked on wartime maps for the United States Strategic Bomber Force. We tasted the wine of the Rhine and we pounded the pavements of Rome, and neither the Rhine nor Trastevere has ever been the same for me since little "Chim" died.

The king of the profession is Henri Cartier-Bresson, the gentle Frenchman who captures life in the raw and his subjects unaware, unposed and uninhibited as they struggle for survival in the maelstrom of their fates—the refugees, the hungry, the helpless, the primitive, whose monuments are Cartier-Bresson's classic pictures. We were in Berlin together, and Henri roamed the streets for hours in search of subjects. ("Always walking the streets, like a whore!" joked Capa.) The result was a gallery of Cold War portraits that has not been equaled. Arthur Miller deprived photography of an outstanding practitioner when he married Inge Moerath, whose camera lent verisimilitude to several of my own reports, and advertising almost swallowed up my favorite London photographer, Joseph McKeown.

With so many photographers at my side I was bound to end up with an inordinate number of pictures of myself taken in the line of duty. Many of them now fill me with a mixture of nostalgia and nausea. One shows me in a miner's helmet and overalls, going down the worst mine in Britain on my hands and knees; others, on night patrol with a Welsh police force or inspecting prisons in Scotland; by way of contrast I can be seen strolling down the Champs-Elysées with Sugar Ray Robinson, meeting Marlene Dietrich at London Airport, or lolling with Françoise Sagan on the Riviera sand.

Rather tactlessly I allowed myself to be photographed in

British uniform with Vienna's House of Parliament in the background; and, rather embarrassingly, arm-in-arm with a Soviet sergeant in front of the Soviet War Memorial in Berlin. Indulging in a brief delusion of grandeur, I am steering a Rolls-Royce through the English countryside, or hovering at the side of Mr. Herbert (now Lord) Morrison to hear the results of the 1945 election, which Labour won, looking as pleased as he, though it was no concern of mine. With Lord Longford, a former Labour minister, I am examining some papers on his desk; and with Field Marshal Lord Montgomery I am strolling and chatting on the grounds of the converted mill which is his country home. I am mingling with the British and Commonwealth delegations on their trip from London to the Paris peace conference of twenty-one nations in April, 1946, among them Mr. Gladwyn Jebb, who as Sir Gladwyn Jebb and Britain's representative at the UN acquired fame by television and ended up as Lord Gladwyn—far from his radical beginnings.

In the company of Pietro Nenni, Italy's foreign minister at the time, I appear on the balcony of the Palazzo Chigi, from which Mussolini used to harangue the Italian populace. The time was 1946, the period of Europe's postwar degradation. In Italy it was the era of the unfortunate *Sciuscia* ("Shoeshine boys") those pathetic, roaming, stealing, pimping children. One sidled up to me in a Naples street and pointed to a little girl, somewhat younger than himself, leaning against the wall on the other side of the street; he whispered in American-accented English, with only the slightest Italian accent: "Want to screw my sister? Takes off all clothes, stays all night." I saw a ten-year-old, with three companions, jump on to the back of a moving Allied food lorry and throw as much of its load as he could get hold of to his accomplices in the street who hurriedly made off with the loot while the boy fell, wounded from the shots of an exasperated soldier whose unit had lost thousands of rations to such juvenile pilferers. For a long time nobody bothered to stop to help the injured child. In Italy in those days orphans were as expendable as stray cats—and as numerous. That Italy would develop an admirable, highly industrialized society from such poor postwar beginnings was difficult to foresee.

Yet another picture shows me gorging myself on delicious *moussaka* in an expensive Athens restaurant while on an inquiry into the postwar problem of UNRRA supplies which were *not* reaching the starving Greeks. What a mess Greece was after the civil war! Destruction and hunger everywhere. To this day I am haunted by the memory of a beautiful but emaciated little girl squatting lethargically at the entrance to her village; the children, potbellied, with swollen limbs, did not get enough to eat to have sufficient energy for play.

Arriving at midnight in Lamia after a nightmarish drive along the pockmarked mountain road from Athens, I relaxed in the square outside my Inn with a bottle of ouzo before taking to my unappetizing bed. I had hardly touched the bottle when a man approached, proudly holding up a piece of paper for me to inspect: "Corporal Jones" of such-and-such a regiment "testifies that the holder, Mr. Zarafides, is a loyal friend of Britain. . . ." Within ten minutes a dozen "loyal supporters of Britain" (as attested by British N.C.O.'s) had joined my table and were sharing my ouzo. Two hours and three bottles later I fell into my bed in a room at the end of a corridor in which men were sleeping on the floor side by side like sardines; and yet another two hours later I woke up, my bare body covered from head to toe with a moving mass of busy, brown, bloodthirsty bugs. A few years later, when I returned to Greece, she had pulled herself up by her bootlaces to offer tourists modern amenities to match her ancient attractions.

A place of honor in my bulging portfolio is reserved for the pictorial memento of breakfast with M. Jean Monnet at his thatched English-style country house at Montfort, near Paris, because it recalls the occasion on which "the Father of the Common Market" unfolded for my benefit his glowing vision of a united Europe, then still in an embryonic stage. What Monnet, the wealthy French winegrower who inspired Winston Churchill, described was a Europe to which Britain, including the Commonwealth, could adhere and which would readily cooperate with the United States in an Atlantic Community. Of all the difficulties ahead, what Monnet did not seem to anticipate was a Common Market which Dr. Adenauer and General de Gaulle would try to turn into an autarkic, anti-Anglo-American organization. There was as yet no hint of a Europe rotating on a Bonn-Paris axis, so like a modern version of the 1931 Long-Name-Association's (and Hitler's) key to the German domination of Europe. When I saw Monnet again a few years later, he put a brave face on just such developments but was evidently saddened by the distortion his concept had suffered at the hands of the aging advocates of a "Little Europe" who were more concerned with separating Britain from her Commonwealth and reducing her power as the world's top trading nation than with his original vision of harmony and peace.

There are three criterions by which to judge prominent figures: their public personality, the immediate impact they make on those who meet them for the first time, and the impression they create on closer acquaintance. Only the general public is likely to accept the first as a genuine reflection of the man—or woman; reporters rarely reach the third stage in their relations with celebrities, but they soon develop an instinct which enables them to see through facades. What we discover can be bitterly disappointing. But by the same token, and in spite of a nondescript public personality, Jean Monnet was one of the most genuinely impressive men I ever met.

My visits to Monnet were made on behalf of Sir Edward Hulton, whose famous *Picture Post* I joined in 1956. Son of a great North of England publisher, Edward Hulton, long after his father's death and the dispersal of the family holdings, founded the first modern British picture magazine. With the shadow of war obscuring the immediate future, his was a very courageous enterprise. As his editor, Edward Hulton chose Stefan Lorant, a Hungarian of German journalistic antecedents. Lorant, who was editing the *Münchner Illustrierte* when I saw him in Munich on the eve of Hitler's advent to power, was arrested by the Nazis a few days later but was soon released. He wrote *I Was Hitler's Prisoner* at a time when his fate was not as yet shared by millions. The book became a best seller.

In London, Lorant first went to work for John Dunbar, from whom he received little intellectual response. It was Edward

Hulton's appreciation of the Hungarian's talent that resulted in the introduction of a new style of picture journalism into Britain, although I could recognize how much it owed to the general approach and presentation of pre-Hitler Germany's *avant-garde* publications in this genre. Sensing the impending upheaval—international, economic, social—Hulton, English to the tips of his fingers, and Lorant, with his *Fingerspitzengefühl*, welded *Picture Post* into a unique publication which, from its first issue, commanded interest, respect, and a very considerable readership. It was not long before the weekly magazine was exerting a profound political influence.

When war conditions made it difficult for Lorant as a foreigner to edit a British magazine (he went to America, where he became a successful author), Hulton once more demonstrated his sure touch by picking as his successor the only indigenous magazine journalist to demonstrate Lorant's flare, Tom Hopkinson. But conflicts became inevitable when Hopkinson insisted on the supremacy of the editor over the Proprietor—a dying tradition in British journalism. A few years later, when most British newspapers were edited by the management, it was difficult to remember why there should have been so much excited comment when Hulton and Hopkinson ceased seeing eye-to-eye and parted company. Some people felt that Hulton had committed the ultimate sin by attempting to exert an influence over his own publication. It was, in the long run, an academic argument. The days of mass-circulation British picture magazines were numbered. By the time I came to *Picture Post* the distracting influence of television and the waning interest of advertisers in general magazines had in effect ordained their ultimate extinction.

My old friend Len Spooner had joined Hulton's from Odhams, where the spirit of Dunbar survived the man himself. On the eve of his appointment as executive editor of *Picture Post*— with Hulton reserving the title of editor in chief for himself— Spooner asked me to join him. I was happy to resume our old association.

I had a big office, a carpet (status symbol), and a secretary, and was wildly enthusiastic. But the majority of the staff regarded the newcomer as an intruder. At conference on the first day a row of cold eyes looked at me across the table. My suggestions were met with stony silence; they were clearly unworthy of comment. My requests were ignored. Leaving this first confrontation, I encountered little groups of inmates whose conversation evaporated as I approached. Walking down the long, lonely corridor, I had the eerie sensation of invisible knives being rammed into my back. But the blades buckled rather than pierced my extremely tough skin and fell to the floor with a clatter.

Although I am not prone to persecution mania, it is possible—indeed, quite likely—that I imagined many of these hostile manifestations, and it is only fair to explain that (almost) everyone associated with them in my lively imagination has since become outstanding in his or her respective career, and many are now friends of mine. Among them is Trevor Philpott, one of Britain's great television reporters, whom I suspected in those days of representing the hard core of *Picture Post* chauvinism and in whom I saw the leader of the resistance prepared to fight the alien intruder in the corridors and in the conference room, and determined never to surrender the magazine to the vulgarizing *Illustrated* upstarts. But I had no complaints. As often before in my life, I was thriving on all this hostility, real or imagined. Anyway, if I could get Trevor Philpott out of the way, I figured, I could handle the situation, and I was confident that I could get rid of him.

"Trevor, my friend," I said, approaching him soon after I had laid my plans, "what baffles me is that a man of your writing ability should concern himself with all this silly administrative work. . . . If I were you I would get out into the wide world—travel . . . write!"

Philpott, though he cared deeply for the medium of picture journalism, did not have much stomach for internecine warfare. A fine and sensitive writer, he naturally enjoyed getting out and about and seeing for himself, as most writers do. "But would they let me go? Would they spend the money?"

"Leave it to me," I said, "Go anywhere you like for as long as you like and as soon as you like. . . ."

"I'd be most grateful if you could persuade the editor!"

A week or so later Trevor was on his way. How luck and

merit combine is never apparent to the fool, but he was in Budapest when the 1956 revolution broke out, and the result was one of the finest pieces of descriptive reporting I have ever seen. On his return he devoted his considerable energies and talent to the production of a special issue on Hungary which earned a small fortune for the victims of the revolt. Trevor Philpott never fully resumed his executive duties.

Picture Post ceased publication in 1957, but two years later I received a call from Sir Edward Hulton when he was planning to reenter the hazardous field of magazine publishing. He wanted me to edit a new paper under his direction. It was only now that I came to know this charming and erudite man better—and Lady Hulton too. Nika Hulton, daughter of Prince Yurevitch, a chamberlain at the czarist court, quick-thinking and impatient, seemed richly endowed with the impressive, formidable, and overwhelming qualities of her race. She is a lover of the arts in the tradition of the European aristocracy, an art collector of great acumen (her collection of Paul Klees is one of the largest in private hands), and a generous patroness of young artists. Inevitably, with a brain requiring more than womanly pursuits to occupy it, Lady Hulton has always taken an active part in the administration of the family fortune, and has always shared her husband's predilection for publishing. It was Nika who negotiated a new contract with me. Oh, yes, I should have added that she is also very beautiful.

After dinner *à deux* in her library with a Braque, a Picasso, a Chirico, a Monet, and several Klees looking down on us, she settled herself opposite me on a couch. She was dressed in one of her usual revealingly décolleté gowns: "Well, how much do you want?" she asked briskly. She likes decisions to be made quickly. I hemmed and hawed. "Tell me your figure," she demanded again.

"Lady Hulton," I answered, "while your own figure obtrudes I cannot think of any other!"

The contract was highly satisfactory.

When I had nursed the new venture to the verge of publication, Sir Edward called me into his office. From his expression it was not difficult to deduce that my dreams of editorship were ended before the new magazine had even appeared. "I have en-gaged an editor" Sir Edward told me. "I hope you will cooperate as loyally with him as you have done with me."

The door opened and a tall, distinguished figure approached to shake hands. "This is Guy Schofield," Sir Edward said. "I ex-pect you two will get on well together."

He bundled us quickly out of the room. Schofield suggested we discuss the situation over a drink. "Look here, Frischauer," he said when we had reached El Vino's in Fleet Street, "I've read your work over the years. . . . Excellent stuff . . . What I cannot understand is why a man with a pen like yours should want to occupy an administrative position. Now, in your place, I should want to travel . . . write . . . see things for my-self. . . ."

Ah, well, those who live by the dagger die by the dagger!

The new paper was not a success anyway. It folded after a few months. Fleet Street entered a period of vast changes. Hulton had already sold the bulk of his publishing interests to Odhams Press, which in turn was taken over by the Mirror Group. *Illus-trated* did not survive *Picture Post* for long; a new type of maga-zine gained popular support, glossier, more precious, "way out" and "with it" or whatever other ugly cliché fits the new prod-ucts. Another prop of my rickety world was in the process of disintegrating.

Association with the Hultons heightened a dilemma from which I have suffered all my life—an inclination toward snobbism combined with very progressive views. My own habits are Syb-aritic and extravagant, although politically I regard such attitudes not only as indefensible but as self-defeating. But I am incapable of practicing what I preach. Or rather, dare not preach what I think so as not to lay myself open to the accusation of hypocrisy. No real insincerity involved—just pitiful human weakness.

Wealth naturally fascinates me, although I have encountered very few rich people whose intellectual stature impressed me. If I were rich my ambition would be to convince my fellow mil-lionaires that the safest way to retain wealth for ourselves and our children would be to support public policies which truly spread prosperity, rather than live in the false hope that pretense and propaganda will do the trick. "The rich man in his castle is not secure if he is surrounded by abject poverty," I wrote years ago. The principle has since been accepted, but implementation lags far behind. Although Conservatives all over the world have adopted many Socialist ideas (welfare, planning, internationalism), they continue to fight a sham battle against Socialism which is fast becoming meaningless, while Socialists seem incapable of taking human nature into account, which puts them out of business as fast as they succeed because it turns prosperous Socialists into Conservatives.

One of Sir Edward Hulton's friends asked me to lunch one day at the Beafsteak Club, one of the many not so secret headquarters of the British Establishment. It was in the early days of my second tenure of Hulton office and, knowing that Sir Edward used the club, I was not anxious to expose myself to the criticism of some of his friends. ("Big fat fellow, foreign accent, strange views, not-one-of-us" sort of thing.) I declined the invitation.

Later that day my millionaire friend was on the telephone: "What a pity you did not come to lunch," he said. "It was a wonderful occasion." He was rapturous: "Edward Hulton was there . . ." (£5 million, I thought) "Harry Pilkington . . ." (another £10 million) "Lionel Fraser . . ." (at least another £5 million). He enumerated one or two others before continuing: "We were sitting there before luncheon, enjoying a glass of magnificent old sherry when who should come in but the prime minister! He sat down among us. . . . Talked quite freely. . . . Let his hair down. . . . You know, that's what I call *democracy!*"

The daughters of the great Greek shipowner, the Livanos sisters, were much in the news—Tina Onassis, as she then was (she has since become the Marchioness of Blandford), and Eugenie Niarchos, wife of another shipping tycoon. I traveled to Paris and Saint-Moritz to talk to them. Tina in particular I thought delightful, a little thing with an uninhibited, naturally girlish manner, quick repartee and a sharp tongue, with a most captivating touch of self-deprecation, the very opposite of pomposity. Having often listened openmouthed to working-class women discussing their neighbors, cousins, the publican's wife, the girl behind the grocer's counter—inarticulately picturesque triviality—I was fascinated to be an ear-witness to an upper-class version of the same practice, the well-known names of the jet-set (never a duke, never a marquise, never a contessa, always Teddy, Yvette, Carla) replacing old Fred, Liz, and Daisy. Fascinating, too, to observe how busy these people manage to be doing nothing—though the Marchioness of Blandford (as Tina Onassis) did a splendid job bringing succor to the Greek islands after the 1956 earthquakes. She went ashore and helped to distribute supplies herself; she would, I am sure, always jump at an opportunity to do something useful if it arose. Eugenie Niarchos was less gregarious, and as mad about skiing as the wives of British aristocrats are about horses.

By comparison with the late Stavros Livanos, Onassis and Niarchos (or, for that matter, the Marquess of Blandford), the young Duke of Kent was, of course, a pauper—and appropriately more reticent. He was on very friendly terms with one of my *Picture Post* colleagues, Alexander Koziel (son of the Polish Count Poklewski), who was Princess Marina's model for her "Painting of a Young Man." Returning to the *Picture Post* office after lunch one day, I saw the duke waiting in the hall, looking a little lost. "Can I help you, sir? Are you waiting for Alex?" I asked.

"I am, as a matter of fact," he said, glancing at his watch. "He said he would be here at three."

"Come upstairs, then," I suggested, and introduced myself.

For half an hour, while he waited, the duke watched operations in my office. It was a busy time, but I made sure that no aspect of the frantic newspaper activity escaped the young duke (photography was his hobby at the time). I called Paris and Rome, and happened to receive a call from New York. Shoals of pictures were shoved onto my desk, and office boys came in relays to collect manuscripts. I talked to the editor on the intercom and summoned the art editor, who looked bewildered when I insisted on discussing a layout which had already been passed for the press. By the time Alex Koziel arrived, the duke was so immersed in the hectic atmosphere, I thought he would there and then ask to join the staff.

"Why on earth did you not take him upstairs?" I later asked the commissionaire at the door. He shrugged his shoulders uncomprehendingly. "The Duke of Kent! So that's who it was. I thought he was just a Mr. Kent. He *said* his name was 'Kent.' "

In 1954, in cooperation with Robert Jackson, I wrote a war book, *The Navy's Here* (United States title: *The Altmark Affair*), about the floating prison of seamen from ships sunk by the Nazi pocket battleship *Graf Spee*. The *Altmark* was eventually cornered by the British Navy in a Norwegian fjord. Ever since that book's great success I had been searching for a similar subject with the same ingredients—Germany and the war—which suited my qualifications and the public's taste. I thought I had found the right mixture when I came across the story of a brothel in Normandy frequented by officers from a Wehrmacht High Command stationed in the local château. The long and short of the story was that a British commando expedition was sent to bring the whole establishment—Madame and girls—back to Britain and extract from them the German secrets they were bound to have overheard in the line of their duties. The British Service departments had helped me readily with research on Goering and the *Altmark*, and I turned to them once more in the hope of getting some official information.

Negative! Entirely negative. All the people I questioned were highly amused but none was able or willing to help. The project was too good to abandon. If the book could not be done as reportage, the subject lent itself ideally to a piece of fiction. Because I had not written a novel before, and had no inclination to try, I came to an arrangement with Jerrard Tickell, who had successfully tackled similar topics and turned them into best-selling novels. He did not fail me. He wrote a splendid book, *Villa Mimosa* that went into many printings, was sold in the United States, and reprinted as a paperback. The film rights were snapped up. Without having done a stroke of work, I made a great deal of money. I was rushed to Hollywood, where I told the producers all I knew about the wartime Wehrmacht, which was plenty. Three years later they had not even started shooting.

New York—the great cosmopolis. Had not one of my first excursions taken me to the Congo crisis session of the Security Council, I should still have felt enveloped by the United Nations, which seems to me an ideal symbol for New York. New York, I guess (how catching the language is), could supply a home-grown delegate for each of the United Nations—and, incidentally, no need to study the statistics to realize that there are more Jews in New York than in Israel.

Luckily, the immigrants have brought their cuisine with them and handed their native culinary arts down to their Americanized children. I ate scampi and cannelloni with fresh Parmesan, golden brown Wiener Schnitzel, delicious real goose liver (on which Strassbourg's paté de foie gras does not have a patch), shashlik with rezina vine leaves (better than in Piraeus), gefilte fish, Chinese sweet-and-sour pork, gorgeous unpronounceable Japanese hors d'œuvres . . . otherwise I would have starved. Native American food looked as if it had come straight from the glossy advertisement pages of their magazines. Alas, inevitably, it came from the "freezer" where all taste is left behind. No wonder New York gourmets clamor for air-mail Dover soles. Struggling with half-a-dozen clams (so as not to offend my host) at Sherman Billingsley's Stork Club, I visualized myself making a fortune, American-style, by organizing an instant-import service of Southend whelks. Compared with these clams they are truly ambrosial.

The food for thought, however, was excellent. The spiritual experience of freedom and human dignity which Britain communicates to the individual wherever he comes from is always with me. So are the claustrophobic frustrations and tensions caused by the London traffic congestion. The first mile's drive from Idlewild Airport along the six-lane highway, the even flow of the multicolored taxis unimpeded by crossroads or red lights, was real liberation and true exhilaration. It immediately conveyed the vastness of the United States, the victory of technical design over the obstruction of overcivilization, the power and speed of the machine age. I might have turned back there and then—I should still have taken with me the feel of America.

Second thought: Americans like to think of their country as the cradle of modern advertising, the Eldorado of high-pressure public relations. Why, then, do they allow a public image of the United States to become fixed in the minds of millions which is positively insulting—and false? How often I have been told that the Americans are materialistic, uncultured, and politically immature, nervous and harassed, borne down by guilt complexes and rude, dictatorial masters and unwilling servants, condescending Bourbon-swigging nabobs or violent paupers, sharp elbows in your ribs, painted faces and hearts of stone, always pushing to the head of the queue, panting in the ratrace until they drop dead from coronary thrombosis. . . . At best they are supposed to be as superficially glossy as *Life* magazine, as simple and fluent as a cover story in *Time*.

Conditioned as I am by many years' diligent perusal of both *Time* and *Life*, I wanted to meet one of these principal purveyors of Americana, fully expecting to come face to face with some brash, bustling, superhygienic, crew-cut ex-college-cum-junior-executive type whose big business happened to be *Time-Life* journalism. Instead, I met a modest, pleasant, good-looking, leisurely, dreamy intellectual whose literary erudition and conversational dexterity would quickly earn him a place by the side (somewhat to the right) of Sartre and Sagan even though he *would* have to plead guilty to being rather more hygienic than the orthodox inhabitants of the Left Bank.

One of his colleagues, rather high up in the Luce hierarchy, invited me to visit him in his home. Period furniture from Paris, silver from Mappin and Webb, mercifully civilized tots of Rémy Martin, a hostess with the allure of Madame de Staël. He treated me to a sober and frank exposition of international affairs which made me feel like asking Walter Lippmann to move over and let my friend share his lonely pedestal. At the *Life* premises one editor revealed his yearning for the great outdoors by the artificial ivy he had stuck to the glass and metal walls of his office; another was studying Gjon Mili's pictures tracing the origins of Greek civilization.

In the event, I found that *Time* and *Life* had prepared me better for my American visit than any of America's frivolous detractors. Always out to make an honest penny, I seemed much more materialistic than the average American. When I lost my way in Manhattan's rectangular maze of streets and avenues, half-a-dozen of the harassed and nervous passersby took time off to put me to rights; two proceeded to tell me about their background, their families, and their jobs, another wanted me to tell him my life story, a fourth (an ex-G.I.), on hearing that I came from England, insisted there and then on repaying some of the hospitality he had received in Great Britain during the war.

I dined with one of those fabulous American millionaires—no condescension, no bourbon—and was served by waiters so polite I was surprised that they were not Viennese. Harlem at night was peaceful, and the slum sections were far less noisy than the *West Side Story* I had recently seen at Her Majesty's Theatre in London. The Statue of Liberty was shrouded in mist and fog, which no doubt came over from England with the *Mayflower*. At the night police court, a homely judge was scientifically clinical and socially conscious to a degree in his dealings with a posse of prostitutes.

What survived most vividly in my mind after a week's tour of New York was the Museum of Modern Art, with Pablo Picasso's "Guernica"; the fabulous construction of the Guggenheim Museum, which overshadows the exhibits; Wall Street, which struck me as a City of London on stilts, and the man-made range of the Manhattan Alps on which I looked down from the Empire State Building. Times Square and Broadway were disappointing—they look more impressive in Hollywood's movies. At Washington Square, Greenwich Village, I got involved in an open-air chess game. . . .

On another visit to New York I hardly left the Waldorf-Astoria, which happened to be the subject of my reportage (covering some of the world's "Grand Hotels" for the *Sunday Telegraph*). It is not a bad place in which to study America. The lobby was teeming with delegates to two or three different conventions. Outsize name labels attached to the lapels of their coats, hundreds of typical honest-to-goodness, average Americans struggled to maintain their identity in the milling crowds, joyfully and noisily greeting each other. Some of them looked as if they had come to some Ruritanian function or—more likely— to a fancy-dress ball, wearing strange and gaudy uniforms, elaborate decorations, giant stars, and ribbons. They turned out to be members of the Society of Foreign Consuls, and inevitably got mixed up with the members of the Quarter-Century Club of the First National City Bank of New York—staffers who have held their jobs with the bank for twenty-five years or more and who were also celebrating. Yet another conspicuously bemedaled crowd of a thousand-odd people surged toward the Grand Ballroom to attend a dinner of the Society of the French Legion of Honor.

A visit to the hotel's Marco Polo Club, which admits only presidents, chairmen, and distinguished figures within companies with an annual profit running into high figures, took me back fifteen years to Cairo's Shepheard's Hotel and its famous Italian-born bartender, "mine host" in the grand manner (off-duty hobby: big-game hunting), exquisitely refined in an immaculate white dinner jacket, assisted by a dozen tense waiters, their big dark frightened eyes riveted on their chief, who, acknowledging his clients' orders with charming urbanity, would direct one attendant after the other with a lordly gesture toward the relevant bottle. As the big bar filled up and orders came thick and fast, the busy barman's gesticulations mounted to a crescendo, his arms waving quickly and incessantly, his fingers pointing rapidly in all directions while he complemented his silent instructions with darting glances from his eloquent eyes. He never touched a bottle or a glass with his own manicured hands. I could hardly tear myself away from this spectacle, which for excitement rivaled the performance of a Toscanini or a Klemperer. The spectacle was in every way intoxicating.

Impossible to forget the man—and here in New York, fifteen years later, I met him again. Jo Scialom—"Jo of Shepheard's"— was manager of the Marco Polo Club. Nasser threw him out of Egypt presumably because of his British associations; Conrad Hilton, who acquired control of the Waldorf in October, 1949, took him on. "I worked for Mr. Hilton in Puerto Rico and in Havana. A couple of revolutions later I asked him to transfer me to a quieter place. . . ."

Of the many stories about the Waldorf, the one about the visit of Queen Elizabeth and the Duke of Edinburgh amused me most. Apartment 35-A of the Waldorf Towers is known as the Presidential Suite, and is let on the understanding that it must be vacated when it is required for heads of state. But when the queen and the duke announced their visit, 35-A happened to be occupied by Prince Feisal of Saudi Arabia. Would he be good enough to move to another apartment for a day, for one day only? The queen was due in New York at 11:00 A.M. She was scheduled to attend a lunch and a dinner and would depart before midnight. . . . Prince Feisal was sorry; he was not feeling well; he could not move; he would not move.

There was nothing the management could do. Hurriedly, Apartment 28-A was made ready for Her Majesty. This was the apartment of the Duke and Duchess of Windsor, who happened to be out of town. Considering that the queen and the duchess were not on speaking terms, it was a piquant arrangement. Mr. Dell 'Agnese, manager of the Waldorf Towers, is not unaccustomed to such dilemmas. On one occasion, five heads of state (crowned and uncrowned) were due to arrive at the same time— but there were only three flagstaffs available. How to avoid offending some of the distinguished visitors? Mr. Dell 'Agnese's answer was to display no foreign flag at all, and hoist the Stars and Stripes instead. It is not a bad symbol for the Waldorf-Astoria.

My next American trip was devoted to research into another American institution—the phenomenon of American foundations, whose number had grown from 7,000 in 1954 to (a conservative estimate) 13,000 in 1961. I talked to presidents, vice-presidents, executives, secretaries of the great foundations—to every type of "philanthropoid"—but also to lawyers, tax experts, economists, and professors. There was hardly a sphere into which the tentacles of foundation activity did not extend. The assignment consisted largely of looking a gift horse closely in the mouth—the wealthiest society on earth being also the most generous, six thousand of the largest foundations giving away the staggering total of $779,000,000 in 1963.

Foundations, I found, are many things to many men. What is a foundation? "A large body of money surrounded by people who want some" was Dwight MacDonald's version (and the early Ford Foundation headquarters in Palm Springs was known as "Itching Palms"). "Private Wealth for Public Purpose" was how Mr. F. Emerson Andrews defined it—he is the head of the Foundation Library Center in New York, and America's leading authority on foundation facts, figures, and history. (Typically, the Foundation Library Center, as all research into the subject of foundations, is financed by—foundations.)

Those who have taken up the cudgels of the late, unlamented Senator McCarthy to pound the antifoundation drums assert that, by their generosity, America's multimillionaires are doing things for people that the people should do for themselves, introducing the Welfare State and Socialism by the back door and thereby changing the psychological and political climate of the United States: "Greeks bearing gifts," they hint darkly, and make it look as if American high finance was anxious to give comfort to Mr. Khrushchev. What was more to the point—as an attorney specializing in foundation work put it to me—"the crux of the whole foundation business" is the section of the United States Internal Revenue Code which authorizes the Treasury to grant tax exemptions to foundations and their sponsors.

That seemed to be the burden of antifoundation criticism. But charity is as old as faith and hope—and religion—and official encouragement of charity in the form of tax exemption is as ancient as taxes themselves. Nor has our civilization a monopoly on charity, which was also known to Hindus and Buddhists. *Wakuf*, the Muslim version, was partly responsible for the collapse of the Ottoman Empire; so much land and property was tax exempt as *Wakuf* that there were no money left for the state to collect. Henry VIII dealt with the wealth the Church had accumulated in England through charity; and it was Benjamin

Franklin who imported the idea of charitable trusts or foundations from England to America. ("I wish to be useful even after my Death, if possible," he wrote.)

Of course, I found cases of wealthy taxpayers who, by giving away part of their capital and considerable income, were actually better off than they would have been had they kept the money, and it is quite true that the tax collector would, on an average, take about nine-tenths of any amount the top-income brackets allocated to a foundation. But thousands whose names were associated with foundations are simply motivated by an impulse which is as deeply rooted in the British as in the American character. Whether it springs from a rich man's guilt complex (Edmund Burke said, "Foundations are the useful fruit of late penitence"), from a Puritan aversion to opulence, or from plain generosity, the result is a wholly admirable virtue. "A man who dies rich dies disgraced," said Andrew Carnegie, and created his foundation which still distributes unstintingly of his wealth. "Your fortune will crush you!" the elder Rockefeller was warned, and he responded by setting up his famous foundation.

Much of my time was spent studying the *Directory of Foundations* (edited by Miss Ann D. Walton and Mr. F. Emerson Andrews), which currently lists 6,000 foundations with assets of $14.5 billion, the American equivalent of the *Almanach de Gotha*, enormous wealth replacing aristocratic ancestry as a badge of entry. For weeks I lost myself in the undergrowth of impressive figures as I studied the balance sheets of the "Top Ten" foundations, each controlling assets exceeding $100 million, and of the 750 in the next category whose assets are one million dollars or over.

The lovable freaks who sail gaily in the wake of immeasurable wealth: Dr. Coles, for instance, who set aside $1,000 for the "Dr. Coles Trust Fund for Ice Cream for the Pupils of Scotch Plains and Fanwood, New Jersey" with instructions that the income be used for the stated purpose one day a year until the ending of the world; and Emma A. Robinson, who established "The Horses Dinner Trust Fund of Kansas," a $10,000 bequest to provide 200 horses with Christmas feasts of oats and corn every year. (While the funds of some foundations are nearing exhaustion, the Kansas Fund, I was told, was in grave danger of running out of horses.) No less startling to the uninitiated was the part foundations played in the origin of such projects as The Kinsey Report, *Sexual Behaviour in the Human Male,* which burst upon the astonished world with the impact of a Gypsy Rose Lee striptease act in Madison Square Garden. It was financed with a Rockefeller grant.

I had a long talk with Dr. J. George Harrar, Dean Rusk's successor as president of the Rockefeller Foundation, a solid, earthy scientist who formed a living link with the organization's pioneering days when, touring Mexico by mule, motorcar, train, and airplane, he devised an agricultural method which has since become a model for schemes to increase the yield of vital crops. How little one knows about the many fine achievements of foundations! In 1943, not far from the area where British troops were engaged in battle with the Afrika Korps, a Rockefeller medical staff was working in Egypt to dam up an outbreak of malaria which had already claimed 135,000 lives, and the troops never knew about the epidemic. The Rockefeller Foundation donated the site by New York's East River on which the United Nations building stands.

"Philanthropoids" employ a language all their own which I had to learn in a hurry. The Ford Foundation has been accused of "scatteration"—of spreading its net too widely. It was described to me as "problem-oriented" rather than concerned with practical operations. The "synergic" result, they said, was difficult to determine—"synergic" meaning a synthesis of several energies. Taking their cue from Mark Twain ("Training is everything; a cauliflower is just a cabbage with a college education"), Ford executives have made education their principal objective. With their support for RAND (Research and Development) they created an ideas factory unique in the history of the world. I came to the conclusion that Ford funds (as also Carnegie efforts), liberally distributed around the world (this side of the Iron Curtain), and particularly in Asia and Africa, have helped to shift the source of intellectual supplies from London to Washington. But not political influence, which seems to have been lost in transit altogether. Educational schemes begun by the British in many parts of Africa have come to rely on American financial support. A few years ago I would have said that American finance could never supplant British know-how in the former colonial areas. But since the Americans have sent out their foundation emissaries and their Peace Corps missionaries to live and work among the natives while imparting to them the blessings of American education, organization, research, and medical care, the human element has been catching up with the dollar sign.

If the influence of American foundations on European institutions is much less obtrusive, the credit often goes to men like Shepard Stone, the big, friendly, polished director of the Ford Foundation's International Affairs Program. Some years ago, for instance, in the course of one of his frequent visits to London, Mr. Stone, whose personality reflects his continuous contact with the elite of many nationalities, invited some of his friends—The Thoughtful Men of England, he called them—to a "bogsat": *b*unch *o*f *g*uys *s*itting *a*round a *t*able—to discuss pressing problems and what could be done about them.

From such informal meetings Mr. Stone reports back to the trustees of his foundation, who then decide whether a grant should be made to fill any need the "thoughtful men" may have discovered. It may be a medical scheme, a research project in the humanities, a fellowship plan, or finance for a new institution. In the case Mr. Stone described to me, what eventually emerged from these conversations was the Overseas Development Institute. A British board was set up and a grant made; the rest was up to the board. Mr. Stone is usually aware of the identity of the man likely to be chosen to head a new project but, strictly speaking, it is not for him or his trustees to decide. The man chosen as director of the Overseas Development Institute was Mr. William Clark, a journalist on the staff of the London *Observer*.

Women figure prominently in the Foundation aristocracy. Two I met were the handsome Miss Flora Rhind, who has been associated with foundations throughout her working life (*Who's Who in America* devotes thirteen lines to her); and Miss Florence Anderson, Secretary of the Carnegie Corporation, among whose duties is the signing of the foundation's checks. The biggest she ever signed was for $1,500,000, and it went to the Institute of International Education.

The entanglement of the foundation bureaucracy with American government service—the State Department supplies the foundations with some outstanding servants, and vice versa—the flow of grants and other aspects of the great foundation saga occupied my interest, but publication of my research will have to await another occasion. No inquiry into any other field of American endeavor could have given me a better insight into the range of America's intellectual life and the unparalleled generosity and selfless skill that helps to distribute invaluable benefits over wide areas of the world.

II | *Back to the Womb*

"Ihr naht euch wieder, schwankende Gestalten,
Die früh sich einst dem trüben Blick gezeigt.
Vermag ich wohl euch diesmal festzuhalten?
Fühl' ich mein Herz noch jenem Wahn geneight?"
                                        —GOETHE, *Faust*

*I*t took me fifteen years and more than half-a-dozen visits after the war to analyze my reactions to Vienna. I feel at first very much like coming home to my old house, yet it is strange, as if it had been occupied by a series of turbulent tenants, burgled, stripped, half destroyed and rebuilt—after a fashion. It is difficult for me to realize that I ever lived here. The new housekeeper, too, thinks of me as a stranger.

The first thing that strikes me is that we—my fellow Viennese and I—no longer speak the same language. Mine is the language of the middle thirties, which makes me sound as if I belonged to some lost tribe that had become separated from the main body of its people. The trouble is that while I was away, Hitler was here. The Germans have played havoc with the language of the Viennese. Just as I used to do twenty-five years ago, I asked for a large dollop of *Schlagobers* (whipped cream) with my coffee.

296

To me *Schlagobers* and Vienna are synonymous. The young waiter automatically repeats my order: *"Schlagsahne?"* This is a German's German such as no self-respecting Viennese would have used in my day. Besides, the war has created a phraseology which is utterly alien to me. I feel like a Londoner who has only just heard the R.A.F.'s English for the first time.

When I left, Vienna was unstable, jittery, plagued by political extremism within. . . . Now Vienna is the prosperous, sedate, unruffled, even complacent capital of a small country which positively enjoys the neutrality imposed on it by the State Treaty of 1955. But if Vienna is becalmed, it has also lost something of its sparkle and its fighting spirit. The atmosphere is provincial. We angry young Austrians of the early thirties used to discuss the danger of the *"Ver-linzerung Wiens"* (Linz is a provincial city, and its name was invoked as symbolic of the creeping provincialization of Vienna). Well, it has happened. The clothes people wear—*Lederhosen* and rough *Loden* jackets—are more suitable to the mountains of the Tyrol than to the once stylish capital. We used to be proud of Vienna, embracing two-thirds of the country's 6,000,000 inhabitants, being different from "the rest." Now it is truly representative of the rural, agricultural hinterland.

There is obviously something missing. Much of the distinctive flavor has evaporated. No, it is not that there are fewer Czechs, Hungarians, Romanians here. There are, perhaps, even more of them, mostly refugees from East European Communism. It is something else—like eggs without salt. In Hugo Bettauer's novel, *City Without Jews*, the Jews return to Vienna in triumph. That has not happened. No more than a handful have survived, and I sorely miss the Jews to whom Vienna owed much of its cosmopolitan outlook and international reputation.

Time—and Hitler—have decimated their ranks. Vienna's coffeehouses have been undermined by the natural process of changing times and habits—I fear forever. The pace of life is slower in Vienna than anywhere else I know of. But few people now make their business appointments in coffeehouses rather than in their offices as they used to do. No doubt the Viennese work harder than before the war, but strangers still find it well-nigh impossible to relate their leisurely mode of life to the spectacular economic progress of the country and the all-pervading prosperity. There can be only one explanation, one German observer suggested: "These people are working surreptitiously!"

But what disturbed me most was an embarrassing barrier between myself and some of the people I used to know, the question unasked yet inescapable, though we tried to suppress it because the answer was bound to widen the gulf between us: "And what did you do in the war?" There is no need to ask an old friend whose artificial arm speaks for itself, a dreadful reminder of the frozen wastes of Nazi-ravaged Russia in 1942. . . . What is obvious in the case of a German comes as a shock when it applies to a Viennese: he fought for Hitler. Unwillingly, perhaps under duress, yet . . . yet . . . "so you live in London," he says, and looks up at the sky, as if London meant nothing to him except a base for wartime R.A.F. bomber squadrons. We are separated by the greatest emotional experience of our lives, the war through which we lived on different sides of the fence.

Much of this is probably a projection of one's own imagination; but, imagined or real, it looms large.

Early in 1946. An army car took us—Peter Waugh, pleasant, ex-army type turned magazine photographer, and myself—from Trieste (trouble spot, likely cause of Yugoslav-Italian conflict, the spark that could set off another world conflagration—that sort of assignment) across the Austrian border to Klagenfurt of happy, youthful memories, now the British Army of Occupation's H.Q. town. . . . I was fourteen or fifteen years old and on a holiday visit to Father and his gasworks, when he decided to take me to Venice for a week. After a night's train journey we arrived at the Lido, moved into a small pension, and went straight to the beach, where I fell asleep. Two hours later I woke up with sunstroke. Next morning I was back in Carinthia. Father never forgave me for preferring Klagenfurt to Venice, and I cannot say I blame him. . . .

Now, twenty-five years later, I lunched at the British Officers' Mess—the Hotel Moser of yore—and drove out to the lake, where senior British officers sailed their boats. A strange homecoming, eerie, unreal. Somewhere along the road I must have made up my mind to regard this trip as just another assignment. As far as I was concerned, I might never before have set foot in Klagenfurt.

The same cold, strange aloofness accompanied me to Vienna, where I moved into the Army's Public Relations Mess in the charming little Palais Salm. It was very much like Berlin, only worse. The remoteness of Vienna from the Western center of my interests complicated the confrontation. Soviet soldiers lounging on benches in the Ringstrasse; Mongolian youngsters in sheepskin hats and fixed bayonets guarding the Danube bridges; the huge hammer-and-sickle adorning an entrance to the Hofburg, where the Soviets had installed an officers' club; the devastation; the dirt; the quiet despair. . . .

It was almost impossible for me to recognize the city of my birth, the city—nothing corny about this—of my dreams. I went through the motions of covering a story. I was shocked (most un-Viennese of me!) when an Austrian official told me of the extensive plans for the restoration of the Opera, and said not a word about the tens of thousands of homeless in the city. I drank a great deal in the Mess and in nightclubs. I embarrassed and enraged the British public-relations chief when, stranded in an outer district of the Soviet Zone in the middle of the night, I used his name to persuade a British Army driver to collect me. I had a brief talk with friends of my parents, who tied their handkerchiefs in knots as they tried to explain how little they were able to do for them. I went back to the U.K. as fast as I decently could.

When I returned a year or so later, some of the old Viennese spirit had reasserted itself. The Soviets were already the bogymen of the world; they had certainly not made themselves very popular in Vienna when they ransacked the Workers' Settlements, whose spacious, solid, well-furnished apartments they mistook for the homes of the idle rich. After that, the Communists never had a real chance in Austria. But while the Western Allies and the Soviets quarreled everywhere else in the world, the Four-Power Allied Control Council of Austria, officiating in the leisurely, good-humored atmosphere of Vienna, at least observed the civilities. The Soviet colonel in charge was a native of the Bronx—and talked like one; the British colonel had first seen the light of day in Shanghai; the setup was truly international.

I toured Vienna in a jeep of the International Military Patrol, which kept the peace in the central international district of Four-Power-occupied Vienna—peace among the four occupying Powers, that is, who used to quarrel violently whenever any of their troops misbehaved and landed in each other's cooler. The Viennese looked upon these jeeps, each manned by an American, a British, a French, and a Soviet military policeman, with benevolent good humor. The principle of the "Four Men in a Jeep" patrol was promptly explained to me with characteristic Viennese insouciance: "The French poilu drives, the American G.I. twiddles the knob of the radio, and the British Tommy sits on top of the Soviet Ivan to keep him from shooting. . . ." The Viennese had a wryly witty story for every contingency. The occupation troops and the Viennese girls? "The Americans buy them, the French seduce them, the Soviets rape them, and the British marry them!"

Behind the smokescreen of casualness the Austrians were working hard—for liberation from the Allied "liberators." Now Austria, I was told, was paying for Schuschnigg's failure to offer resistance to the Nazis in 1938; had but a few Austrians fought the invading Wehrmacht, Austria would have earned the right to a government-in-exile and liberation without occupation. I disagreed. Austria, the fair and peaceful country, suffers from the geographical handicap of an extremely important strategic position in Europe; it was too valuable for the Soviets to let it slip into the Western orbit without the safeguard of militarily enforced neutrality.

Unlike Germany, Austria, though occupied, had the advantage of a national government which, however restricted by the occupation Powers, enjoyed a measure of authority over the country as a whole from the beginning. It was a coalition of the Right-wing, Catholic "People's Party" and the Socialists, whose leaders picked up where they had left off before Dollfuss. Heading the coalition government as chancellor was Leopold Figl, a shrewd and amiable Catholic engineer whom the Nazis had held for years in Dachau concentration camp (where he cunningly and courageously sabotaged the construction of incinerators and was, on one occasion, punished with twenty-five strokes on his bare back). But the brains behind Austria's shrewd and patient post-war politics was a farseeing Catholic statesman, Julius Raab, who eventually succeeded Figl as head of the coalition government.

When I complimented Raab on the apparently smooth working of the coalition, he gave me his formula for success: "We have reversed the old practice," he said. "We quarrel in public and work in harmony behind the scenes." It seemed to satisfy the Austrian people, who thrived on their daily ration of angry party political quarrels while the government functioned smoothly in the background and the country prospered. The Austrian inclination toward compromise nurtured some curious phenomena, like the system of proportional distribution of jobs which permeated public life and even private industry. It did not necessarily make for efficient administration, but it has worked for twenty years and withstood all strains and stresses—and elections.

Inevitably, my heart warmed to Austria again. What I could not forgive in a German did not shock me so deeply where an Austrian was concerned. There had been some bad Austrian types: as Seyss-Inquart rose in the Nazi hierarchy he collected a gang of Austrians around him who accompanied him when he became Nazi Protector of Holland and left an ugly legacy of hatred behind; Norway, too, suffered from Austrian troops and administrators, but the wounds have now healed; but the deeds of the Lublin arch-exterminator, Gauleiter Odilo Globocnik, besmirched the good name of Austria. Everything in Austria, as was said of the Habsburg tyranny, was mitigated by *Schlamperei*, which is a typical Austrian happy-go-lucky, couldn't-care-less untidiness and laissez faire. That Austrian Naziism had no such redeeming feature but was mercilessly and efficiently vicious and cruel stamps it as an alien importation: "made in Germany."

At one stage, in 1954, when my affairs were not prospering in England, I accepted an invitation to become adviser to a group of Austrian publishers who proposed to start a modern, illustrated, popular evening paper in Vienna. Six months or a year away from London, I thought, might reverse a streak of bad luck, and what could be better than to spend it in Vienna, working? I packed my things, and with my extremely English wife and daughter in tow, made for Vienna. They were both delighted. The weather was wonderful. The food was delicious. The people were kind and hospitable. The cafés were ideal for idling the time away. The architecture was enchanting. The little hotel was cozy. They were extremely happy.

Everything was fine—except that I was miserable. That difference in outlook which separated me from most Austrians extended also to the professional field. These men, experienced and successful newspaper operators in Austria, simply did not know what I was talking about. Nor could I follow their train of thought. In theory and in practice, technique and ideas, the approach to things Austrian and foreign—we might have belonged to different worlds. Or, maybe, it was not that at all but . . . Someone raised, as he thought, tactfully, the question of my wartime writings in London. Had I not helped to incite the Allied bombings of Austria?

A story by an air correspondent which could so be interpreted had indeed been published during the war, and, this being a Continental subject, a subeditor had mistakenly associated my name with it. Now my Austrian employers warned me that this could develop into a nasty affair with undertones of treason. What nonsense! I wholly endorsed the idea underlying the publication: if a cancer was eating away my mother's vitals I would wish it to be cut out to save her. If the Nazis put Mother Austria's industry at the service of aggressive war, the industries which aided Hitler's war effort had to be cut out. With not so much as a whisper did the liberated people of Metropolitan France condemn de Gaulle whose Free French airmen, flying from London, flew over France attacking strategic targets so that France could be liberated. . . . Those Austrians who considered this sort of thing treason were themselves traitors to Austria, and with the Nazis in spirit still, if no longer arm-in-arm.

I had had enough! I was gripped by a violent longing for Britain, where the political air was not contaminated by the poison which affected consciences wherever the Nazi jackboot had crushed genuine patriotism underfoot. Fortunately, these people were as eager to get rid of me as I was to leave them. The Austrian adventure lasted barely three weeks. Yet, however happy I was to go back to London, I was far from cured. Vienna, the city of my dreams, still beckoned me.

Year after year I go in search of it. Year after year something jerks at my heartstrings. Call me a fair-weather friend, but I almost fell in love with Vienna again when the burden of occupation was finally lifted in 1955. Julius Raab was the architect of Austria's independence. As the price of independence, Austria agreed to anchor neutrality in her constitution. The Austrian Peace Treaty—in spite of the Allied Control Council's hard and patient labor in hundreds of meetings—might not have materialized had Raab not acquired the knack of dealing with Khrushchev and established a friendly working relationship with the Soviet leader. Against much opposition, Raab responded to Soviet overtures and accepted an official invitation to send an Austrian delegation to Moscow. From this slender thread of early contact he spun a solid agreement which suited Soviet Russia, the Western Allies, and Austria herself. Although the Kremlin was disappointed in its hope that neutral Austria would serve as a model for an all-German solution, and extracted inordinate reparations from her, the Soviets kept their political bargain and left the country alone—the only territory from which they have voluntarily withdrawn their troops.

Austrians went to work with much enthusiasm engendered by the restoration of their independence, which they duly celebrated with a gala performance of *The Marriage of Figaro* in the rebuilt Vienna State Opera. I was not certain whether it was the new Opera House or the new independence that made the deeper impact on the people. They never looked back—economically. Psychologically, however, the urge to look back was growing greater every day. Freud would have diagnosed it as a feeling of insecurity, creating a desire to return to the womb. It is something which Austria and Britain—and I—have in common. Although both countries get a little tired when foreigners constantly link them with a bygone era, both glory in their past and the traditions which spring from it.

The last time I had seen Baron Eugene Rothschild was in the hectic days of the abdication, when the Duke of Windsor went to stay at the Rothschild estate in Enzersdorf near Vienna. In 1961 I saw the baron again, still tall and lithe, a little harder of hearing now, but elegant and aristocratic in the best sense of the word. With his English-born wife he was dining at Sacher's, as one always imagined him doing, and the air was vibrant with the attentive voices of the waiters: *"Jawohl, Herr Baron," "Sofort, bitte sehr, Herr Baron!"*

Hotel Sacher! We used to call it "Hotel Habsburg" because its damask-lined, ornate yet intimate *séparées* (small private dining rooms) were the playground of young Habsburg archdukes and their girl friends of the Opera Ballet next door. In those elegant little hideaways history was made when Cabinet ministers and diplomats displaced the lovers, seeking the seclusion of the *séparées* for discreet meetings with their political associates. Here, before the turn of the century, Father's brother Berthold Frischauer used to plead the cause of Crown Prince Rudolf against the stern old Emperor while enjoying the Sacher cuisine in a *séparée;* thirty years later, Mother's brother Ernst Klebinder was a habitué of the *séparées,* to which he enticed embattled politicians for clandestine meetings. Both uncles, I am told, had also been observed sneaking into *séparées* in the company of ladies who were not their wives and who certainly did not look like politicians.

Presiding over this unique establishment, where the food was glorious (it still is) and the service better, was Frau Anna Sacher, who smoked cigars and held court sitting in a wicker chair outside the hotel entrance. She was a Viennese institution. The only social status symbol in those days was a greeting from Anna Sacher. Those whom she did not acknowledge were beyond the pale. After the collapse of the monarchy, when Sacher's dining rooms were besieged by the *nouveau riche* and, worse, by foreigners, Frau Sacher gave instructions to serve these "upstarts" only after all her old aristocratic customers had been catered to, even though they no longer had the money to pay for their exquisite meals. In 1945 the British Army, with a fine sense of taste and tradition, chose Sacher's as their "A" Mess. I am afraid some of the old waiters still shudder when they recall this "gin-and-tonic period" in the hotel's history. Frau Sacher, whose life story I wrote in the late twenties, has been dead for a long time now (since 1934), and Sacher's is crowded with foreign tourists who are made very welcome, but the table next to Baron Rothschild was occupied by a member of the world's new aristocracy, a scion of the House of Hollywood. "A traveling player," Frau Sacher would have called him. I doubt whether she would have let him in.

Relaxing in the lounge of Sacher's, one cannot escape the imperial ghosts that haunt the hotel. Ghosts? In the dim light of the Blue Bar on a Sunday morning not long ago, I was having a drink with Prince Fuerstenberg, eighty-six-year-old head of his ancient family, and his nephew Prince Tassilo Fuerstenberg, the father of Princess Ira. "I have to go, Uncle," Prince Tassilo said. "We are lunching early. Karli is off to thank the Emperor personally for having bestowed the Golden Fleece on him. . . ."

Has the world stood still? It is well over forty years since the Habsburgs lost their throne, but at Sacher's one still refers to the man whom the world knows as Dr. Otto von Habsburg (the Austrian Pretender) as "the Emperor"; and "the Emperor" still invests Austrian nobles with the Golden Fleece, which was, and still is, the Order of the Habsburgs.

That day Prince Fuerstenberg decided to lunch at Sacher's. Inevitably, we talked of his tour of service at the Austro-Hungarian Embassy in London before 1914. How long was it since he first came to Sacher's? "Well, our estates were in Bohemia and we went mostly to Prague, but Father often promised that if he went to Vienna he would take me with him and give me *Tafelspitz* [the famous Viennese boiled beef] at Sacher's. . . . It did not happen, however, until we bought a *Schloss* in Vienna. . . . Let me see . . . that was in 1886. On the first Sunday after our arrival, Father took me to lunch at Sacher's and, of course, I had *Tafelspitz.*"

Seventy-five years ago! The Habsburgs, the First World War, the breakup of the Austro-Hungarian Monarchy, the Austrian Republic, the *Anschluss* of 1938 and Hitler, the last war, liberation, Four-Power Occupation and the Russians ravaging the old imperial city, independence at last in 1955 . . . *Plus ça change, plus c'est la même chose.* The Prince still regularly eats *Tafelspitz* at Sacher's. . . .

At about the same time, by way of contrast, Mr. Khrushchev made a state visit to Vienna which I reported on for London's *Evening Standard.* Two sentries were on guard at the Ballhausplatz chancellery, where Metternich had presided at the time of the Congress of Vienna. I asked the sentries whether their carbines were loaded, and they looked at me uncomprehendingly. I could not blame them. This was the spot where a quarter of a century earlier the Nazi raiders had brushed aside the military guards with their traditional rifles.

Frau von Schirach had told me how Hitler had sent her American-born husband, Gauleiter Baldur von Schirach, to Vienna as *Reichsstatthalter.* Schirach immediately moved into the Ballhausplatz. For good measure he also had an office in the Hofburg, where he and his guests ate off the priceless historic Habsburg gold plate. Now I watched Mr. Khrushchev entering the Hofburg, which has become the residence of Austria's federal president.

As a child I was privileged to accompany Mother to the Opera on special occasions, and she, with hushed awe, pointed out to me the members of the imperial family in the imperial loge. Who would have thought I would live to be invited to a performance in honor of "His Excellency the Chairman of the Council of Ministers of the Union of Socialist Republics, Herrn Nikita S. Chruschtschew"! I can see a grim logic in this strange twist of my personal history, for I feel that it could not be a bad thing if Austria could maintain her equilibrium somewhere between the Habsburgs and Mr. Khrushchev. That should not prevent a Habsburg restoration—with a difference. Dr. Otto Habsburg might persuade the Austrians to elect him president of the republic. A Habsburg republic! That would be something worth seeing!

To paraphrase Josephine Baker: *"J'ai deux amours, mon pays et—Londres!"* For thirty years I have nursed a theory about Britain and Austria and what they have in common. My view was reinforced—if reinforcement were needed—when, not long ago, one of the *nouveau vague* intellectuals, those slick English youngsters with the quick, all-round, surefire judgment who have replaced the doubting, questing minds of their predecessors, brushed through Austria and summed up the little country's efforts to come to terms with the political and economic realities of the times with the sneer that the Austrians would soon be content to make cuckoo clocks like the Swiss. Did I discover here the attitude of a British imperialist manqué who, incapable of adjusting himself to the loss of the empire, must sneer at a fellow sufferer in order to serve his own self-esteem? Like Austria a generation earlier, Britain is going through the psychological and political pangs of a painful and slow readjustment.

This, in many ways, is where I came in.

In October, 1962, I was working on a series of articles about Dr. Adenauer's West Germany. Taking my cue from a leading article in the *Frankfurter Zeitung*, which was critical of political standards in Bonn, I called the series "The Rotten Reich" (the *Frankfurter* had said there was "something rotten in the state"). The series was based largely on reports in the West German press which honestly portrayed a disturbing situation. Writing about West Germany as a hotbed of spies and Cold War traitors, I was soon borne out by Dr. Adenauer speaking in the Bundestag. I described vice in Frankfurt and Munich and recalled a nasty court case involving the frivolous sexual habits of the new West German upper crust. A final installment was devoted to the Nazis in high and low places as exemplified in the rash of prosecutions (in the wake of the Eichmann Trial in Israel) against hundreds of "respected" West German citizens as ex-concentration-camp murderers and extermination experts.

No sooner had my manuscript been delivered for publication than the Hamburg weekly magazine *Der Spiegel* was accused of giving away NATO secrets by revealing serious flaws in the Western defense. The Security Group of the West German police invaded the offices of *Der Spiegel* magazine, Gestapo-fashion, in the middle of the night. (A little later the police commander of the raid was suspended, while his wartime activities as a Nazi S.S. officer were being investigated.) Without legal authority a Cabinet minister engineered the arrest and extradition of a *Spiegel* editor who was vacationing in Spain, and deceived the Bonn Parliament about his part in the affair. Altogether, eleven people were arrested, all but three *Spiegel* editors. Rudolf Augstein, the courageous publisher, was held in prison for three months. And all this because of a spurious accusation. Most of the so-called NATO secrets had previously been printed in other publications. It looked like, and was generally held to be, a political act of revenge by a government and a Cabinet minister whom *Der Spiegel* had consistently and rightly criticized.

My moral indignation fed on the memory of conditions in Austria thirty years before, a memory on which I had been happy to turn my back. But looking around me, Britain of the 1960's did not seem a good pulpit from which to preach to the Germans. The printer's ink had hardly dried and the posters announcing my series still looked down from the billboards when a London treason trial brought in its wake the kind of disclosures, imputations, and accusations (justified or unjustified) that I had only recently reported from Germany. Presently two Fleet Street journalists were behind bars. It was another *Der Spiegel* scandal, British version.

To match the rapacious materialism of West Germany's booming economy, Britain's stagnating economy seemed to provide a hundred inflationary get-rich-quick opportunities. The little men were queueing up outside gambling shops at every street corner, and the idle rich frequented the posh casinos where fortunes changed hands every night; notorious call girls replaced the more pedestrian prostitutes (the case of the murdered "Girl Rosemarie," a Frankfurt prostitute whose clients included leaders of the West German society had a British counterpart, albeit nonfatal, with disastrous consequences for the country's reputation); protection rackets flourished not only in London but in every provincial city worthy of its underworld; dope peddlers hawked marijuana instead of the old-fashioned cocaine. All these things were symptoms of a turbulence of mind caused by the winds of change. It is in such a climate that political freaks and gangsters invade the legitimate arena to incite low instincts and deficient minds, causing commotion, noise, and violence, and drag a country downhill.

Yet, as has been well said, it is not for its virtues that one loves a country, but in spite of its faults. It is how a nation reacts in a crisis that proves its mettle. I remember the worldwide criticism of the United States when Senator McCarthy made a mockery of the democratic process of a Senate investigation, and arrogated to himself what has been described as the prerogative of the harlot—power without responsibility. Overnight McCarthy disappeared into oblivion, and the United States, assimilating its excesses without poisoning the body politic, was rehabilitated. Again, when it looked as if an American general might defy the civil power, President Truman reasserted its supremacy, and prevailed. However distressing the violence accompanying integration may be, by upholding the principle of racial equality (even though the practice may lag behind), the President of the United States, against strong odds, rises above the turmoil and confusion of the hour to point the path of justice. It may be a long road, but the goal is clear.

Britain's Dunkirk spirit operates along similar lines. Though often maligned and misunderstood, it represents the innate moral, social, and political strength of the United Kingdom. Having put every ounce of its strength on the line against Naziism to achieve victory, the country emerged from the war much weaker than it cared to acknowledge, and had to face social and international changes much broader and deeper than it had anticipated. Yet, while the French and the Belgians took their overseas territories to freedom through a sea of blood, Britain nimbly plucked her colonial leaders one by one from prison to install them, each after a safe interval, as rulers of their own nations (Gandhi, Nehru, Nkrumah, Banda, Kenyatta . . . I have a fellow feeling for this band of men who emerged from British prisons as friends of Britain). And the Commonwealth cast off the outmoded regalia of empire and stepped into the ring in modern dress to buttress Britain as a force to be reckoned with.

Written in London while Britain is in the throes of a social and political crisis of Dunkirk proportions such as was bound to accompany the painful adjustment to new international conditions, these lines cannot fail to reflect the day's problems, which are really the problems of my life and times. The new generation will have to grapple for quite some time yet with the scandalous years through which I have lived. How will it cope? Is it a moral, a social, or ultimately a political issue? I have every confidence in Britain's unique powers of recovery and survival as a great nation—if she does what will have to be done. I mean that, above all, she must take a lead in reconstructing the framework of some of her ancient (too ancient and unchanging) democratic institutions which seem no longer equal to the burden of society's changing needs.

What may well be required are modifications in the time-honored Westminster model of democracy—in Britain's case the provision of a second chamber of eminence and expertise as represented by "The thoughtful men of England" to illuminate the minds of baffled, bewildered, often utterly confused ordinary people. The creation of such a chamber should be preceded by a worldwide study of democracy in our time, and an educational campaign to expound the true meaning, the requirements, the advantages and the dangers inherent in modern democracy. Unless democrats do it, there may be no democracy left to restore and explain.

Nothing has shocked me more than listening to the comments of the "man in the street" (or woman, as the case may be) which television interviewers collect from time to time to present as *vox populi* on topical political subjects. The fatuities, the ignorance of basic issues, the cocksureness based on insufficient knowledge or complete misunderstanding are most painful manifestations of the Age of the Common Man—and tend to make nonsense of a third of Lincoln's ideal of government of the people, by the people, for the people.

We are living in a state of war with forces stronger than any that mankind has ever encountered (and I am not referring to Communism, which is itself reeling under the impact of a similar onslaught). The speed of progress threatens to overtake our mental capacity to appreciate much of what is happening around us and our physical ability to adjust ourselves to the new dimensions (we have not even coped with such obvious phenomena as earlier puberty as a source of grave and self-perpetuating moral and emotional complications). The crushing advance of technology, the rapid march of science, the inevitable specialization as a result of the vastly extended frontiers of knowledge, the failure of the philosophers to throw much light on the rapidly accumulating enigmas—all this adds up to war on many fronts involving all of us. A world that seems fit only for the Huxleys and Toynbees finds most of us utterly unarmed. It makes fools of all of us, however eminent some of us may be in our own little niches.

It was Talleyrand who said that war is much too serious a thing to be left to military men. The implications are far-reaching, but I have already heard it said, on the Right wing as well as on the Left, that democracy in our age is much too serious a thing to be left to the uninformed.

And therein lies our problem—and our duty.